'And *then*
I met...'

ALSO BY JAMES E. ROGAN

My Brush with History (contributor, 2001)

Rough Edges: My Unlikely Road from Welfare to Washington (2014)

Catching Our Flag: Behind the Scenes of a Presidential Impeachment (2011)

JAMES E. ROGAN

'And *then* I met...'

STORIES OF GROWING UP, MEETING FAMOUS PEOPLE,
AND ANNOYING THE HELL OUT OF THEM

 WND Books

'And *then* I met...'

Published by WND Books®, Washington, DC, WND Books is a registered trademark of
WorldNetDaily.com, Inc. ("WND")

Unless otherwise credited, all photographs appearing in this book were taken by the author.

Book designed by Mark Karis

WND Books are distributed to the trade by:
Midpoint Trade Books, 27 West 20th Street, Suite 1102, New York, New York 10011
WND Books are available at special discounts for bulk purchases. WND Books, Inc.,
also publishes books in electronic formats. For more information call
(541) 474-1776 or visit www.wndbooks.com.

First Edition
Hardcover ISBN: 978-1-936488-38-4
eBook ISBN: 978-1-936488-46-9

Library of Congress Cataloging-in-Publication Data
Rogan, James.
"And then I met..." : stories of growing up, meeting famous people, and annoying the hell out
of them / by James E. Rogan. -- First edition.
pages cm
Includes index.
ISBN 978-1-936488-38-4 (hardcover) -- ISBN 978-1-936488-46-9 (ebook)
1. Rogan, James. 2. Legislators--United States--Biography. 3. United States. Congress. House-
-Biography. 4. Republican Party (U.S. : 1854-)--Biography. 5. Politicians--United States--
Biography--Anecdotes. 6. Rogan, James--Friends and associates. 7. Rogan, James--Childhood
and youth. 8. Mission District (San Francisco, Calif.)--Biography. 9. United States--Politics
and government--1945-1989. 10. United States--Politics and government--1989- I. Title.
E840.8.R594A3 2014
328.73092--dc23
[B]
2014012365
Printed in the United States of America
14 15 16 17 18 19 MV 9 8 7 6 5 4 3 2

To my mother, Alice,
who forgave all the times I ditched school to meet politicians

And to my kid brother, Pat,
who always handled the dirty work

CONTENTS

INTRODUCTION

"**S**ix degrees of separation," a theory developed in the 1960s, holds that everyone in the world connects to everyone else by no more than six people. For example, even though we have never met, I once met someone who met someone who met someone . . . who met you (eventually). Thus, by this concept, we are "connected in the chain" by no more than six people between us.

I don't know if this notion has any validity, but it intrigues me because, according to it, I am only one degree from Marilyn Monroe and Rudolph Valentino; from Winston Churchill and Theodore Roosevelt; from Babe Ruth and Charles Lindbergh; from Buffalo Bill and Chief Crazy Horse. On the darker side, just one person stands between me and Charles Manson, Al Capone, and Adolf Hitler. When it comes to "no degree of separation," meaning the people I've met whose stories once populated the headlines, the list is endless. Their ranks include presidents (and the men they vanquished to win the White House), great political leaders in their day, movie stars, astronauts, and sports legends. I had one friend who costarred in *Gone with the Wind*, and another who danced with Judy Garland in *The Wizard of Oz*. I was "attacked" by an Indian who witnessed General Custer's massacre at Little Big Horn; I've "sparred" with Muhammad Ali; I've played practical jokes on both the first man on the moon and Pope John Paul II.

A congressman meeting famous people is no big deal; in fact, it goes with the turf. The difference between me and the other members of Congress with whom I served is that I met most of the ones in this book when I was a kid, and I did it under very unlikely circumstances. No, they weren't the friends of my wealthy or connected parents: I grew up as the illegitimate (and oldest) child of a single mom on welfare and food stamps in the hardscrabble Mission District of San Francisco. By the time I was a young boy, Mom was a convicted felon with three other kids. I got expelled from high school in the tenth grade and never went back to finish. I spent my teens hanging out with car thieves and dopers and thugs; I sold vacuum cleaners door-to-door to the local whorehouses; I bartended in various Hollywood strip clubs; I carried a gun, and sometimes I used it. How I went from this backdrop to university graduate, lawyer, state court judge, legislator, congressman, author, husband, and father–instead of ending up on a police blotter or morgue slab–is a great story, but it's not one for this book. You'll have to dig up a copy of my recently rereleased book, *Rough Edges: My Unlikely Road from Welfare to Washington*,[1] to learn about that wild ride (but don't read it if you're faint of heart or easily offended!).

So, how did I stay out of prison? The short answer is that as a young kid, and despite all the swirling dysfunction around me, I developed an insatiable appetite for history, government, and politics. I dreamed that I could climb out of the old neighborhood and one day serve in Washington as a congressman. It took me thirty years of hard work, but I did it. Of course, once I got there, I made an absolute nuisance of myself by demanding that we respect the rule of law rather than the polls and the focus groups. It's funny: voters always say they want politicians who will do what is right instead of what is popular–until they get it, and then they get mad at the guy who didn't do what was popular! That's another great story, and you'll find it in my second book, *Catching Our Flag: Behind the Scenes of a Presidential Impeachment*.[2]

This book, *"And Then I Met…,"* is the story of how that nuisance gene first manifested in me, and how I used it to foster a lifelong interest that changed my life forever (it even let me end up being a small player in history). By the way, a few of the stories were told in my previous works, albeit in abbreviated form. I'm including them for two reasons: first, I can tell the story more completely here; and second, they're just great stories worth retelling.

---

1   James E. Rogan, *Rough Edges: My Unlikely Road from Welfare to Washington* (Washington, DC: WND Books, 2014).

2   James E. Rogan, *Catching Our Flag: Behind the Scenes of a Presidential Impeachment* (Washington, DC: WND Books, 2011).

. . .

Readers of my earlier books know I am at heart a political buff, a lifelong collector of campaign memorabilia, and (mostly) a wannabe historian. I started meeting famous people to ask for advice (generally politicians, but they covered the gamut of fame-dom) when I was twelve, and I brought my camera and notebook to memorialize each encounter. My photo albums and diaries over the last forty-plus years cover the greats, the near greats, and the former greats now long forgotten. They remained buried in storage until early 2013, when I became the last person in America to join a social networking site to keep in touch with family members (memo to as-yet-unborn readers in future generations: "social networking" was a prehistoric invention from the digital Paleozoic Era, designed for people to meet and chat with one another without meeting or chatting the way God intended). Once I joined, my daughters urged me to pull out some of my old photo albums of pictures I'd taken of famous people from decades past and post a sampling of them. After I started, friends and family e-mailed and asked me to share the stories that went with the pictures. I started doing this for a while, and–voilà! Another book idea was born.

In writing this book, I read old diary entries I hadn't seen since writing them–some more than forty years later. As one might expect, at times I found that the vivid stories I've told over the decades had more color than some hastily scrawled, bland, ancient notebook jottings. The dilemma: how to harmonize the dull written source and my storyteller's memory? The 1962 film *The Man Who Shot Liberty Valance* helped resolve the question. The movie opened with aging US senator Ransom Stoddard (who built his career on the reputation he earned as a young lawyer in the Old West for killing outlaw Liberty Valance) returning to the small town of Shinbone for the funeral of the town drunk. When the reporter from the Shinbone "*Star*" demanded to know why America's most distinguished statesman had come back for the burial of some old sauce bag, the movie faded back to the past for the true story. The film ended with the senator confessing to the reporter that the drunk, and not he, had killed Liberty Valance, and that Stoddard had built his entire career on a lie. After hearing the confession, the reporter tore up his notes. When the senator asked why the reporter refused to write the true story, the reporter replied: "Senator, this here's the West. And in the West, when truth conflicts with legend, we print the legend."

. . .

Finally, a word to anyone present with me at any of the stories I recount in this book: if your version conflicts with mine, I recommend to you President Harry Truman's account of growing up on a Missouri farm. His father brought young Harry to the local Democratic Party annual county picnic, where by tradition Colonel Crisp (Truman described him as a colonel "by agreement") ended the affair each year by standing on a picnic table and delivering an oratorical presentation of his Civil War experience at the Battle of Lone Jack. At one such picnic, after the colonel finished his tale, a soldier who had actually fought at Lone Jack rose and gave a point-by-point contradiction of the colonel's account. At the conclusion of the heckler's outburst, Colonel Crisp spat out a reply to this attack on his veracity: "Goddamn an eyewitness anyway. He always spoils a good story."[3]

Like old Colonel Crisp, when I'm invited to share recollections of famous people I've met or known, it takes little coaxing to get me to climb atop the picnic table. And unlike that Shinbone reporter, I've done my best to be faithful to the truth over legend.

---

3   David McCullough, *Truman* (New York: Simon and Schuster, 1992), 63.

1

Homework Assignment

When I was in seventh grade in 1969, I spent untold hours at the Daly City Public Library, looking up the addresses of retired government leaders so I could write them for both autographs and advice on entering politics. Getting former president Harry Truman's address came in handy for one particular middle-school project, although not without causing some indigestion along the way.

That year my history teacher, Mr. Puhr, assigned us to write a biography of a historic person. This was my first long-term homework assignment: our paper had to be typed, researched, and at least seven pages long. In the pre–personal computer era, few twelve-year-olds were keyboard literate, so Mr. Puhr gave us three months to complete this monumental task. "But you'd better have it ready to turn in on the due date," he warned us ominously, "or there will be consequences."

For my subject, I picked the eighty-six-year old Truman, who was then two decades removed from his White House service. I approached my task in earnest, and instead of spending three months on the project, I finished it in three days. With so much time to spare, and having learned during my research that Truman once said his only obligation in retirement was to answer personally the letters he received from young people, I decided to mail my report to Truman and ask him to look it over. Long before readily available copy machines (and the invention of hard drives), I had no duplicate of my homework. It never dawned on me that Truman wouldn't return it.

Months passed; when the paper came due, I was empty-handed. Mr. Puhr rejected my explanation: he called me a liar in front of the class, accused me of never doing the report, and gave me an F. "Besides," he announced to everyone, "Truman's dead–I watched his funeral on television twenty years ago!"

More months went by, and I forgot about the incident. Then one afternoon, I returned home from school and found a large envelope postmarked from Independence, Missouri. Inside I found my report returned, an autographed picture of the great man, and this letter:

HARRY S TRUMAN
INDEPENDENCE, MISSOURI

April 29, 1970

Dear Jim:

I was very pleased to have your letter and manuscript. I am sorry I cannot help you with it, as I have a rule against working on another author's paper.

It is clear, however, that you did your home-work well.

With best wishes for success in your life,

Sincerely yours,

Harry Truman

Jim Rogan
25 Poncetta Drive - Apt. 110
Daly City, California

President Harry Truman's letter to me, April 29, 1970

The next day in class, I walked up to Mr. Puhr's desk and placed on it silently my proof. His face reddened as he looked over the documents.

"Take your seat," he said sternly.

"Is that all you have to say to me, Mr. Puhr?" I asked in surprise.

"I said, take your seat."

After humiliating me earlier, Mr. Puhr now refused to acknowledge his mistake. I fumed over this injustice for the rest of class. When the recess bell rang, I exacted my own vindication: jumping from my desk, I rushed to the door and blocked the exit. Holding aloft my treasures, I called to my classmates, "Hey, if anybody wants to see the letter and autographed picture I got yesterday from the *late* President Harry Truman, I'll show it to you on the playground!"

Despite my protests, Mr. Puhr refused to accept my paper. I went to the principal, Mrs. Zenovich, and presented my case. Marching me back to class, Mrs. Zenovich confronted Mr. Puhr and ordered him to accept it.

Later, Mr. Puhr handed back my paper in front of the entire class and announced that he marked me down for "repeated punctuation errors" because I kept failing to put a period after Truman's middle initial "S." I told him the omission was intentional, because the *S* didn't get a period—S was his middle name. Mr. Puhr grabbed volume T of the *Encyclopedia Britannica*, turned to Truman's entry, and cackled aloud, "The encyclopedia lists him as Harry S-with-a-period Truman! What do you say to that, Mr. Rogan?"

From the tomb: Engraved portrait autographed for me by former president and Mrs. Truman, signed some twenty years after Mr. Puhr supposedly watched Truman's "funeral" on television!

"The encyclopedia's wrong."

Mr. Puhr chortled, "So! The encyclopedia is wrong and Mr. Rogan is right! My, aren't we lucky to have such a brilliant student in our midst!" Students laughed as Mr. Puhr mocked me for the rest of class. For days afterward, he called on me to "confirm" facts, like our first president was George Washington, or that Columbus discovered America in 1492 ("Or was it in 1493, Mr. Rogan?"). Growing tired of the abuse, I took matters into my own hands:

"Dear President Truman," my new letter began, "You won't believe this teacher of mine . . . ." I asked Truman to settle the issue.

Sadly, the school year ended without any reply, and again I forgot about it. Then one day, as my 1970 summer vacation ended, another letter (see opposite page) from Missouri arrived.

Now, for the first time, I noticed Truman's engraved letterhead: sure enough, it bore the name "Harry S Truman" with no period after the middle initial.

On the first day of the new school year, I tracked down my former teacher. Mr. Puhr looked baffled when I entered his classroom, as if I had made another mistake. I walked to his desk and showed him the second Truman letter. Again he refused to re-grade my report, but changed his mind when I threatened him with more Mrs. Zenovich therapy.

As I walked away, Mr. Puhr called to me sharply: "Rogan," he said, "I'm very glad you won't be in my class this year."

. . .

Former president Harry S Truman died at age eighty-eight on December 26, 1972.

In the early 1990s, *American Heritage* magazine first published my story about Harry Truman helping me with my homework. A few years later, I gave *Reader's Digest* permission to republish it in its April 1995 issue, which coincided with the fiftieth anniversary of Truman's presidency.

A couple of weeks later, while on a trip to Missouri, I toured Truman's house in Independence (now a national historic site). The guide led about twenty of us to the rear porch and said, "Here's where Mr. Truman sat each morning, answering his mail. In fact, in this month's *Reader's Digest*, there is a story of how he helped a young boy with his homework. This porch is where he would have read the boy's letter and wrote his reply."

HARRY S TRUMAN
INDEPENDENCE, MISSOURI
August 19, 1970

Dear Mr. Rogan:

I was glad to autographed your engraved picture of
the White House and it is being returned to you
herewith.

The "S" in my name stands for the first letter of
the first name of each of my grandfathers. In order
to be strictly impartial in naming me for one or the
other, I was given the letter "S" as a middle name.
It can be used with or without a period after it.

I appreciate your very kind comments and send
you best wishes,

Sincerely yours,

Harry Truman

Mr. James Rogan
25 Poncetta Drive
Apt. #110
Daly City, California 94015

In this second letter to me, Truman settled a lingering historical question

When the tour ended, I mentioned to the guide that I was the author. He
asked me to wait while he called his wife (who worked at the nearby Truman
Presidential Library). A few minutes later, a couple of cars arrived with staff
and docents from the library. They led me back to the porch and asked me to
recount the entire story for them, and it pleased me greatly to do so.

Some years later, I attended a weekend legislative retreat with fellow members of Congress. The guest speaker was one of my generation's preeminent historians, David McCullough, who wrote a Pulitzer Prize–winning biography on Truman. When I asked McCullough to autograph my copy of his book, I mentioned with a grin that I was pleased to meet a fellow Truman "scholar." He asked me in seriousness what Truman work I penned; I laughed and told him about my little story of Truman helping me with my homework when I was a boy.

McCullough's eyes brightened. "The 'homework' story in *American Heritage*!" he said. "Truman wrote you back about the *S* in his middle name! I not only read it–it helped me win a bet on that *S* issue!"

It seems that when Harry Truman took the time to help a young admirer long ago, both David McCullough and I came out winners.

2

KGO's Gift

In 1960s and 1970s San Francisco, newsman Jim Dunbar's AM show on station KGO was a staple of local morning television. From 6:30 to 8:30 a.m., Dunbar hosted a live call-in program with news makers. While watching the station one morning in 1971, I heard an announcement that senators Hubert H. Humphrey and Edward "Ted" Kennedy—two of the most recognizable political titans of their generation—would appear with Dunbar the following Monday morning. I called my classmates (and fellow political junkies) Dan Swanson and Roger Mahan. Together we concocted a plan to cut eighth grade classes and try to meet Kennedy and Humphrey when they arrived at KGO.

Writing this story over four decades later, I am mindful that with each passing year, Hubert Humphrey's name registers with fewer people. That was not true when I was young. A political heavyweight for decades, Humphrey first won election to the US Senate in 1948. He ran unsuccessfully against John F. Kennedy for the 1960 Democratic presidential nomination. Four years later, President Lyndon B. Johnson tapped Humphrey as his running mate. As the 1968 Democratic presidential nominee, then vice president Humphrey lost the White House to Richard Nixon by a whisker. After recapturing his old Senate seat two years later, and with the 1972 presidential campaign around the corner, Humphrey itched for a Nixon rematch.

Humphrey was more than a mere political figure to me—he was an early inspiration. As a fifth grade boy during his 1968 presidential run, I read a *Life* magazine profile on him. It told of his experience as a young Midwestern pharmacist making his first visit to 1930s Washington and the newfound passion for politics he found there. One night, after an exhilarating tour of the monuments, Humphrey rushed off an excited letter to his fiancée back home; after pleading with her not to laugh, he wrote that if he applied himself, maybe he could return one day as a congressman. She didn't laugh; they married, and along the way, he helped shape almost every landmark law of his era. That magazine profile on HHH showed me that if an ordinary Midwestern druggist could accomplish such great things through politics, then maybe one day I could do the same. Once I connected those dots, I set my compass.

Senator Edward Kennedy was the surviving heir of the famous political dynasty. Perhaps the most popular politician in the 1970s, Kennedy topped all presidential preference polls despite his reluctance to bid for national office after losing two brothers to assassination. To party activists, however, his hesitation was of no moment: many viewed Kennedy's presidency as inevitable.

. . .

Well before daybreak one morning in 1971, Dan, Roger, and I caught the trolley to downtown San Francisco. To get to KGO, we walked many long blocks down dark streets while passing hobos sleeping in doorways and winos urinating in the gutter. It was a spooky journey for three kids, but we arrived at KGO in one piece, and a kindly doorman told us where to wait for Humphrey's and Kennedy's arrivals.

Whenever I saw political leaders on television, they always seemed to have Secret Service and police wedged between them and the throngs of news cameras and people pushing forward. Expecting this type of greeting for Kennedy's and Humphrey's arrivals, I strained my ears at the sound of every passing siren to await the expected procession. When an unassuming blue sedan pulled in front of the studio, I paid no immediate attention to the man reading the morning newspaper in the front passenger seat. A second, closer look at his familiar features prompted a shock of recognition. I drove an elbow into Dan's ribs and whispered, "There's Kennedy."

Kennedy climbed out of his car and walked toward the entrance. We were so nervous that we almost let him pass without meeting him. Once he realized our purpose, he proved very gracious in signing autographs and suggesting we have a group picture made. Kennedy took my camera from his nervous fan, conscripted an aide for photography duty, and then started giving him stage directions: "Cock it . . . Cock it . . . Now, move in a bit *closah*." Kennedy gathered us about him, and the aide snapped the shot. While standing next to Kennedy, I noticed the "PT-109" tie clasp he wore. I knew from reading history that President Kennedy gave these out as souvenirs commemorating his World War II service. Kennedy shook our hands, thanked us for waiting for him, and then entered the studio for his interview.

We were ecstatic that we had succeeded in our long-shot mission; in all the excitement, we almost forgot there was more to come.

Despite Kennedy's stealth arrival, I still expected a motorcade scenario for Humphrey's entrance, but was also determined not to be caught off guard again. I studied every passing car, looking for Humphrey, and was ready when another plain sedan double-parked in front of the studio. When the passenger door opened, I raised my camera and snapped a picture of Humphrey as he stepped unescorted from the car.

Senator Edward Kennedy with (from left) Dan Swanson, Roger Mahan, and me outside KGO Studio, May 16, 1971

Humphrey bounded toward us with a broad smile and outstretched hand. He signed autographs and showed a genuine interest in our trio: he wanted to know our names, where we lived, and where we went to school. When he heard we loved politics, he beamed with enthusiasm, sharing his joy of public service and encouraging us to keep up our studies and plans to join him one day in Washington. I was so tongue-tied that I couldn't do much better than mumble back my thanks and admiration as he wished us luck before disappearing inside KGO.

I don't think I ever had a bigger thrill as a boy: here was my inspiration in the flesh—a man who almost became president—encouraging us to get into politics! The experience left me breathless. Meanwhile, back at school, our chutzpah in meeting Humphrey and Kennedy became the stuff of classroom legend. It so impressed our government teacher, Mr. Robert Lasley, that he ran personal interference to clear our unexcused truancy.

· · ·

Over the next few years, Dan, Roger, and I became regular fixtures outside KGO Studios. Whenever newsman Jim Dunbar planned to interview any national political figure, we rode the predawn trolley into town, ran the gauntlet of

street derelicts, and waited outside to get autographs, take pictures, and get advice on entering politics. We met almost every notable making his or her way through San Francisco in the early- to mid-1970s. We became so familiar to Dunbar and the KGO crew that they started letting us inside the studio to watch the interviews from the control booth.

Each visit to KGO was memorable, and making these connections with national leaders taught me an important lesson beyond autograph collecting: in

I snapped this photo of former vice president Hubert H. Humphrey as he stepped from his car at KGO Studio, May 16, 1971 sizing up so many of them personally, I developed at a young age the confidence that someday I could do this too.

. . .

Decades later, when Ted Kennedy and I served together in Congress, I showed him our 1971 KGO photograph during a chat on the Senate floor. He let out a hearty laugh when he saw the old picture. Kennedy grabbed my arm and dragged me around the chamber as he showed the picture to every Senate colleague he could collar.

During that same period, when I served on the House Judiciary Committee during President Clinton's impeachment and Senate trial, I repaid the KGO debt. My press secretary, Jeff Solsby, fended off the scores of daily interview requests from the national and international media. Despite my backbreaking schedule and my very limited time to accommodate interviews, Jeff knew to put through every request from Jim Dunbar (still broadcasting at KGO almost thirty years later) or any reporter from that station.

. . .

After the assassination of his second brother (Senator Robert Kennedy in 1968), Ted Kennedy remained an emotional Democratic presidential favorite, but (like Humphrey) it was not to be. Kennedy tried for the White House only once, but lost a bitter campaign for the presidential nomination to incumbent Jimmy Carter in 1980. He resumed his legislative duties in the Senate for the rest of his life. When he died of brain cancer at age seventy-seven on August 25, 2009, he was the fourth-longest-serving senator in American history.

As for Hubert Humphrey, I'll have more stories about him later in the book.

3

The Indian and the Preacher

Short of the apostles, Billy Graham may be the greatest evangelist ever. For more than sixty years, his worldwide "crusades" led untold millions of people to faith in Christ. When he came to the Bay Area in July 1971 for a weeklong appearance at the Oakland Coliseum, classmate Roger Mahan and I again braved the early-morning streets of San Francisco to meet him when he did a scheduled interview at KGO. Just like when we met Hubert Humphrey and Edward Kennedy there a few months earlier, we waited outside the studio for the guest to arrive.

A car turned onto Golden Gate Avenue and parked by the entrance. Suddenly, six men jumped out and hustled past us toward the door. We tried to determine if one of these men was Graham, but it was impossible: all six men wore dark glasses, hats, and overcoats—in the middle of summer! By the time we figured out which one was Graham, he was inside the lobby, behind locked doors, and heading to the elevator. We decided to remain and try meeting him on the way out. It was during this lull that I had one of the most unexpected confrontations of my boyhood.

Soon after Graham's incognito entrance, the lobby door opened and out shuffled a grizzled old man in full Indian costume and headdress. As he exited, impulsive curiosity led me to raise my camera and take his picture. The Indian's pale red eyes glowered in anger as he hobbled in my direction, made a sudden lunge at me, and demanded I surrender my camera to him. Startled, I drew away and held my plastic Kodak out of reach as he kept grabbing for it. "Give me that camera!" he hollered. "My photograph is copyrighted by Congress!

Give me that camera so I can destroy your film!"

I backed up against the advancing, shouting, and grasping Indian. Speechless, I managed to protect the offending instrument from his destructive clutches. Eventualy, the Indian lowered his arms and stared silently at me. I stood frozen and mute, too bewildered and frightened to say anything. The old Indian grunted, turned, and trundled down Golden Gate Avenue toward Hyde Street.

Roger and I looked at each other in disbelief, unsure what to make of the bizarre scene that had just unfolded. Having watched the commotion, the KGO doorman called me over to explain the significance of the encounter.

"Hey, don't you know who that is?" he asked. "That's Chief Red Fox! He was born in 1871, and he's in town promoting his autobiography." The doorman then explained that Chief Red Fox, 101 years old and a nephew of Crazy Horse, was now the last surviving Sioux to witness the massacres of both General Custer and his troops at the Little Bighorn (1876) and the battle of Wounded Knee (1890). Before the turn of the century, Red Fox joined Buffalo Bill's Wild West show and worked for him for many years; in 1905 he even "scalped" Great Britain's King Edward VII during an exhibition show in England and was one of the original models for the old Indian Head/Buffalo nickels (first struck by the US Mint in 1913).

The offending snapshot: Chief Red Fox leaves KGO, July 20, 1971

Imagine hearing that story as a thirteen-year-old boy! The news left me thunderstruck. Besides, how lucky can a kid get? If Chief Red Fox tried scalping the King of England, imagine what he might have done to me?

I looked down Golden Gate Avenue and watched the chief still lumbering away in the distance. Curiously, dozens of people passed him; not one person gave the old Indian in full regalia a second look.

Oh, well, I thought. *It's San Francisco.*

· · ·

Chief Red Fox died at age 105 on March 1, 1976.

4

The Happy Warrior

As I mentioned earlier, during my youth former vice president Hubert Humphrey (the 1968 Democratic presidential nominee) helped dominate the political stage in the 1960s and 1970s. He also was a personal favorite of mine; only Ronald Reagan matched him in kindness when meeting fans too young to vote for him.

I met Humphrey many times during his campaign swings through San Francisco in the 1970s, and for you old-time political aficionados out there, here are a few more memories of the man dubbed "the Happy Warrior."

Vice President and Mrs. Hubert Humphrey with Senator and Mrs. Edmund S. Muskie, accepting the Democratic presidential and vice presidential nomination, 1968 Democratic National Convention, Chicago

. . .

Since my classmate Dan Swanson and I had had luck meeting Humphrey the morning we cut school and traipsed to KGO studio in May 1971, we tried to renew our fortune a few months later when Humphrey paid a return visit to KGO shortly before declaring his presidential candidacy for the third (and final) time.

Early that morning, Dan and I stood outside the studio, shivering in the cold, when a 1950s-style limousine arrived. Humphrey looked dour as he stepped from the rear seat and ran past us for the entrance. I asked for an autograph; in a moment of brusqueness, he waved me off, saying he was in a hurry.

As he walked by, I saw his eyes fix on the small "Humphrey for President" badge pinned to my sweater. Then Humphrey stopped dead in his tracks: a big smile crossed his face as he exclaimed, "Of course I have time to sign an autograph!" With that, Humphrey grabbed Dan and me by the arm and escorted us inside the warm studio lobby.

I handed Humphrey a small White House card signed previously by Richard Nixon, the man who had beat him in 1968. As he signed his name with a flourish to the card, he asked where I got it. "I wrote him a letter," I replied. "When you're president, I'll write you a letter." That proved to be the winning answer. Humphrey's face lit up: the candidate in a hurry suddenly became the candidate with lots of time on his hands.

Good answer! White House card signed (eventually) by the 1968 Republican and Democratic Party nominees for president and vice president: Richard Nixon and Spiro Agnew; Hubert Humphrey and Edmund Muskie

"Now, what else can I sign for you boys?" he insisted. Dan and I looked at each other as if we'd just discovered an unattended cookie jar. We started passing Humphrey all the photos, cards, and 1968 campaign mementos we brought. HHH boldly penned his signature on each, all while stating repeatedly that we were "Fine young boys! Fine young boys!" and adding, "I'm mighty proud of you both."

Humphrey threw his arm around my shoulder and instructed Dan to take our picture. Dan followed orders. "Let's have another!" HHH insisted. Dan took the second snapshot, and then handed off the camera to me so I could return the favor.

Humphrey continued ignoring an aide's plea to keep on schedule. "Now," Humphrey said, "is there anything else I can do for you boys?" There wasn't, since Dan and I had no more autograph-able items. Humphrey pumped our hands heartily as we thanked him; he waved good-bye and then stepped into the lobby elevator. As the doors closed, HHH thrust his arm between them. The doors caught his arm, and then they popped back open.

"Are you boys sure I can't sign anything else for you?" he called out. When we assured him we were satiated with HHH autographs, he again waved good-bye. As the doors closed, we could still hear him telling the doorman, "I am so proud of those boys! What fine young boys!"

If America had enfranchised twelve-year-old boys back then, Humphrey would have had my vote. By the time those elevator doors closed, I'd begun to think I had his.

Hubert Humphrey and me at KGO Studio, September 27, 1971. Note the very helpful HHH campaign button pinned to my sweater.

...

Humphrey was a formal candidate for the presidential nomination the next time I saw him during a San Francisco campaign swing on March 24, 1972. My kid brother, Pat, and I grabbed our cameras and waited for the candidate outside station KPIX on busy Van Ness Avenue. Remembering the positive response my little Humphrey campaign button had generated at KGO six months earlier, I doubled down on that strategy: Pat and I each pinned to our jackets two jumbo-sized HHH for President badges.

Humphrey exited the studio and waved to the assembled, cheering crowd. When he saw Pat and me wearing the badges, he made a beeline for us, exclaiming, "Oh, boy! Am I for you!"

I had brought a typescript quotation from one of Humphrey's major 1968 campaign speeches for him to sign, but he went us one better. Ignoring the increasingly frantic pleas of his Secret Service agents to return to the safety of his car, Humphrey led Pat and me down to the corner so he could use the nearby mailbox as his writing desk. Humphrey took several minutes to write out in slow and careful longhand the quote I'd only hoped to have him sign. Unhappy and fidgety agents nervously watched the nearby rooftops, passing cars,

and gathering spectators with good reason: two weeks earlier, a would-be assassin pumped four bullets into Alabama governor George Wallace as he campaigned for the 1972 Democratic presidential nomination. Tossing aside safety concerns, HHH created what remains one of the sentimental favorites in my political memorabilia collection.

Later that evening, Pat and I snuck into Humphrey's private reception for his national convention delegation slate in the Fairmont hotel's Crystal Room. After making a brief campaign speech, and while

HHH worked the room, a group of pretty young stewardesses peeked inside the doorway and recognized him. Sheepishly, one of them asked a campaign aide if they could come in and shake hands with the candidate. Humphrey looked over and saw their group; not waiting for his aide to grant permission, HHH bolted to the door and escorted them personally into the reception. After shaking hands and posing for photos with the women, Humphrey announced he had a gift for them. Reaching into his pocket, he pulled out a fistful of brass "HHH" pins that fastened to clothing with a removable butterfly clutch. "These are our special campaign pins we give special friends," Humphrey told the flight attendants, "and I would like to give one to each of you!"

The first giggling stewardess reached out her hand to receive the gift. Humphrey ignored her outstretched palm and said, "Here, let me pin it on you!" With the practiced speed of a teenage boy in the backseat of an old Buick, Humphrey slid his hand down and inside the young woman's blouse while he fastened the pin clasp. The startled stewardess blushed through saucer-sized eyes, but her giggling smile never wavered. Some onlookers chuckled while others exchanged nervous glances. HHH ignored both his whispering aide and the potential social breach as he moved down the line, pinning each attendant's top with intimate, unfettered gusto.

As Humphrey fastened the last pin, someone in the crowd called out, "Muriel [Mrs. Humphrey] will give you hell for this!" Humphrey ignored the crack and completed the task. As the last flushed attendant straightened her disheveled blouse, Humphrey looked over at Pat and me and gave us a wink.

"Ahh," he exclaimed with a grin, "the joys of running for president!"

. . .

Not everyone in San Francisco was glad to see Hubert Humphrey's campaign come to town. In late May, just days before the 1972 California Democratic primary, Humphrey made an outdoor campaign appearance. His motorcade pulled up to the world-famous cable car turntable at Powell and Market Streets; HHH

Before the stewardesses distracted him: Hubert Humphrey speaking in the Crystal Room of the Fairmont hotel's March 24, 1972 leaped from his car and plunged into the sizable crowd, crisscrossing busy Powell Street, trying to shake every hand as he made his way to Union Square.

I learned from attending previous campaign events like this that TV camera operators will do whatever it takes to get their shot: swinging heavy equipment into innocent bystanders is considered inflicting necessary collateral damage to accomplish their task. While trying to take pictures at earlier events like this, I came away trampled and bruised from these aggressive photojournalists. In the now-huge crowd pressing forward to meet Humphrey, it became difficult for anyone with a camera to get a decent photo. Looking around for an assist, I spied a tall concrete tree planter on the sidewalk. Climbing atop it quickly, I now had a perfect bird's-eye view of Humphrey as he passed.

In fact, the view was too perfect: a cameraman from station KTVU decided he wanted my spot and tried to yank me off the planter. I kicked him as he grabbed me; only the sudden shouting of an irate, horn-honking motorist stuck in this street gridlock interrupted our battle.

"Damn you, Humphrey!" the driver screamed out the window while leaning on his horn. "Get outta my way—I'm late for an appointment! Get outta my way, you damn Humphrey! Move, you dirty bastard reporters . . . !"

My attacker and a few nearby TV cameramen exchanged momentary, knowing glances, and then they rushed toward the angry driver's car. Clambering atop the car with their heavy equipment, they trained their lenses on Humphrey as he passed their way. The sound of bending metal could be heard from the car hood, roof, and trunk. The driver screamed like a banshee to the point that I thought he might have a stroke. The cacophonous sounds of the cheering crowds—and the driver's piercing horn blasts—nearly drowned out the trapped motorist's profane screams.

As the Humphrey parade passed, the cameramen jumped off the car and chased their quarry toward Union Square. As I followed the entourage up the street, I could hear a faint, distant cry above the din:

"Hummmmm-phrey! Damn you, bastard! Hummmmm-phrey . . . !"

. . .

When I visited Washington, DC, for the first time in 1975, Humphrey invited me to his Senate office for a chat. After arriving for my early afternoon appointment, one of his aides apologized and said a late-scheduled legislative luncheon had delayed him. While waiting for his return, she gave me a tour of the vast collection of memorabilia decorating his walls. In the middle of one hung a huge color photograph of Humphrey and his running mate, Senator Edmund Muskie, acknowledging the cheers of the delegates before the 1968 Democratic National Convention.

After forty-five minutes, she answered a phone call. When she hung up, she grabbed me by the hand. "Come on, Jim," she said. "Let's go find the senator." We took the subway to the Capitol and then walked to the private Senate Dining Room. On the way there I tried to beg off, saying I didn't want to disturb his meeting. She brushed off my concern and said Humphrey wanted to see me. I waited in the foyer, pacing nervously, while she fetched him.

A few minutes later, Humphrey exited the dining room and approached with a wide smile. When I apologized for interrupting his lunch, he dismissed my concern. "Oh, nonsense to that lunch, Jim," he exclaimed as he pumped my hand, "I'm glad to see you."

Humphrey took my camera and passed it to his aide, with directions to take our picture. As we posed, he pointed to her and said to me, "We've got the prettiest photographer on Capitol Hill."

"Nonsense to that lunch": Senator Hubert H. Humphrey and me, US Capitol, September 12, 1975.

After she took a couple of photos, I urged him to return to his lunch. Humphrey would have none of that. Rather than dismiss me summarily, he questioned me at length about my first impressions of Washington and all of my activities since arriving. No wonder I loved Humphrey: he treated me like an old friend, not like a young nuisance.

When I told HHH that I would start college next week and hoped to go on to law school and (someday) politics, he beamed. "That's wonderful!" he exclaimed. "That's just wonderful. I know exactly how you feel." Humphrey closed his eyes and rubbed his temples, as if conjuring a distant memory, and then shared with me this recollection:

"My first trip to Washington was in 1935, and I spent a week here on the Hill, like you, just looking all around. As I sat in the Senate gallery one day, I decided that's what I wanted to do in my life. I composed all my thoughts and feelings, then sat outside and wrote a letter to my wife, Muriel, back in Minnesota. I told her that I wanted to set my sights on one day running for Congress."

How well I knew that story: I told him I'd read that very account in *Life* magazine as a fifth grade schoolboy in 1968, and that it motivated me to enter politics someday. "Well, Jim," he said with a parting smile, "When you do come back as a congressman, bring honor to the place. That's the obligation of all who serve here."

A few days later, when I returned home to California, a letter from Humphrey arrived. He thanked me again for visiting and reminisced about the story he told me of his first experience visiting DC. After encouraging me in my future endeavors, he closed with this line: "Just remember that you always have a friend here in the Humphrey office."

I knew that without being told.

. . .

For Humphrey fans, 1976 looked to be his year—finally. As Jimmy Carter stumbled in the polls, support for a fourth Humphrey presidential candidacy surged. In every preference poll, Humphrey beat all comers, including delegate-leader Carter. For the first time in his public life, Humphrey resisted the seduction and announced to a shocked political world he would not be a candidate. "I am available for a draft, but I will not run," Humphrey stated. "If my party wants me and needs me, I will answer the call."

The call never came.

After the convention nominated Jimmy Carter for president, the Happy Warrior stumped the nation for the Democratic ticket. His late August campaign visit to San Francisco also had another purpose: to promote his recently published autobiography, *The Education of a Public Man*. When I heard a last-minute radio announcement that HHH would appear that afternoon on KGO Radio promoting his book, I made a quick trip to the studio with old friends and classmates Dan Swanson and Alex Pava to say hello and have him sign copies of his new book we planned to buy. Unfortunately, it was not yet in stock at a nearby bookstore, so we were left with mere congratulations for the author.

When Humphrey arrived, he greeted us warmly and invited us to join him in the studio. Dressed in a jaunty green plaid sport jacket and wearing a small peanut pin on his lapel (Carter's campaign symbol), Humphrey appeared the picture of vitality. A bout with cancer in 1974 had caused initial concern, but HHH had beat back the disease; by 1976, doctors gave him a clean bill of health for a possible presidential run. Humphrey's appearance at KGO confirmed their findings.

A studio employee asked Humphrey to autograph her copy of his new book. She slid next to Humphrey on the sofa as he inscribed it, and he drafted me into photography duty for her.

Our time to visit was brief; Humphrey needed to start his interview, and I needed to return home in time for my after-school job. We shook hands and wished him luck on the new book, and he thanked us for stopping by. HHH then entered the studio elevator, and as the doors closed, he gave us a salute.[1]

I never saw Hubert Humphrey again.

---

[1]   It had been more than five years since Dan Swanson, Roger Mahan, and I made our first trip to KGO. During those years, our visits there provided us the rare, boyhood opportunity to meet dozens of national leaders, as well as fuel our growing interest in government and politics. This trip to see Hubert Humphrey at KGO marked the last time we ever visited the station. Appropriately, we met Humphrey there on our first trip to the studio in 1971. After this final visit to KGO, we channeled our energies in new directions: college and adulthood.

   KGO closed its studio and moved to a new location in 1985. Almost thirty years later, I attended a conference in San Francisco; I walked over and stood on the sidewalk outside 277 Golden Gate Avenue, where, as a boy, I had waited with Dan, Roger, and my brother, Pat, to meet so many great leaders. The building remained vacant and boarded. Scheduled for demolition in 2012, the old structure received a last-minute reprieve from the wrecking ball and is now slated to become a housing complex. With all the history I saw inside and outside that building so long ago, I'm delighted it survives and will soon open its doors once again.

. . .

Humphrey's hearty appearance at that last KGO visit gave no indication of the undetected cancer spreading silently through his bladder. Two weeks after our meeting, Humphrey entered the hospital for a routine checkup. Doctors found the tumor and diagnosed it as terminal. Later news photos of Humphrey leaving the hospital shocked me: I hardly recognized this cadaver-like shell as the same buoyant person who had saluted me on a KGO elevator only weeks earlier.

Still, Humphrey refused to surrender to his disease. "Life was not meant to be endured," he said. "Life was meant to be enjoyed." He gamely resumed his duties in the Senate and helped lead the battle for President Carter's legislative agenda. Despite this brave determination, news clips of Humphrey throughout 1977 depicted a progressively haggard, dying old man.

From his deathbed, Humphrey spent his final days calling old friends and political enemies to say good-bye. He made one such call to the man who had vanquished his dream in 1968, Richard Nixon, and invited him to attend his funeral.

Hubert H. Humphrey died at age sixty-six on January 13, 1978.

In the final letter he sent me a few months before the end, Humphrey encouraged me to press on with my goals for the future. He closed with this advice: "We need good, progressive, honorable young people in government and politics. So, go to it. Work hard; study hard; fight the good fight; and, my friend, be of good cheer."

Even though our political philosophies parted long before I returned to Washington as a congressman, I always tried to live by Hubert Humphrey's advice–and his example.

5

George Who?

On January 18, 1971, Senator George McGovern announced his candidacy for the 1972 Democratic nomination. These days, White House contenders start running many years before the contest, but back then, it was unprecedented for a candidate to announce twenty-two months early. The unknown McGovern needed the extra time: with heavyweight opponents lining up to run, the pundits viewed McGovern's pronouncement as quixotic. And why not? He registered only 2 percent in the Gallup poll, giving him the nickname "George Who?"

When McGovern brought his fledgling presidential candidacy to San Francisco in August 1971, his success looked so unlikely that even my collector friends Dan Swanson and Roger Mahan skipped meeting him. Instead, I conscripted my little brother, Pat, to join me. McGovern's local campaign office sent me a flyer announcing an upcoming reception, but the cost was outside my budget: three dollars a person! If we wanted to attend, we had to sneak into the event.

Pat and I staked out the front door of the hotel, hoping to see McGovern when he arrived. While waiting, we met his aide, who spoke freely about the problems of running a campaign nobody took seriously. He said McGovern usually stayed in private homes during these trips because their treasury couldn't sustain the expense of hotel accommodations.

As we spoke, a weathered station wagon pulled up to the entrance; the aide whispered, "If I tell you something, can you keep a secret? There he is now." McGovern stepped from the car with two young staffers, combed his thinning hair, put on his jacket, and greeted Pat and me as he entered the hotel. There was no danger of breaching the aide's "secret," because as McGovern smiled and nodded to the people he passed in the lobby, nobody showed any hint of recognition. Pat held the elevator for McGovern, who rode it upstairs to freshen up for his event.

Presidential candidate George McGovern walks unrecognized through the Rodeway Inn hotel, San Francisco, August 29, 1971.

The aide we befriended earlier kept riding up and down the elevator to check on the reception turnout, and then report upstairs to McGovern. He offered to get McGovern's autograph for me; I handed him a card, and the aide went back up the elevator. He returned a few minutes later with the requested signature. I asked him what McGovern was doing when he signed it. The aide smiled. "Truthfully," he replied, "he was standing naked in the bathroom, shaving."

The next time I saw McGovern, eight months later, the dynamic shifted dramatically.

· · ·

QUESTION: When is the winner the loser, and the loser the winner?
ANSWER: When the winners and losers are presidential candidates.

The above riddle is a phenomenon of politics, where expectations often count more than votes. The 1972 Democratic presidential primaries are a perfect example of this conundrum. As the gun sounded for that marathon nomination race, Senator Edmund Muskie of Maine had remained the decided frontrunner for three years leading up to 1972. Everyone expected a Muskie win in the first primary state of neighboring New Hampshire. George McGovern had remained largely unknown after over a year of campaigning, and he straggled in the polls. On primary night, Muskie did well, winning the state with almost 50 percent of the vote in a field of five contenders. McGovern lost, but his grass-roots campaign did better than expected: he came in second, with 37 percent. Immediately the pundits and network anchors proclaimed the results in their version of algebraic logic:

Muskie won, but not by whatever we define as "enough"

+

McGovern lost, but did better than we expected

=

Muskie lost the New Hampshire primary; McGovern won

The following morning, it was McGovern's name–not Muskie's–that splashed across the headlines. Next, in the pivotal Wisconsin primary, McGovern parlayed his New Hampshire momentum into a stunning first-place victory. This catapulted the near-anonymous candidate only days earlier into the acknowledged position of front-runner.

The day after his Wisconsin win, McGovern brought his now-energized campaign back to San Francisco. For weeks his local headquarters couldn't give away tickets to his scheduled fund-raising dinner at the Hilton hotel; only minutes after Wisconsin voted, the event sold out.

Today, we live in an era where tickets to political events cost thousands of dollars. It's hard to conceive that in 1972 the price tag for admission to a sit-down dinner for the leading presidential candidate at a major hotel cost twenty-five dollars. Yet, for my brother Pat and me the price may as well have been $25 million. We had no money to buy a ticket, but that didn't dissuade us from trying to get in to hear and meet McGovern.

We made the two-hour bus ride from the East Bay (where we now lived) to San Francisco, arriving at the Hilton three hours before the dinner began. We sat in the lobby, hoping to meet McGovern when he arrived. Not long after we parked ourselves, I saw a chunky man with a buzz haircut and wearing a Hilton blazer staring at us from across the room. He approached, identified himself as hotel security, and demanded we account for our presence. I explained we had taken the bus from Pinole to see McGovern in person. Once he learned we had no dinner ticket, his already unpleasant attitude became downright nasty.

"Let me give you boys some advice," he said sarcastically. "Get back on your bus to Pinole and get the hell out of here. You aren't meeting anybody in this hotel tonight."

Before we knew it, we were on the sidewalk.

Pat and I didn't surrender easily. We snuck back inside the hotel at another entrance, but the sentry grabbed us within minutes. Tossing us out once again, he warned that any further entry would result in our arrest.

I had an idea. Finding a pay telephone, I called the hotel switchboard, dropped my voice to the deepest baritone a fourteen-year-old could muster, and commanded the hotel operator to put me through to Senator McGovern's suite. To my surprise, she routed the call.

Dick Dougherty, McGovern's national campaign press secretary, answered the telephone. I explained our situation, and Dougherty proved sympathetic. He arranged for us to get freelance photographer passes and complimentary dinner tickets at the press table. Dougherty told us to have the hotel security guard call him directly if he gave us any more problems.

We returned to the hotel and waited. It didn't take long: the guard grabbed our arms and started yanking us across the lobby, saying the police were en route to arrest us for trespassing. When I told him to call Dougherty, he refused. Amid the yelling and the tugging, the hotel manager rushed over to investigate the disturbance. After hearing our explanation, the manager walked over to a courtesy phone in the foyer and called the McGovern suite. A few moments later, the manager summoned the guard to join him over in the corner. I couldn't hear their discussion, but I saw the guard's face redden as the manager spoke with him angrily while poking an index finger into his chest. The guard stalked away; the manager rejoined us, saying, "Personal guests of Senator McGovern are always welcome in this hotel."

With the event still two hours away, and while we continued our lobby stakeout, I saw McGovern strolling from the elevator bank alone and unrecognized. Pat and I introduced ourselves, and the candidate (in no apparent hurry) settled into a high-backed lobby chair and invited us to visit with him for a few minutes. "I was just going to take a walk around the block," McGovern said with a chuckle, "so I've got some time to kill." When we told him the story of the guard and Dick Dougherty, McGovern laughed. "So you're the boys, eh? Dick told me about your enterprising effort to join us tonight. We're glad to have you."

I asked McGovern about his sudden vault to the front of the presidential pack. He said he felt reluctant to claim front-runner status yet. However, he said the Wisconsin result gratified him, and he hoped the momentum would continue.

Before resuming his walk, McGovern obliged an autograph request: on an index card, he wrote out in longhand and signed his campaign slogan for me: "For Jim, I make one pledge above all others–to seek and speak the truth. With kindest regards, George McGovern."

Presidential candidate George McGovern puts his campaign pledge in writing for me, April 5, 1972

After thanking him, we watched as McGovern rode the escalator down to Geary Street. Nobody in the hotel lobby gave the Democratic front-runner a second look.

Later that evening, and shortly before the dinner began, two couples chatting nearby called us over: one man in the group said they saw us in the lobby with McGovern earlier, and he asked if we had succeeded in getting his autograph. We showed him the quotation McGovern wrote; they each looked at it and then congratulated us. It wasn't until they introduced themselves that we realized with whom we were speaking: movie star Jack Nicholson, along with fellow actors Warren Beatty, Julie Christie, and pop singer Michelle Phillips from the Mamas and the Papas.

Following the dinner, Congressman Don Edwards (D-CA) introduced McGovern to the packed, enthusiastic ballroom. I moved from the press table to the podium to snap a few photographs as the candidate urged his supporters to help him win the California primary and clinch the nomination.

At the end of McGovern's dinner, and as the crowd departed, I saw California state assemblyman (later congressman and Democratic state party chairman) John Burton; he wore on his lapel a type of McGovern campaign button I'd never seen before (or since). After introducing myself, I told him I collected political memorabilia and asked for the badge. Burton didn't want to part with it, but my youthful zeal wore him down and he relented.

By the way, as the years went by, Burton went to Congress, retired, and then in later years regained his old seat in the California legislature. Twenty-four years after he gave me the badge, Burton and I served together in the State Assembly as colleagues. One day I wore his old McGovern button and struck up a conversation with him in the chamber, waiting to see if he recognized my vintage treasure. Sure enough, after a few moments he asked about the McGovern pin on my coat. As I recounted the story, Johnny got a distant, almost wistful look on his face. When I finished, he sighed and lamented, "Those were the good old days."

I sought to draw him out: "You mean the good old days when liberalism was on the rise? You mean the days of energized college students forming grassroots armies for the Democrats? You mean the days when liberals believed they could solve the ills of the world?"

Presidential candidate George McGovern, the San Francisco Hilton, April 5, 1972

Johnny looked at me as if I were an idiot. "No," he snapped. "I don't mean any of that shit. I mean the good old days—when we could take money out of the Assembly Rules Committee budget and print up our fuckin' McGovern buttons!"

By the way, writing this memoir over forty years after Dick Dougherty helped create a fond memory for two grateful boys crashing the San Francisco Hilton, I thought he might enjoy this story, and I wanted to send him a copy

"The Good Old Days": Congressman John Burton's McGovern campaign button given to me on April 5, 1972, San Francisco Hilton

of this recollection as renewed thanks for his courtesies long ago. I looked for his address on the Internet and found this entry, dated January 2, 1987: "Richard Dougherty, . . . former New York bureau chief of the Los Angeles Times . . . [and] press secretary for Senator George McGovern . . . died of lung cancer Tuesday at a hospital in Southampton, N.Y. He was 65."[1]

Thanks again, Dick. As you can see, I never forgot your kindness.

. . .

A few years after McGovern's presidential campaign ended, I attended his speech on Cuban-American relations before the San Francisco Commonwealth Club. To a sold-out audience, McGovern called for lifting the longstanding embargo against Cuba, describing it as a "foolish sanction that has weakened [Cuban president Fidel] Castro, but forced a stronger Cuban reliance on the Soviet Union." McGovern also described his recent visit to Cuba, saying that he and Castro made an impromptu visit to the local marketplace: "The warmth of the reception given Castro was enough to bring envy to the heart of every American politician," he said.

Following his prepared remarks, he took a few questions from the floor. When asked if he might seek the presidency again in 1976, he smiled and said, "I knew that question was coming." Then he shook his head and replied, "The chances are a hundred to one against my running again. In all candor, I have

---

1   John J. Goldman, "Richard Dougherty, 65; Ex-Times Bureau Chief," *Los Angeles Times*, January 2, 1987, http://articles.latimes.com/1987-01-02/news/mn-1489—1—richard-dougherty.

no plans to run again. I have sought the advice of a few close friends as to what role I should play in the 1976 elections, whether I should speak on behalf of other candidates or whatever, but I will not be a candidate again."

Senator George McGovern, the Sheraton Palace Hotel, San Francisco, July 2, 1975

Another questioner noted that Alabama governor George Wallace, a former segregationist running to the far right of other Democratic prospects, led most Gallup polls for the 1976 nomination. When asked if he would support Wallace for the presidency if the Southerner won the Democratic nomination, McGovern's response was emphatic and brief: "No."

At the end of the lunch, McGovern spoke with me about his 1976 decision; I asked under what circumstances he might reconsider his withdrawal. "Oh, I don't know," he said with a shrug. "I'll just have to wait and see what these other guys do."

Three years earlier, as the Democratic presidential nominee, reporters and security guards had crowded every inch of McGovern's path. Now, just as I saw with so many other also-rans, McGovern left the ballroom and walked through the lobby—alone and anonymous.

· · ·

Later that year, I made my only teenage trek to Washington, DC. Before leaving, I dropped McGovern a note to let him know I would be in town; he invited me to visit him. A delay in floor votes pushed back our scheduled meeting by two hours, so I waited in his office. Finally, his secretary told me he had returned. She took me into the public hallway, unlocked an unmarked door, and escorted me into McGovern's private quarters.

McGovern sat behind his desk at the far end of the room. Dressed in a cream-colored suit, he rose from his chair and welcomed me to Washington, offering repeated apologies for keeping me waiting so long. "When you do the people's business," he said with a smile, "sometimes the people aren't in a big hurry to get matters brought to a vote!"

McGovern was full of questions about my trip and my impressions of the capital, putting me at ease with his friendly and unhurried manner. We talked about the upcoming 1976 presidential race, as well as his decision to not run again. He said the main reason he had opted out of running was because his 1972 candidacy had caused deep divisions in the Democratic Party, and he felt

Senator George McGovern and me, US Capitol, Washington, September 9, 1975

it needed a unifier in 1976. "I'm not sure that my being a candidate, and being nominated, would do that because several factions of the Party were alienated by my candidacy in 1972," he said, shaking his head in sorrow. "So I do not expect to run for president again."

I mentioned to McGovern that I had recently seen a post-Watergate Gallup poll (taken a year after Nixon clobbered McGovern) finding that, had the 1972 election been held then, McGovern would have prevailed handily. A smile crossed McGovern's face; he stepped back and leaned against his desk. "Yes, I saw the poll when it came out," he said. "I was very gratified by it. Do you know why? Because it vindicated me." Then he dropped his voice to a whisper and looked out the window as he said it again, almost whistfully: "It vindicated me."

I brought with me the photograph I had taken of McGovern at the Commonwealth Club a few months earlier (see page 31) and asked him to autograph it. He took the photo from me, sat behind his desk, slid on his reading glasses, and studied it carefully. "You took this?" he asked with a touch of surprise at my youthful effort. "You know, it's a very, very good picture!"

As McGovern began to inscribe it, I raised my camera to take a couple of candid photos while he signed. When McGovern noticed my camera, he quickly slid off his reading glasses and placed them on his desk. Apparently, even with a quiet, humble man like McGovern, vanity prevailed over good penmanship.

. . .

I stayed in touch with McGovern over the years. In 1994, after I won a seat in the California legislature, McGovern remembered his old campaign volunteer of long ago and called to congratulate me on my victory. Later that year we reunited at a couple of conferences hosted by ALEC (the American Legislative Exchange Council), a national forum

Senator George McGovern signing a photograph I had taken previously (note the reading glasses tossed hastily on his desk), US Capitol, September 9, 1975

for conservative state legislators. The liberal McGovern proved an unlikely but very popular speaker before this group.

In August 1994, at one of these conferences, McGovern joined Newt Gingrich (still a relatively obscure Georgia congressman but destined for political superstardom two months later, when he led Republicans to seize control of the House of Representatives for the first time in forty years). More than a thousand conferees crowded into the breakfast, with many there out of sheer curiosity as to why ALEC had paired this leading American liberal with a black-belt conservative champion.

A Democratic legislator (one of the few at the conference) introduced McGovern, who joked about the dearth of liberals in attendance: "I am pleased to be introduced by one of the select few at this conference who voted right in 1972!" McGovern then related a story about his presidential run:

> One of the joys of running for president is that it gives one the opportunity to visit every state in the Union. In 1972 I carried only one state, but I fell in love with all of them. Pardon me if I say I carry a special place in my heart for Massachusetts [the only state McGovern carried], but I love them all. I remember a time during the 1972 Florida primary when I was to fly in for a large airport rally. When we landed, only a few mechanics were on the tarmac. We later learned that our problem was that we landed in the wrong town. As one of my rivals later noted, "If McGovern can't find the right town, how can he run the country?" America will never know! My parents were old-fashioned conservatives who believed that the least government is the best government. I have often wondered if they had lived to 1972 whether they would have voted for me. I am sure they might have been sympathetic, but it would have been a hard sell!

Alluding to his famous bent for liberalism, McGovern recalled the last time he had addressed an ALEC conference: "When last I spoke at one of your conferences, I had my arm in a sling. I had fallen down on a slippery Washington street outside the Avalon Theater on a rainy day and broke my shoulder. A Republican neighbor asked me what shoulder I broke. I told him it was my left shoulder. He said, 'McGovern, you're so liberal you can't even fall to the right!'"

After the laughter subsided, McGovern told the story he had come to share: after leaving the Senate in 1981, he'd bought a small hotel in Connecticut with his life savings. Eventually the hotel failed, despite his hiring an experienced manager:

The experience taught me that a small businessman faces a plethora of federal, state and local regulations. My manager burned the midnight oil not trying to make the hotel profitable, but to keep up with the compliance requirements of regulations. I was also sued over an injury at the hotel. A drunk left the hotel bar and got into a fight in the parking lot. He was hurt and he sued me, saying the hotel should have provided him more security. We did have a security guard and lights outside, but a small business cannot afford to station the Marine Corps in its parking lot. We won the lawsuit, but not without a large expenditure of money. I was later sued when a lady tripped and broke her hip. These fraudulent and frivolous lawsuits are hurting small businesses.

McGovern called for comprehensive tort reform and suggested three ways it might occur: "The first way would be for self-correction by the American Bar Association, but I do not expect that to happen [laughter]. The second alternative would be for Congress to enact it, but I am not optimistic that will happen. The third route is tort reform in the states, and this is where it has to happen. These excessive lawsuits take the civility out of society. When I fell and broke my shoulder, it was an accident. It never occurred to me to sue someone over it."

McGovern's partial reversal from his previous endorsement of big government and more regulation was greeted with a standing ovation. When Gingrich was introduced, he shook his head in disbelief and said, "I never thought I would hear myself say this, but I agree with everything George McGovern just said!"[2]

Later, McGovern greeted me warmly and wanted to know how I liked the legislature over being a trial court judge. He was full of questions about my new life in politics, and took some measure of pride in the fact that I'd started off as a kid working on his campaign a quarter century earlier. However, when McGovern told my new colleague, assemblyman Curt Pringle (then assistant Republican Assembly leader and later Speaker) that I was one of his favorite Republicans, it caused Curt to question my conservative bona fides–forever!

---

2   At the conclusion of the seminar, a colleague introduced me to Gingrich. He said he heard about my replacing his old friend Pat Nolan in the legislature and wished me luck. Newt and I didn't know each other yet, but that would change in a couple of years when I joined him in Washington.

I wanted Curt Pringle in this picture so he couldn't tease me before GOP colleagues about my friendship with George McGovern! From left: Assembly GOP assistant leader Curt Pringle, me, and former senator George McGovern, Hyatt Regency hotel, Tampa, Florida, August 6, 1994

A few months later, McGovern and Gingrich brought their act on the road to the ALEC winter conference in Washington, DC. This time Gingrich received a reception reserved normally for rock stars: after having delivered a crushing defeat to House Democrats a few weeks earlier, Gingrich prepared to become the first GOP Speaker since 1954. McGovern reiterated to the audience his change of heart on tort reform, and cited his failed hotel venture in Connecticut as the policy wake-up call he received. Then, shifting his tone, he took Gingrich to task over comments the Speaker-designate had made recently: "Newt and I have become good friends," McGovern said, "but I was bothered when he recently called President and Mrs. Clinton a couple of 'counter-culture McGovernites.'

> "Over the years," he continued, "I have heard people accused of being radical liberals called 'McGovernites' or 'McGoverniks.' I started as a noun, and now I am an adjective! I must confess I never really understood it. I served in World War II and flew thirty-five bombing missions. I have gone to war, I was the son of a Methodist minister, and I have been married to the same woman for fifty years. I do not feel I am part of any counterculture."

McGovern then joked about the results of the Republican sweep of Congress a few weeks earlier. "Judging from your broad smiles," he told the conservative audience, "I can tell most of you enjoyed the results of November 8!"

When I saw the results of this election, I felt pretty much as I had in 1972, when I lost forty-nine of fifty states. The first Senate colleague I'd run into after my defeat was Barry Goldwater, the 1964 Republican presidential nominee, who had also lost in a landslide. Barry later sent over a cartoon to me with the caption "If you must lose, lose big!" I'd thought it was a joke, but Barry later told me he was serious. When next we saw each other, Barry had explained what he meant by the cartoon. "In 1960 Dick Nixon lost the presidency to John F. Kennedy by less than a hundred thousand votes," he had said. "Nixon spent the next eight years torturing himself, saying things like, 'If only I had gone to Chicago that last weekend instead of Alaska, I might have won.'

"George," Barry had comforted me, "in our case, it wouldn't have mattered how many times we went to Chicago!"

At the end of his speech, McGovern remained at the head table, signing autographs and posing for pictures. Before leaving, he called me over and said he heard I might be running for Congress in the next cycle. "You know, Jim, if you run, as a Democrat I won't be able to endorse you," he said apologetically. "But the fact I can't endorse you doesn't mean I can't take great pride in you if you win."

That meant much more to me than an endorsement.

. . .

When I went to Congress in 1997, McGovern and I saw each other occasionally. My favorite visit with him was when he invited my family to his office, but that and other tales must wait for my next book, on stories from Congress.

I last saw McGovern—of all places—when he spoke at the presidential library of the man who had beaten him in 1972: at age eighty-eight, he gave a talk and did a book signing at the Richard Nixon Library in 2009. As an elegant touch, all the Nixon Library employees and docents wore old "McGovern" campaign buttons on their lapels to welcome the aging former candidate.

. . .

George McGovern died of natural causes in a hospice facility at age ninety on October 21, 2012. Although my reputation in Congress was as a conservative Republican, I always considered it an honor and a blessing to know this kind man and devoted public servant.

Senator George McGovern and me, 1995

6

Mr. Conservative

I f US senator Barry Goldwater didn't invent the modern conservative political movement, he brought it out of the shadows and started its march to the mainstream. As the 1964 Republican presidential nominee, he railed against New Deal liberalism and argued for a constitutional paradigm of individual responsibility and personal freedom. Although Goldwater led the GOP to a landslide defeat against Incumbent President Lyndon B. Johnson that year, from these trenches charged an army of young conservative warriors that learned how to organize, fight, and (eventually) win. The DNA of Barry Goldwater's 1964 effort runs through the 1980 victory of his ideological heir, Ronald Reagan.

As a young boy, I met Goldwater several times. The first was at the California Republican Party State Convention in 1972, when Goldwater spoke at the two-day event also headlined by New York governor (later vice president) Nelson Rockefeller, senator (later 1996 GOP presidential nominee) Bob Dole, and California governor Ronald Reagan. At age fourteen, I snookered the state GOP media officer into giving me full press accreditation, which included complimentary meals and tickets to all events at the St. Francis Hotel conference in San Francisco.

In the Grand Ballroom, awaiting Goldwater's arrival for the evening banquet, I saw seated at the head table Edgar Bergen, the famed ventriloquist who, with his dummy Charlie McCarthy, had been one of the biggest stars of radio's "Golden Age." I introduced myself to Bergen, a kindly gentleman who seemed impressed to have a fan born long after his fame had ebbed. He signed a couple autographs for me; alongside one he sketched a small picture of Charlie McCarthy, complete with top hat and monocle.

At 8:15 p.m. Goldwater entered the ballroom to great applause. When everyone had settled down to dinner, I approached the head table and introduced myself to Goldwater, who was very pleasant–despite my talking him into signing nine autographs for me on various photos and 1964 campaign items. While he signed, I asked him what it was like to be the presidential nominee of a major party. He stated he had just finished writing an article on that subject and offered to send it to me, adding that the main lesson from his experience was this: "You've never been beaten in your life until you've been beaten for the presidency of the United States." When I asked if he might ever run again, he shook his head and said, "No, I'm too old now."

The program began with Bergen as master of ceremonies. He entertained the audience with stories about his years in radio and working with great comedians such as W. C. Fields. Although he didn't bring his famous wooden sidekick, the old showman needed no crutch to entertain the delighted audience.

Bergen introduced Goldwater, who received another standing ovation. I moved from the press table to the podium and knelt directly under Goldwater to take pictures. I wanted to use my new 8-millimeter home movie camera, but the hum of its motor proved so loud that Bergen (no longer the kindly gentleman) put his finger to his lips, gave me a cross look, and said, "Shhh!" I turned off the camera and skulked back to my seat.

Goldwater waved the audience to silence, adjusted his eyeglasses, and then read a greatly abbreviated excerpt from his prepared speech. He apologized for cutting short his remarks, explaining he had to catch a flight back to Washington that night for an important (but unexpected) Senate vote the following morning. However, he didn't relinquish the microphone without both whacking the Democrats and delivering a ringing endorsement of the Nixon administration. Then, with a brief wave, Goldwater disappeared out a side door.

Card signed for me by Senator Barry Goldwater and comedian Edgar Bergen (and Charlie McCarthy), St. Francis Hotel, San Francisco, May 13, 1972

. . .

On the tenth anniversary of Barry Goldwater winning the 1964 Republican presidential nomination at San Francisco's Cow Palace, Goldwater returned to the city of his convention victory to commemorate it with a speech to the annual Young Americans for Freedom (YAF) conference. Comprised of young conservatives, YAF members viewed Goldwater's nomination as their political high-water mark; now they looked to California governor Ronald Reagan as their hope for the future. Once organizers announced that both Goldwater and Reagan had accepted invitations to speak, the conference sold out in an hour.

With a ticket to the event in hand, I arrived at the Sheraton Palace Hotel for the kickoff of the forum. Concession booths outside the banquet room sold vintage Goldwater-Miller campaign buttons from 1964 and "YAF Backs Barry" badges. The hottest-selling badge, however, read simply, "Goldwater in 1976." Other big sellers were bumper stickers lambasting current Democratic leaders, like Edward Kennedy and George McGovern ("Teddy Kennedy–Unsafe at Any Speed,"[1] and "Acid–Amnesty Appeasement; Vote McGovern").

In a cavernous ballroom packed with YAFers and reporters, I overheard a panicked discussion between two conference officers: Goldwater's flight from Washington was delayed; they might need to cancel his much-anticipated appearance. By 8:30 p.m., dinner was over and Goldwater remained a no-show. However, the crowd remained patient: I suspected the YAFers might stay all night if necessary to see Goldwater.

Two hours after waiters collected the empty dinner plates, an excited voice down the hallway cried out, "Here he comes!" Klieg lights and flashbulbs went off as Goldwater entered the room to a hero's welcome. The YAFers jumped to their feet, chanting "We want Barry! We want Barry!"

Admirers besieged Goldwater as the escort committee brought him to the head table; he took his seat, with cheers still ringing throughout the room. Congressman Sam Steiger introduced him as "the greatest living statesman this country has ever had." With the audience again roaring for him, Goldwater

---

1   A reference to Kennedy's 1969 controversial traffic accident, where a young, single woman drowned in his car when Kennedy drove it off a bridge at Chappaquiddick after leaving a late-night party with her.

walked to the podium. A Hawaiian hula girl placed a lei around his neck and kissed him on the lips. Goldwater turned to the whooping throng, smiled, and shook the lei up and down (splashing water drops all over the front of his light-gray suit).

Senator Barry Goldwater, the Sheraton Palace Hotel, San Francisco, July 18, 1974

After motioning the crowd to silence, Goldwater thanked everyone for waiting for him to arrive. Then he reminisced about the night ten years earlier when he had waited in a small anteroom to be introduced to the convention "as the nominee for an office I knew I could not win."

Goldwater departed from his prepared text to add a personal observation about the Republican Party, which was now reeling over the current Watergate scandal engulfing the doomed Nixon administration: "We have been going morally downhill for thirty or forty years. I thought we'd have something like this [Watergate scandal], but I thought it would be under someone else's administration–and I won't mention his name. But we'll survive it. Our people are tough. This country is so tough that not even the *New York Times* or the *Washington Post* can hurt it."

. . .

After his speech I met Goldwater and had the chance to talk with him briefly. Although he again said he'd never run for president again, he expressed the hope that his 1964 effort might pave the way for another conservative candidate to win the White House in 1976 or 1980.

"By the way," he said to me, "I understand Ronald Reagan is speaking here tomorrow."

. . .

During my first trip to Washington, DC, I saw Barry Goldwater occasionally while I roamed the Capitol building. He turned me down politely each time I asked if I could meet him for advice on getting into politics (his busy legislative schedule didn't permit it). As far as asking for his autograph, I didn't need another: in 1973, when his mood proved more receptive, he wrote out and signed for me his famous (or, to Democrats, infamous) quotation from his 1964 GOP convention acceptance speech. Although Democrats jumped on the phrase to show Goldwater was an "extremist," he never backed down from the sentiment (as his willingness to memorialize it for me shows):

Presidential candidate Barry Goldwater's famous phrase from his 1964 Republican nomination acceptance speech: "Extremism in the defense of liberty is no vice; moderation in the pursuit of justice is no virtue."

. . .

Barry Goldwater retired from the US Senate in 1987. Even out of office, he remained active in politics for another decade until suffering a massive stroke in 1996. He died at age eighty-nine on May 29, 1998.

In late 1978, comedian and ventriloquist Edgar Bergen announced his retirement after fifty-six years in show business. He played a farewell engagement at Caesar's Palace in Las Vegas; later that night, he died in his sleep at age seventy-five on September 27, 1978. His sidekick of over five decades, Charlie McCarthy, today is on display in the Smithsonian Institution.

7

My Governor

I was a young boy growing up in San Francisco when Ronald Reagan became my state's governor. I met him many times before he left Sacramento to chart his course that led to Washington. Just a few of my recollections from those early encounters follow.

The first time I ever saw Reagan in person was also the first time in my life that I ever saw someone famous. It was June 26, 1970, when I was in the seventh grade. Hundreds of international dignitaries had come to San Francisco for the twenty-fifth anniversary of the signing of the United Nations charter at the old Opera House (where the original charter was signed on that date in 1945). My classmate Jon Jacobs and I talked his father into driving us downtown and dropping us off near city hall. From there we were twelve-year-old boys on our own for the entire day to explore the City and the ceremony, without parental supervision (and also without admission tickets to the event).

When the opening ceremonies convened at the Opera House, Jon and I schemed on how we might sneak inside, circling the outer perimeter of the building and looking for a chink in the security armor. After several failed attempts, we prepared to give up. While standing in defeat, with our noses pressed against a large iron gate, I saw a few men exit through a side door and enter a black limousine; the car then circled and passed slowly in front of us. An old man standing nearby yelled out, "Well, hello-o-o, Ronnie!"

I looked up and saw the ruggedly familiar features of Governor Reagan, who smiled and waved to Jon and me as his car rolled past us slowly. My reflexes were too slow to have my camera in position, so I contented myself with a returned wave. It was only a brief glimpse, but I spent days telling anyone willing to listen how Governor Reagan had waved to me personally.[1]

Governor Ronald Reagan's surprise gift after my Opera House encounter, 1970

A couple of weeks later, I wrote Reagan and recounted our Opera House sighting of him, and lamented that Jon and I hadn't had the presence of mind

---

1   Eventually, we coaxed two bored delegates from India into giving us their admission tickets; we got to watch the rest of the ceremony from their reserved seats.

to flag him down to shake his hand and get an autograph. Soon thereafter a package came from Sacramento: inside was a letter from Reagan's secretary saying the governor enjoyed my message; enclosed were two large, inscribed photographs of Reagan–one for Jon and one for me. He asked me to deliver the extra photo to Jon on the governor's behalf.

That proved easier said than done: between seeing Reagan and getting the photographs, we moved and I lost track of Jon. We didn't reconnect again until thirty years later–after Reagan's presidency had come to an end. I turned over the treasure to Jon as instructed decades earlier. As they say, better late than never. Truthfully, it proved a little painful to let the picture go: Jon ended up a lifelong Democrat!

. . .

I first met Ronald Reagan on May 13, 1972, when the California Republican Party held its annual convention at the St. Francis Hotel in San Francisco (see the background on this in my previous chapter, "Mr. Conservative").

By the time I arrived at the hotel for the event that Saturday morning, scores of angry protesters had assembled across the street in Union Square and started throwing rocks; police in full riot gear waded into the mob to restore order. I raised my movie camera to shoot footage of the fracas, but before I could start filming, a rock thrown from the crowd bounced off my lens and knocked the camera out of my hands. I might have been pretty bold at age fourteen, but I wasn't an idiot–I hastened to safety inside the St. Francis.

I found a seat in the Grand Ballroom in time to see Governor Reagan arrive for his opening address. The delegates jumped to their feet and cheered madly for Reagan; his brief remarks hit all the right buttons: strengthening and building the GOP base, attacking Democrats as big-spending liberals, and urging President Nixon's reelection in November. At the conclusion of his speech, he waved to the crowd and then stepped from the podium into a thicket of security agents there to escort him out of the hotel quickly. I had hoped to meet Reagan, but given his heavy guard and the crush of so many fans, that looked unlikely.

Reagan made for the exit, and then, suddenly, he changed direction and came directly toward me. As he passed, I saw a crack in his security net; I stepped through the gap and found myself swept inside "the bubble" and directly next to the governor. Reagan shook my hand and greeted me. When I asked him for the autograph, he took my item: "Sure," he said. "Why don't you walk with me while I sign it?" As we strolled together, a phalanx of press photographers kept their cameras trained on us. Although I never received a copy, in newspaper morgue files somewhere are pictures memorializing my first meeting with a man who went on to change the destiny of the world.

Reagan handed back the autograph, shook my hand, and wished me luck in school as he climbed into his waiting limousine. Throughout the rest of the day, convention delegates kept asking me in awe, "Aren't you the boy that was walking with the governor this morning?"

. . .

During Ronald Reagan's last year as governor, the battle to succeed him was in high gear on the Republican side. Shortly before the GOP primary, party leaders organized the "Governor's Dinner," both as a salute to Reagan and a chance for the two leading Republican gubernatorial candidates to put away their knives for an early show of unity.

On March 20, 1974, Dan Swanson, Roger Mahan, and I arrived at the Sheraton Palace Hotel in San Francisco an hour before the scheduled banquet. Taking a page from my earlier playbook, I telephoned Governor Reagan's room and spoke with his assistant press secretary, Rudy Garcia, who (I know—it's hard to believe how many times I pulled off this hat trick as a kid) gave all three of us press passes and complimentary tickets for the dinner with Reagan.

At 7:00 p.m., Reagan and his entourage appeared in the lobby and entered the "Convention Sales and Catering" room. He remained inside for ten minutes in a private meeting with the candidates battling to succeed him. When Reagan reappeared, he saw our young trio and invited us to join him as he entered the ballroom. Talk about three kids making a grand entrance into a political main event!

The program opened with remarks by David Packard, the chairman of Hewlett-Packard. After the obligatory speeches of both GOP gubernatorial candidates, the evening belonged to Ronald Reagan. Packard introduced him to a thunderous ovation. Reagan smiled and waved, and then settled into his half-hour speech. It proved vintage Reagan, who attacked the tax-and-spend Democrats while defending with gusto the accomplishments of his outgoing administration. Stressing the urgent need for California to elect a Republican successor, Reagan pledged his full support to the winner of the primary campaign.

When the dinner adjourned, Dan, Roger, and I approached Reagan at the head table. He autographed a few items for me, most notably an original Turf Cigarette trading card from the 1940s featuring Reagan in a football uniform and listing him as a Warner Bros. star. Reagan put on his glasses to study the card more closely; then he smiled and penned his name to it. "Hey, you've quite a collection here," he chuckled.

I did and each time I got the chance, I let Ronald Reagan add to it!

. . .

In the 1990s, the Flat Stanley Project swept schoolchildren by storm. Students cut out and decorated a paper doll (Flat Stanley). They mailed him to friends and family around the world, asked that they treat him as a visiting guest for a few days, write down his activities, and then return him home with the diary and a photograph taken of him in his temporary city. After collecting enough of these stories, each student wrote a report telling of Flat Stanley's journeys.

I have a piece of political memorabilia that is my equivalent of Flat Stanley, and Ronald Reagan gave it to me. It not only traveled far and returned; it (unlike Flat Stanley) changed my life—and maybe history, as you will see.

On June 13, 1973, Governor Ronald Reagan appeared as guest of honor for a luncheon at the Boundary Oak restaurant in Walnut Creek, California. Unbelievable by today's standards, but back then the cost of attending a private reception and sit-down lunch with Reagan (and speech) at an exclusive country club cost only six dollars. Of course, as a young teenager, I didn't have the price of

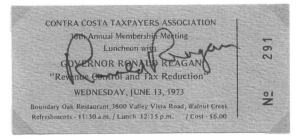

Original ticket to Governor Reagan's reception and speech, Boundary Oak restaurant, Walnut Creek, June 13, 1973. Note the $6 admission price! I found this ticket on a table during the reception and had Governor Reagan autograph it.

Governor Ronald Reagan and me, Boundary Oak restaurant, Walnut Creek, California, June 13, 1973

admission (if you have gotten this far in my book, you know by now how I got in)… By the way, to the hostess who left the entrance door unattended momentarily that day, I send my deepest thanks across these many years.

Reagan arrived at noon and was besieged by admirers. Later, while others ate, he enjoyed little of the lunch served that day. Instead, he spent most of his time shaking hands and signing autographs for admirers like me.

After meeting the governor, and shortly before the program began, Reagan sat at the head table, reviewing his speech notes. While I took pictures, I noticed something intriguing about those notes: they were hand-written (not typed) on a stack of four-by-six-inch index cards. I decided to ask Reagan to give them to me for my collection when the program ended.

Governor Ronald Reagan reviews his speech notes before his remarks at the Boundary Oak restaurant, Walnut Creek, California, June 13, 1973

…

After Reagan finished his speech, his security detail whisked him to a private room elsewhere in the restaurant for a meeting with state legislators. The number of luncheon guests lingering outside waiting for him dwindled gradually over the next several hours. Finally, only two people remained waiting for Reagan: a ten-year-old boy holding a vintage Brownie camera, and me.

Three hours after Reagan disappeared with the legislators, his aide told us that Reagan was about to leave, but not from the entrance where we waited: Reagan's security detail had brought his car to a side entrance by the rear parking lot, and the aide suggested we change to that location if we wanted to see the governor before he departed. As I followed the boy outside to the lot, I saw Reagan entering his car as we hit the exit door. The boy with the Brownie missed his shot. Unaware of our presence, Reagan settled into the rear of his limousine, and the motorcade started pulling away.

Just then, Reagan happened to look over his shoulder and saw the boy holding the old camera, with his young face etched in disappointment. Reagan leaned forward and said something to the driver. The limousine stopped, backed up to where the boy stood, and Reagan rolled down his window.

"Hi, son!" Reagan called out to the boy cheerfully. "Were you waiting to take a picture of me?" The boy's mouth gaped open.

With no reporters or crowd around to witness his act of generosity, Reagan climbed out of the car, greeted the boy, posed for him, and then had an aide snap their picture together. Reagan then turned and looked at me, as if asking silently what I wanted. Here was my chance for those speech notes!

When I shook hands with Reagan, I praised his luncheon presentation, told him about my collection, and then asked about his speech notes: "Governor," I said, "while you were sitting and reviewing them at lunch, I saw they were all handwritten. Did you write them out yourself?"

"Why, yes, I did," he replied. When I asked if I could see them, he pulled them from his coat pocket and handed them to me. While I leafed through the cards, Reagan told me he had written them the night before in his hotel room. He explained that with today's speech at the Boundary Oak, he had formally kicked off his campaign for Proposition 1, a statewide ballot initiative to both reduce state income taxes and place a constitutional limit on the percentage of income the state could take. Calling this the "signature initiative of my administration," Reagan told me he had spent three hours last night working on the speech because of its significance.[2]

---

2   Reagan's Proposition 1 lost at the polls, but it was the precursor for California's Proposition 13, the 1978 Jarvis-Gann Initiative, which passed overwhelmingly and also set off a national copycat revolt.

It was now or never: "Governor, can I have them?"

Reagan grimaced at my request. "Well," he said with a heavy sigh, "you see, I'll need to give this speech more than once, and I don't have another copy of it. My staff will kill me if I don't come back with it."

Sensing my opportunity slipping away and remembering how the sad-faced boy with the Brownie camera had played on Reagan's sympathy earlier, I tried the same ploy. I dropped my head and feigned grievous disappointment. "I know all about the three hours you worked on it," I said with a fake crack in my voice. "That's how long I waited to ask you for them." I wiped a nonexistent tear from my eye.

Reagan shook his head in defeat. "Okay," he exclaimed with sigh. "You win. You may not be able to make heads or tails out of my writing, but here they are."

With my cry-fest ending instantly, I handed back the last note card to Reagan: "These are no damned good if you don't autograph them!"

Smiling and shaking his head at my brazenness, he penned his name on the last card and returned it to me. Reagan then showed me that on each speech card, his handwritten notes were on one side for today's speech, and on the other side were speech notes typed in large black font. Reagan explained that the typed side was his reading copy of a speech he'd delivered earlier to a Cali-

Governor Ronald Reagan's speech notes from the Boundary Oak restaurant, Walnut Creek, June 13, 1973 (Reagan signed the last page)

fornia Highway Patrol audience. Not one to waste paper, Reagan said he used the back of the CHP speech to handwrite his speech notes for today's event. "So you see," Reagan said, "you're really getting two speeches for the price of one."

. . .

The rest of the story:

Eight years later, when voters installed Ronald Reagan into the White House, I was a student at UCLA Law School. A financial crisis hit, and I needed fifteen hundred dollars to pay for tuition and expenses, or else I risked losing my place in school. Knowing of my dire straits, a collector offered me the needed fifteen hundred dollars for Reagan's speech notes. I refused to sell, telling him the president had given those to me as a gift, and I'd never part with them. However, as time ran out for me to come up with the money, and faced with the choice of being kicked out of school or selling the notes, I had no choice other than to part with them. However, I refused to sell the entire set: I kept page 1 of Reagan's notes in my collection, and sold pages 2–8. I used the proceeds to pay my tuition; soon after, I graduated, passed the bar exam, and my career took its course.

Almost thirty years after Reagan handed over to me his speech notes in that parking lot, and after I served as a House manager in the US Senate impeachment trial of President Clinton, I had lunch with Clinton's White House counsel (and my friend) Lanny Davis. We talked about impeachment over hamburgers; Lanny told me that during the House Judiciary Committee hearings, the White House staff called me "the Domino." I asked why; Lanny explained they had identified enough GOP committee members reluctant to vote for impeachment, but those congressmen wanted to watch what I did because I was the only former prosecutor and judge on the committee. He said these reluctant members felt that if an ex-prosecutor and judge looked at the evidence and voted no, it gave them "cover" to do the same: "We knew if we could flip you our way, the others would follow, and we could have killed impeachment in committee." I thought the insight was interesting, but believed it overestimated my limited influence. Nevertheless, Lanny insisted they had the votes to defeat impeachment if their linchpin (me) voted no.

Not long after this lunch, I spent a rare afternoon off the campaign trail and relaxed by sifting through my memorabilia collection. When I came upon page 1 of Reagan's old speech notes, I looked at it for a long time, thinking about what Lanny had told me. If Ronald Reagan hadn't given me those notes at Boundary Oak in 1973, I wouldn't have finished law school, which meant I would never have become a prosecutor, judge, state legislator, congressman, member of the House Judiciary Committee, or House manager in the impeachment trial. Would that changed circumstance have mattered to the ultimate impeachment vote?

Who knows?

Still, as I reflected on this possible chain reaction, and suffering renewed pining over the forced sale of pages 2–8, I hoped that Reagan would forgive me if he knew I'd sold the notes to finish my education and embark on a life of public service. Somehow, I felt he would.

Weeks later, I was flipping through an auction catalog of political memorabilia for sale. I almost fell out of my chair when I turned the page and saw Auction Lot #73: it was pages 2–8 of my old Reagan speech note cards! The original purchaser had died, and his heirs had put his collection up for sale, including the notes I'd sold him. I placed my bid on the notes, and then monitored the bidding by telephone on the night of the auction.

When the sun rose the next morning, Auction Lot #73–Ronald Reagan's Boundary Oak restaurant speech notes from 1973–came home.[3]

---

3   Martin Anderson (a former Reagan adviser who wrote books sourced from Reagan's handwritten archives) told me a few years ago that his research showed my Boundary Oak note cards are the only known complete set of Reagan's famous four-by-six-inch handwritten speech notes outside the possession of the Reagan Library. More important, they are the *only* complete set known to exist anywhere that Reagan also autographed. Apparently, nobody thought to ask Reagan to sign his speech cards before I came along, and nobody bothered to ask after.

8

Valhalla

National nominating conventions are to political junkies and campaign memorabilia collectors what Valhalla is to a dead Viking, so my boyhood dream was to attend one. In early 1972 I got my chance when I received a letter from Thomas Bell, chairman of the Young Voters for the President (YVP) delegation to the 1972 Republican National Convention in Miami. Bell wanted to organize three thousand young volunteers to help staff the convention. For only $280, the GOP committee offered round-trip airfare from California to Florida, hotel rooms and meals for a week, and tickets to the convention to see President Richard Nixon and Vice President Spiro Agnew renominated. However, there was a hitch: the YVP's limited eligibility to registered Republican voters ages eighteen to thirty. I was a fourteen-year-old kid, and a Democrat, to boot, but so what? The Democrats didn't invite me to their convention; the Republicans did.

There was a second hitch: I needed to convince my mother to let me fly cross-country alone and spend a week on the East Coast, with no adult supervision. When I asked for permission, I got the anticipated response.

"Mom," I countered, "I'll be with twenty thousand Republicans–how much trouble can I get in?" Since she couldn't think of an answer, she told me to have a good time.

I scraped together the money and sent it to the Republican National Committee. My application came from "Jim Rogan, Republican, age twenty-six." Soon I received my confirmed reservation aboard the "Miami Special" departing Los Angeles International Airport at midnight on August 18, 1972.

. . .

I was unprepared for the anarchy of our charter flight to Miami. From the moment our plane went "wheels up," passengers jumped from their seats and the in-flight party began. Someone pried open the liquor galley and passed out now-complimentary bottles to all takers. Rock music blasted through the cabin, and people danced on the seats. Recognizing the futility of trying to preserve order, our stewardess crew kicked off their shoes and pillbox hats and joined in the revelry.

Growing up in San Francisco, I always heard you could tell a Republican by his or her hair color: gray for men and blue for women. My traveling companions smashed that stuffy stereotype: they were young, hip, loud, and (within minutes of takeoff) drunk. As I surveyed the raucous scene, I remembered what I'd said to convince Mom to let me go on this unsupervised weeklong escapade. Now I asked myself the same question I had put to her, but the emphasis changed: How much trouble *could* I get into with Republicans?

My late-twenties seatmate–I'll call her Bambi–offered a potential answer to that question. At first, she presented a severe contrast to the other partying passengers. Bambi's old-fashioned blouse buttoned all the way up her neck-high collar; she wore glasses, her hair in a bun, a long skirt, and cloddy shoes. We struck up a friendly but reserved conversation. As the plane reached its cruising altitude, she drank a glass of wine–and then more of them. Soon the upper buttons on her librarian blouse loosened up as much as her previously reserved persona. The bobby pins came out, piles of chestnut locks dropped past her shoulders, and the nurse shoes disappeared.

Somewhere over Kansas, a deeply relaxed Bambi reached over and took my hand. Looking over the top of her eyeglasses at me, she said, "You really seem like a nice guy. You're easy to talk to. May I tell you something?"

"Sure," I said innocently.

"I have a bit of a problem," she teased. After assuring her I could be trusted with her secret, she let it fly: "I'm . . . well . . . I'm a nymphomaniac."

Even at fourteen, I knew what that meant.

Then Bambi leaned toward me and appeared to size me up. "Say," she asked through half-opened eye slits, "how old did you say you are?"

We looked at each other in silence for a few beats before I answered: "Bambi,

I'll tell you the truth. I lied on my application. I wrote back to the national committee and said I was twenty-six because I really wanted to come to the convention. But it's not true."

"So how old are you?"

I cleared my throat: "Bambi, I'm thirty-two."

As a young boy growing up in a pro-union, Democratic, San Francisco household, I couldn't understand why anyone would want to be a Republican. Now, as our airborne jubilee continued winging throughout the night, I recognized for the first time that America did indeed have a vigorous two-party system, and that perhaps I shouldn't be so hasty in deciding which one suited me better . . . .

My security credentials to the 1972 Republican National Convention; here I am depicted at age 14 . . . I mean age 26 . . . I mean age 32 . . .

. . .

Our charter plane arrived in Miami the next morning. Once we landed, organizers packed our time with campaign and convention-related events. Since President Nixon faced no serious opposition, the thousands of enthusiastic Republicans descending on Florida gathered for a coronation, not combat.

Later that afternoon I attended a rally for Vice President Agnew at the Americana Hotel. At the conclusion of the event, and always looking for a chance to add to my collection, I shimmied up a pole mounted near the platform and yanked the convention seal off a speaker's podium. If I met any dignitaries, I thought this might be a unique item on which to collect autographs. As it turned out, I was not disappointed.

. . .

Nautilus Middle School in Miami has a significant bit of unknown historical trivia that might surprise their faculty and students: over a two-day period in 1972, three future presidents of the United States visited their small site. I know because I was there.

August 21 was the first full day of the convention. I boarded an early morning shuttle to Nautilus, now designated as the YVP holding center during convention week. With summer recess, the vacant school proved useful for assembling the army of young Nixon volunteers. Organizers erected a large outdoor tent on the athletic field; we encamped under the tent during convention downtime throughout the week.

At noon, a station wagon pulled up on the grounds. Out stepped a middle-aged man with thinning brown hair, wearing gray slacks and a yellow open-neck shirt–Congressman Gerald R. Ford, the House minority leader. Recovering from recent knee surgery to correct an old football injury, Ford hobbled on a cane over to our holding tent. An organizer summoned the volunteers together and introduced Ford to us.

Many of the YVPs were indifferent to hearing or meeting the rather obscure congressman; while Ford spoke, most volunteers remained in the back of the tent, painting rally signs, blowing up balloons, or napping. For those of us listening, Ford kept his remarks brief. He welcomed the YVPs to Miami and thanked everyone for their efforts on behalf of the Nixon–Agnew ticket. He then urged us to return home at the end of the convention and work very hard to deliver a Republican congressional majority in November. This, Ford added, would bring him his greatest personal ambition–becoming the next Speaker of the US House of Representatives.

Ford mingled with the volunteers, signing autographs and answering questions. His knee pain appeared to aggravate with time: when he signaled his readiness to go, an aide had to assist him back to the car. Ford slid his cane underneath the seat and waved as the station wagon pulled away.

The next day, Miami's brutally hot and muggy weather (combined with no air-conditioning unit under our tent) left the cluster of YVPs increasingly lethargic. Even the free Pepsi concession stand failed to bring much relief, since all the ice melted quickly in the heat. The sluggish spirit evaporated suddenly when a car pulled up to the tent and someone shouted excitedly, "It's Governor Reagan!"

Unlike the reception accorded Congressman Ford, volunteers ran from all corners of the school and crammed underneath the tent to see Reagan as he stepped from his automobile to great cheers.

During convention week, the parade of guest speakers visiting us wilted quickly in the heat: neckties didn't last long, collar buttons loosened unceremoniously, and dress shirts drenched in perspiration. Reagan proved the exception; he looked crisp and fresh throughout. The other speakers generated only mild interest; Reagan's surprise appearance merited a reception accorded a teen idol.

Reagan discussed the Nixon campaign, the important convention efforts of the YVPs, and his own vision for an America free of bureaucratic intrusion into people's lives. When his impromptu remarks concluded, an aide told him it was time to go. Reagan brushed him off and told the crowd of young activists there was no place he'd rather be right now than with them. He took questions for another fifteen minutes; when asked if he would run for president in 1976, the prolonged ovation almost drowned out his answer. Cocking his head and flashing a smile, Reagan demurred. "Well," he replied coyly, "1976 is a long way off."

The crowd mobbed Reagan when he finished. He signed autographs and shook hands as he made his way back to his waiting car. Once inside, he rolled down his window, waved, and thanked everyone for their support as his driver pulled off the field.

A few hours later, another car arrived with an unrecognized dignitary: the United States ambassador to the United Nations, former Texas congressman George Bush (who had lost a US Senate race two years earlier). Wearing slacks, an open-neck shirt, and a security pass hanging from a chain around his neck (similar to the ones we wore), Bush walked around the field, introducing himself and thanking the volunteers. Like Ford and Reagan earlier, Bush gave a brief pep talk to the troops. Also like Ford, he was met with lukewarm enthusiasm. It was less a reflection on his oratorical skills than it was the late afternoon's draining heat and humidity. Besides, Ronald Reagan was a tough act for anyone to follow.

Bush posed for pictures and signed autographs before

United Nations Ambassador George Bush, Nautilus Middle School, Miami, August 22, 1972

leaving. He returned to the school the next day to play in what organizers billed as a celebrity tennis match on the field, but few YVPs showed much interest in the event.

. . .

I turned fifteen on the opening day of the 1972 Republican National Convention, but the birthday blessing proved mixed. Getting inside the hall to witness history was more difficult than expected: thousands of protesters descended on Miami to disrupt the GOP confab. For our security, the National Guard provided a fleet of buses with steel-barred and mesh windows to transport us through downtown Miami. As our caravan barreled down Collins Avenue, I watched as troopers lining the route fought against demonstrators throwing rocks and bottles at our bus. At one checkpoint, a guardsman wearing full riot gear and carrying an automatic rifle boarded and delivered this ominous instruction to us: "There's a lot of tension out there on the streets, and some of these people are very violent. If your bus is attacked, do not try to leave the bus. Stay on board. Your life may depend on it. If any of them break through our lines and attack your bus, everybody needs to lean toward the rioters so they will have a harder time turning the bus over and killing you."

Lean toward the rioters if they break free and try to kill us? The trooper offered no Plan B.

As we approached Miami Beach Convention Center, the scene outside the hall looked just as grim. Police clashed with a huge mob of chanting, screaming protesters; only a bare chain-link security fence separated us from the anarchy. The view unnerved me, but I hadn't come all this way to be deterred. I planned to get inside that hall no matter what.

Gratefully, our bus plowed past the melee and dropped us safely at the entrance. Because security inside the arena was very tight, the line moved painfully slow. The Secret Service required each attendee to pass through two metal detectors and then have all personal items hand-searched. After half an hour, our line had barely moved. As the time approached for the opening gavel, I grew antsy at the thought of missing it.

Watching an impatient reporter at the rear of the crowd gave me an idea. He held aloft his press credentials and pushed his way through to the front of the line, calling out, "CBS News—let me pass, please. CBS News . . ." The thick mass of people moved aside for him without ever looking over their shoulders. If it worked once, it might work again: I held my YVP credentials over my head: "Excuse me," I cried out. "NBC News—let me pass, please. Excuse me, NBC News . . ." Once more, the "Red Sea" parted. I went straight to the security table inside the arena.

Any lingering bus-ride anxiety dissolved when I entered the hall: the sight thrilled me. Neat rows of multicolored state delegation banners atop tall poles sat amid thousands of seats; at the front of the arena stood a two-story, eggshell-colored podium bearing the seals of all fifty states; huge American flags and Nixon banners hung from the rafters. In the skyboxes, network news anchormen Walter Cronkite of CBS, John Chancellor and David Brinkley of NBC, and Harry Reasoner and Howard K. Smith of ABC all looked down from their glass-encased perches. Behind the podium, two large Jumbotron screens flashed a repeated admonition: "Delegates and Alternates: Please be seated." From my spot in the gallery, I watched as US senator Bob Dole brought down the ceremonial gavel and called the 1972 Republican National Convention to order. Little did I dream that twenty-four years later, Dole—as the 1996 GOP presidential nominee—would campaign for me during my three congressional races.

One of the first convention speeches proved to be the briefest: Alf Landon, the 1936 Republican nominee against Franklin D. Roosevelt, approached the microphones and received a standing ovation. The eighty-four-year old former Kansas governor wore a huge sunflower (his 1936 campaign symbol) on his coat lapel. Landon accepted a commemorative plaque, and then delivered a two-sentence address: "We meet tonight in this convention in unity and enthusiasm for the winner of the next election, a great president, a great world leader, Richard Nixon. One good term deserves another."

I was especially delighted to see Landon in person: years earlier, as a young boy, I had wanted him to send me an autographed picture. So when I learned the Topeka telephone directory listed his home number, I decided to call him and ask for it personally. I waited for my mother to leave on an errand, and then dialed PR 2–2460. Sure enough, the former candidate answered the telephone himself, but the results proved frustrating. No matter how loudly I spoke, Landon kept saying we had a bad connection, he couldn't hear me clearly, and told me to hang up and try again. I did–fourteen times. The next month, when my mother received the whopping long-distance bill for fourteen peak-time calls to Topeka, I got a spanking to go with my signed picture from Landon! Decades later, after Landon died, I wrote condolences to his daughter, then US senator Nancy Landon Kassebaum, and shared that story. She wrote back, thanking me for my letter: "I appreciate your story about Dad. It always amazes me to hear how many people have talked with him and remember him fondly. He of course loved the attention, and I am sure he enjoyed your calls as much as you did–and he didn't get spanked for it!"

Landon wasn't the only heavyweight on the program that night. Following that nostalgic appearance, Senator Barry Goldwater (the 1964 Republican presidential nominee), First Lady Patricia Nixon, and Governor Ronald Reagan took their turns addressing the delegates.

The evening also proved memorable for unexpected reasons. During a filmed tribute to Mrs. Nixon, I stepped out of the hall for some fresh air. When I tried returning through the same gate, a guard said my pass didn't authorize readmission there, and he didn't know where to direct me. I walked the outer perimeter of the auditorium, trying other gate entrances, but guards rebuffed me each time. Meanwhile, another violent confrontation erupted between police and rioters on the other side of the nearby, chain-link, makeshift fence. Teargas burned my eyes as it wafted my way, while members of the mob directed profane jeers and gestures at the only visible conventioneer–me. Someone threw a rock that just missed my head. Growing increasingly nervous, and now trapped outside between a convention fortress on one side of me and a riot on the other, I didn't know what to do. Fortunately, a security guard saw my plight: after checking my credentials quickly, he grabbed my arm and pulled me inside just as more rocks and teargas crashed where I had stood moments earlier.

Later that night, on the armored bus ride back to our hotel, I looked out my barred coach windows as screaming rioters still tried to break through police lines to attack us. For the $280 I paid to be in Miami, I was getting far more of a convention experience than I ever anticipated. Still, it was a hell of a memorable way to spend a fifteenth birthday.

...

The next morning, the YVPs piled onto buses for the ride over to President Nixon's arrival ceremony. Thousands of supporters waving flags and campaign signs packed the temporary bleachers on the tarmac at the Eastern Airlines hangar of Miami International Airport. The impressive lineup of celebrity speakers warming up the crowd for Nixon included Academy Award–winning actors James Stewart, Mickey Rooney, and John Wayne.

Cheers arose when the gleaming *Air Force One* came into view on final approach; chants of "Four more years! Four more years!" rang out as the plane taxied to a stop. The clamor grew louder when the cabin door swung open; pandemonium erupted when a solitary figure in a blue suit stepped out and waved.

President Richard Nixon deplaned and walked to the bank of microphones on the tarmac. Flanked by his family, he thanked the YVPs for their welcome and promised to reward their efforts with a November victory. When he finished his brief remarks, he walked along the fence, shaking hands. I reached for him, but his hand moved so fast that it was gone before I could grab it. The Nixon family then boarded the waiting *Marine One* presidential helicopter; it circled the crowd twice before disappearing.

Later that night, New York governor Nelson Rockefeller placed Nixon's name in nomination. During the roll call of the states, organizers corralled our YVP group into a holding area while ushers passed out noisemakers, flags, and Nixon hats. As the balloting neared conclusion, they brought us to the delegate entrances; from my spot near the gate, I saw Congressman Gerald Ford (the chairman of the convention) bang the gavel and declare Richard Nixon the 1972 Republican presidential nominee.

With that, the band struck up patriotic music, ushers threw open the gates, and our YVP group swarmed onto the convention floor as a quarter million balloons dropped from ceiling nets. While fellow YVPs waved flags and tooted noisemakers, I wandered the arena, taking pictures of everything that moved.

Standing near the podium during the floor demonstration, I saw convention chairman Gerald Ford joking privately with vice chairman Bob Dole. The irony of that image returned to me four years later: through the twists of history, these two obscure 1972 convention officials stood before the next national convention as the 1976 Republican nominees for president and vice president.

Photos from the floor of the 1972 Republican National Convention taken by me minutes after Richard Nixon won the presidential nomination, Miami, August 22, 1972

. . .

On the final night of the convention, I sat in the gallery and witnessed the nominees' acceptance speeches. Vice President Agnew concluded his remarks by introducing Nixon, who emerged from behind the stage to strains of "Hail to the Chief" and a wall-shaking ovation. State banners and Nixon signs bounced up and down as the chant again rolled through the arena: "Four more years! Four more years!"

When the speeches ended, Nixon and Agnew wrapped their arms around each other and waved to the delegates as the convention adjourned sine die. Gerald Ford then made the surprise announcement that the Nixons wanted to meet as many people as possible before leaving the hall. I rushed onto the floor and joined the receiving line hoping to meet the president. While waiting, I added more autographs to my convention seal, including Governor (later Vice President) Nelson Rockefeller's, Bob Dole's, future secretary of state Henry Kissinger's, and others.

President and Mrs. Nixon greeted conventioneers in their receiving line for an hour; just as my turn neared, he picked up a microphone and announced it was time to go: "I was just reminded that we have a rather light day tomorrow. To give you an idea of what a 'light day' is for a president: I fly to Chicago and speak at the American Legion Convention; then I fly to Detroit to dedicate the

Eisenhower High School; then I fly to San Diego and speak at a rally, and then we fly by helicopter to San Clemente and speak there."

After the Nixon party left, the convention hall emptied quickly. Workers swarmed onto the floor and began disassembling the arena in preparation for an upcoming sports event. Souvenir hunters grabbed state banners off the poles, tore them into thirds, and divided the pieces. I considered volunteering for the cleanup crew because I assumed I'd find a treasure trove of abandoned campaign memorabilia when the convention ended. Now I combed the empty aisles, looking for discarded historical mementos; I found the only thing a cleaning crew inherited at the end of a national convention was a messy hall.

After joining fellow YVPs for a postconvention party at the Americana Hotel (with a hosted bar), I dragged myself back to my hotel room around 4:00 a.m. Shortly after dozing off, shouts in the hallway awakened me. I dressed quickly and stepped outside to find a young man calling for help. "Get that woman out of my room!" he yelled to the assembling (and very hungover) YVPs. Sounding exasperated, the man said he had come back from the party and taken a shower. As he climbed into bed, a naked woman had appeared from nowhere, demanding he have sex with her.

While he explained his plight, I heard a female inside his room shouting slurred obscenities and demanding that someone "come in and love me." I peeked through the open door: a nude, intoxicated woman stood wrapped partially in the window drapes.

Bambi! It was my seatmate from our charter flight a week earlier.

As hotel security led a crying Bambi from his room, I patted the disoriented guy on the shoulder and offered my assessment: "She's a nice girl once you get to know her."

. . .

By the end of convention week, I returned home to California carrying a suitcase filled with political memorabilia and countless memories (thanks again, Mom, for letting me go!). Those three future presidents I'd met at Nautilus Middle School had each signed the convention seal I swiped from the podium my first night in Miami, as had other dignitaries and (later) President Nixon and Vice President Agnew. Today it still hangs on my wall, framed with my fading security clearance credentials and YVP badge.

Back then I never imagined that in later decades I'd come to know many of the people whose autographs I collected at the convention–including those three future presidents. The family of one invited me to the private interment ceremony when he died; the other two campaigned with me during my 1990s congressional races. Those experiences remained many years in the future, and unimaginable to a starry-eyed fourteen-year-old kid who stepped off a plane in Miami on a humid August morning in 1972.

Podium seal from the 1972 Republican National Convention, autographed for me by four presidents (Nixon, Ford, Reagan, and Bush); two vice presidents (Agnew and Rockefeller); and multiple dignitaries, Miami, August 1972

By the way, that purloined convention seal returns "home" occasionally: I've loaned it to the Richard Nixon Presidential Library to display whenever the archivists request it. I do so without any concerns over legal repercussions.

The statute of limitations on my podium heist expired long ago.

9

You Didn't Wait for Me

By October 1972, Democratic nominee George McGovern's presidential campaign limped along on life support. With polls showing McGovern heading into a massive beat-down by President Nixon in a few weeks, party leaders turned their attention to protecting their majorities in Congress. The Democratic National Committee scheduled all-star fund-raising dinners around the country; the San Francisco installment came to the Fairmont Hotel on October 5.

My twelve-year-old brother, Pat, and I snuck into the Grand Ballroom when a security guard left the entrance unattended temporarily. Within minutes, we had met and collected autographs from former vice president Hubert Humphrey (defeated recently by McGovern for the 1972 presidential nomination) and Senator Thomas F. Eagleton, McGovern's original running mate until McGovern dumped him from the ticket two months earlier (I'll have a few more words about Eagleton in the next chapter). It was easy visiting with both men: they stood around the reception with little attention paid to them. Ironically, only weeks earlier, each man had traveled with an army of Secret Service agents, reporters, photographers, and cheering mobs greeting them at every stop. Events like this showed me at an early age that political adulation for winners is fleeting; for losers, it's nonexistent.

After the program, I hoped to meet one of the guests of honor, House majority leader Hale Boggs. First elected to Congress in 1941, Boggs had served on the Warren Commission that investigated and reported the government's official version of President Kennedy's assassination. Now, with House Speaker

In the rebellious 1970s, teenage boys wore their hair long; I think this photograph of me killed the fad single-handedly. From left: me, Congressman John Burton, House Majority Leader Hale Boggs, Pat Rogan, Congressman Phil Burton, San Francisco, October 5, 1972. Twenty-five years later, when Johnny Burton and I served together in the California State Assembly, this photo gave Burton unending opportunities to tease me mercilessly. (Photograph by Lindy Boggs, but disseminated heavily by John Burton)

Carl Albert's pending retirement, everyone expected Boggs to succeed him.

As the room emptied, I saw Boggs talking privately in a corner of the room with local congressmen (and brothers) Phil and John Burton.[1] Pat and I hung back and waited for their animated conversation to end so we could meet the future Speaker. While we lingered, a diminutive woman tapped me on the shoulder and asked if I wanted to meet Boggs. I told her yes, but I didn't want to interrupt his discussion with the Burtons. Insisting Boggs wouldn't mind, she grabbed my arm and pulled me toward him. As I again voiced my reluctance to intrude, she smiled and assured me nobody would object: "I'm Lindy Boggs–Hale's wife."

Mrs. Boggs (with Pat and me in tow) broke off the Boggs-Burton powwow and introduced us. Then she took my camera and directed our group to pose together for a photograph. Boggs signed an autograph for me after his wife snapped the picture; he urged me to keep up my interest in politics and government. "Maybe I'll see you back in Washington someday," he said.

. . .

Eleven days after Lindy Boggs took our photograph, House Majority Leader Hale Boggs went to Alaska to campaign for Congressman Nick Begich's reelection. Boggs and Begich took off in a small twin-engine plane in Anchorage,

---

1   Technically, at this time Phil Burton was a congressman; his brother, John, was a state legislator. Soon thereafter, John joined Phil in Washington as a member of the US House of Representatives.

bound for Juneau; the plane disappeared somewhere in the Alaskan wilderness. Despite the lengthiest search in US history, authorities (to this very day) never found the plane or the victims' bodies.

On January 3, 1973, the House passed a resolution presuming Boggs dead, which opened the way for a special election to fill his seat. His widow, Lindy, won the race; after she assumed office, I sent her a copy of the photograph she had taken that night at the Fairmont (which turned out to be one of the last pictures of her husband). In my letter, I reminded her of my goal to join her in Congress someday. She responded with a gracious letter, noting that in ten years I would be twenty-five, which is the constitutional age for congressional eligibility.

"I'll wait for you," she wrote.

A quarter century later, after I won a seat in Congress, I tracked down former Congresswoman Boggs's address (she retired after serving almost twenty years in the House) and sent her a copy of the photo she had taken and the letter she had written me long ago. On my new congressional letterhead, I penned this message: "I am so disappointed—you didn't wait for me!" Soon thereafter, she visited me in Washington for a lovely reunion lunch.

A couple of years later, when I was in the middle of President Clinton's impeachment drama, I appeared on the ABC News Sunday show,

A wonderful reunion: Former Congresswoman Lindy Boggs and me in my US Capitol office, September 10, 1997. Two days later, President Clinton nominated Mrs. Boggs as the United States ambassador to the Holy See.

This Week. I broadcast my segment from the Los Angeles affiliate station via satellite. Before airtime, I heard through my earpiece ABC News analyst and program host Cokie Roberts (broadcasting from the Washington, DC, studio) thanking me for coming on her program. While we waited to go live, I mentioned my story about her parents, Hale and Lindy Boggs. Suddenly my earpiece went dead. A few minutes later, we went on the air, and Cokie interviewed me without missing a beat.

Weeks later, over lunch with Cokie, I mentioned the curious "dead earpiece" incident to her. She said the reason my audio feed had gone silent was because she had become emotional at the mention of her father and needed to get composed before airtime: as it happens, that West Coast campaign swing where I met her parents was also the last day she ever saw her dad alive. She added that she already knew the story of my meeting her parents because her mother had shared it with her previously, but until that moment, Cokie hadn't made the connection that I was the congressman of whom her mother spoke.

Here is yet another example that this is, indeed, a small world. Maybe there's something to that "six degrees of separation" theory after all.

. . .

Former congresswoman Lindy Boggs died at age ninety-seven of natural causes on July 27, 2013.

10

The Eagleton Question

Once George McGovern locked up the 1972 Democratic presidential nomination, speculation arose over his choice for vice president. Back when nominees gave potential running mates only a cursory vetting during the convention, McGovern chose a Senate colleague he'd only met twice: first-term senator Thomas F. Eagleton of Missouri. Before tendering the offer, McGovern's campaign manager asked Eagleton if he "had any skeletons in his closet." Eagleton said no, McGovern approved the selection on July 13, and the convention delegates ratified his choice later that night.

A few days after the convention, news reports surfaced that Eagleton had suffered previously from emotional and psychological problems. On July 25, Eagleton admitted multiple hospitalizations in the past for nervous exhaustion and depression, and that he had undergone electric shock therapy. Party leaders demanded Eagleton resign or that McGovern drop him. On July 26, McGovern announced "I'm behind Tom Eagleton 1,000 percent." With McGovern's renewed blessing, Eagleton hit the campaign trail, trying to salvage his nomination as well as the troubled McGovern-Eagleton ticket.

Along with my brother, Pat, and classmate Wyn Sorensen, I took the bus to San Francisco, hoping to see Eagleton during his July 28 blitz of the city. Well-wishers, protesters, police, and Secret Service agents encircled "Number 1 California Street," the building where Eagleton had scheduled his first major press conference to deal with the controversy dogging his candidacy. When Eagleton's motorcade arrived, he stepped from the car quickly as he waved to supporters and ignored hecklers. Mayor Joseph Alioto took his arm and rushed him inside.

As a sudden mass of reporters and security surged into the building, we let their wake absorb and sweep us inside with them. We got as far as the entrance to the press conference when a Secret Service agent stopped us. He put his hand on my shoulder and said sternly, "Come with me." Luckily, the agent recognized Pat and me from our previous trips to see political leaders. Instead of ejecting us from the building, he led us to a side door and slipped us inside to witness what Eagleton called the largest press conference of his campaign.

Not stepping down: 1972 Democratic vice presidential nominee Thomas Eagleton insists he will not resign from the ticket, press conference, San Francisco, July 28, 1972

I squeezed my way to the front of the pack and stood only a few feet from Eagleton, who faced hostile questioning centering on his personal life and political survivability. Eagleton perspired heavily under the hot lights and intense interrogation, and mopped his forehead frequently with a handkerchief. Through it all, Eagleton stood firm: "I'm on the ticket to stay," he insisted, "and I won't step down. George McGovern and I will win in November, and I'm going to be a good vice president."

After the press conference, as reporters ran for the telephones to file their reports, Eagleton stood strangely alone, as if looking for a familiar face in an unfamiliar setting. Remembering the opening quip from his recent acceptance speech, I introduced myself and said, "Senator, I have to hand it to you–you sure did give Roger Mudd one heck of a beating!"[1] Eagleton threw back his head and

---

1   During the vice presidential roll call vote, one delegate cast his ballot for CBS newsman Roger Mudd. Later that night, when Eagleton stepped before the microphones to accept the nomination, he opened his remarks by saying, "Well, I sure gave Roger Mudd one heck of a beating!"

roared with laughter, telling me, "I sure did!" When I told him he'd handled himself well at the press conference, he put an arm around my shoulder and thanked me for my encouragement. Eagleton then signed a few McGovern campaign items already autographed for me by his running mate.

I liked Tom Eagleton: he was a kind man. In politics, however, kindness doesn't always count for much. Two days after meeting Eagleton in San Francisco, McGovern dumped him as the vice presidential nominee and replaced him with former ambassador R. Sargent Shriver.

. . .

I met Eagleton one more time: a few months after resigning from the ticket, he attended a fund-raiser for Democratic congressional candidates at the San Francisco Fairmont Hotel (see my previous chapter, "You Didn't Wait for Me"). Because donors at that dinner tended to ignore him and instead focused their homage on other rising luminaries, Pat and I had a lengthy chance to visit with him. In fact, at our request, he wrote out in longhand and signed a quotation from his vice presidential acceptance speech for my collection:

"For my friend Jim: We know all is not well–we know that. But it is not because, as some would have us believe, that we Americans have lost our way. All we have lost is the leadership to show us the way. With best wishes, Tom Eagleton, US Senator."

Decades later, when I served in Congress and Eagleton had long since retired to Missouri, I dropped him a note thanking him for his kindnesses to me when I was a young boy fascinated by the political process. Against my better judgment, I sent him a copy of the photograph taken of us at the Fairmont Hotel in 1972, which showed me with the very regrettable long hair I sported as a teen, in surrender to the fashion of the era. I thought he would find the picture amusing, especially since I had now made a name for myself in conservative Republican circles.

Senator Thomas F. Eagleton and me, San Francisco, October 5, 1972 (photo by Pat Rogan; autographed in 1974)

Eagleton sent me a charming reply that read as follows:

Dear Jim:

BURN THAT PICTURE! It will cost you votes. Let me tell you a VP/San Francisco story. I was staying at the Mark Hopkins Hotel. On my way out of the hotel one morning, a very nice kid came up to me and asked if I would autograph two cards—one for him and one for his brother. I signed the two cards. Later that same day, I went back to the hotel, and the same kid came up to me and asked me to sign two cards for his sisters. I said, "Young man, how many brothers and sisters do you have? He paused and then said, "Senator Eagleton, would you be mad at me if I told the truth?" I said, "I won't be mad; tell me the truth." He said, "Senator Eagleton, I do not have any brothers or sisters. If I have four of your signatures, I can keep one and trade the three others for a Willie Mays." I signed the cards.

Many politicians, at one time or another, get carried away with their own importance. I think I was one of those. It is very healthy to have someone—like the kid in San Francisco—bring one down to earth.

After I lost my seat in Congress over my role in the Clinton impeachment trial, thousands of nasty letters cascaded into my office telling me, in various degrees of incivility, good riddance. A rare complimentary letter found its way to my desk, and it arrived as I packed my congressional office:

November 20, 2000

Dear Jim:

I know you were Target # 1. I read somewhere about the millions of dollars being spent on both sides in your district. Although I personally did not favor impeaching Clinton, I thought that you and [Congressman and fellow prosecutor Asa] Hutchinson were the "class acts" on the Republican side....

I left the Senate in '86. It was beginning to get mean. Since then, it has gotten dreadfully mean. I had some great friends on the Republican side, e.g., Mark Hatfield, Mac Mathias, Ted Stevens (his first wife and my wife were best friends), Paul Laxalt, and others. We went to dinner together. We came to each other's house. We kidded about politics. I am told that most of that camaraderie is gone. It's war! It's one side against the other! It's "shoot to kill." SAD! SAD! SAD!

You are a man of character and ability. I wish you the very best in the years ahead. I am most sincere when I say, best wishes,

Tom Eagleton

. . .

In the decades since Tom Eagleton stood before the cheering delegates for his brief moment in the sun, his name has become synonymous with the notion of full disclosure. In 1985, just before tendering a job offer to me as a deputy district attorney for Los Angeles County, assistant DA Curt Livesay conducted my final hiring interview. Livesay instructed me to reveal any factor about my life that might embarrass the office if he hired me. He told me, "That's the last question I ask in every hiring interview: I call it 'the Eagleton Question.'"

. . .

After retiring from the Senate, Thomas Eagleton returned home to Missouri to practice law and teach. He died at age seventy-seven of heart and respiratory complications on March 4, 2007. In a farewell letter he wrote to friends and family, he said his dying wishes were for people to "go forth in love and peace, vote Democratic, and be kind to dogs."

11

Speaking of Dog Lovers . . .

As mentioned earlier, I spent countless hours as a boy looking up the addresses of long-retired national leaders to write for autographs and advice on political life. Many proved receptive in hearing from a young person born years (and sometimes decades) after their influence and fame had waned. When I learned that one such figure lived nearby, I set out to meet him.

By 1973, few remembered that the obscure publisher of the *Oakland Tribune*, William F. Knowland, had been a political powerhouse in his day. A former state legislator, Governor Earl Warren (R-CA) had appointed Knowland to the United States Senate in 1945 following the death of Hiram Johnson. Twice elected in his own right, at age forty-four Knowland became the youngest Senate majority leader in history (his minority leader counterpart was future president Lyndon Johnson). With his eye now on the White House, Knowland challenged incumbent Governor Goodwin Knight in the 1958 Republican primary. Knowland won the bloody battle (and then convinced Knight to run for his vacating Senate seat). However, when the dust settled in November, both men were defeated soundly. Knowland never again sought elective office; he returned to his family's newspaper and became publisher of the *Oakland Tribune* upon his father's death in 1966.

Knowland proved an elusive quarry. I sent him many letters when I was a boy, but each went unanswered. Finally, I took a more direct approach. With classmate Roger Mahan along, we took the bus to Oakland and walked to the Tribune building. I called Knowland's secretary from the lobby, told her of our purpose, and asked if we could come upstairs and meet him. Without checking with her boss, she put us on his calendar for 11:00 that morning.

To kill time, Roger and I rode up the Tribune Tower elevators to view the beautiful panorama across the Bay. A security guard grabbed us: "What are you kids doing hanging around here?" he demanded. When we told him we had an appointment with Senator Knowland, he shook his head in disbelief as he pulled us toward a telephone. Once he confirmed the meeting, he grew respectful very quickly.

When our time drew near, Roger and I presented ourselves in the lobby and passed through several layers of protection before a guard escorted us to a private locked elevator that ran directly to the fourth floor. I couldn't understand all the security precautions involved in meeting a man almost two decades out of the public eye.

The elevator opened in Knowland's outer office. We waited by his secretary's desk for over ten minutes, listening to her pick up a frequently buzzing telephone and responding, "Yes, Senator . . . Yes, Senator . . . ." Finally, after another loud buzz, she led us toward two large wooden doors: "Senator Knowland will see you now."

The unsmiling man behind a large desk rose and offered a perfunctory handshake. He motioned for us to have a seat. An uncomfortable silence filled the room, with Knowland glowering at us and saying nothing. I thanked him for letting us come up to get his autograph. "Okay," he replied, and waved me behind his desk to collect a signature. He posed for a quick photograph, and then ushered us to the door.

Here's your autograph–what's your hurry? Autograph of Senator William F. Knowland, August 13, 1973

Political memorabilia crowded all of Knowland's office walls; I wanted him to show it to us, but Knowland had no interest in prolonging the visit. Just as he was scooting us out the door, I saw a large photograph hanging on the wall of two Saint Bernards. I pointed to it and mentioned that I had a Saint Bernard. He stared at me and then asked intently, "You have a Saint Bernard?" I opened my wallet and showed him a photo I carried of Pumpernickel, our family pooch.

Knowland's demeanor changed from dour to almost grandfatherly. His eyes grew moist as he spoke of his two dogs (one had died and the other was fourteen). With this newfound interest in his guests, Knowland gave us the grand tour. He showed us all his gavels, plaques, signed photographs, and other mementos of his role in history, and pointed with pride to framed photographs of him with luminaries such as Robert A. Taft, Dwight D. Eisenhower, and Lyndon Johnson. He pointed out his certificates of election to the United States Senate and as majority leader (the latter bearing the faded brown signature of Vice President Nixon), his commission from President Eisenhower appointing him a delegate to the United Nations, and an original oil portrait of Lincoln painted by Eisenhower as a gift to Knowland.

After making our "dog connection": a smiling Senator William F. Knowland and me, Oakland Tribune building, August 13, 1973

A large color photograph of Knowland swearing in Richard Nixon as vice president hung in the center of the room. "Nixon served two terms as vice president, but I swore him in three times for the job," Knowland said. "Do you know why that is?" I did, but I didn't want to ruin a good story. Knowland related that Inauguration Day 1957 fell on a Sunday, so Eisenhower and Nixon followed tradition and had a private oath ceremony at the White House that day, and then held a public ceremony the next afternoon.

It was half an hour later when his secretary tried rescuing Knowland from his fans with a reminder of another meeting. He shooed her away; when she returned a few minutes later insisting that he needed to keep to his schedule, he wrapped his arms around our shoulders as he strolled with us to the security elevator. He shook our hands, thanked us for visiting, and didn't leave until the elevator doors closed behind us. For a man who hadn't relished seeing us when we arrived, he seemed genuinely sorry to see us go.

Apparently, the later warmth he showed us was out of character. His biographers, Gayle B. Montgomery and James W. Johnson, wrote that even as a senator, "Knowland was uncomfortable in close contact with people . . . Although he could mesmerize a room full of admirers with his speeches, a one-on-one talk with the senator was painful for both parties. His son, Joe, said once, 'The hardest thing I have to do is carry on a conversation with my father.'"[1]

When I read that passage, my experience with him made sense. After our meeting, I came away thinking that for all his power and position, William F. Knowland was the loneliest man I ever met.

. . .

Six months after our visit, Knowland spoke at the *Oakland Tribune*'s one hundredth anniversary party. A reporter covering the event described him as tired, emotional, and losing weight.

Two days later, on February 23, 1974, Knowland drove alone to his vacation home in Guerneville. He went to the rear of his house and climbed down the steps leading to the edge of the Russian River. After wading waist-deep into the water, he raised a .32-caliber revolver to his right temple and pulled the trigger. Divers found his body later that afternoon.

Knowland left no suicide note, but later, investigators learned of his crumbling private life. After divorcing his wife of forty-five years, Knowland married a woman twenty-five years his junior (they separated shortly after the wedding). In debt and fearing financial ruin, Knowland also developed a security phobia. After the recent kidnappings of *Atlanta Constitution* editor Reg Murphy and

---

1   Gayle B. Montgomery and James W. Johnson, *One Step from the White House: The Rise and Fall of Senator William F. Knowland* (Los Angeles: University of California Press, 1998), 80.

Patty Hearst (granddaughter of publishing magnate William Randolph Hearst), Knowland believed he was next on the hit list. This explained the protective maze we navigated to get in and out of his office. With multiple stresses pressing in on him, he found his escape on the bank of the Russian River.

When I heard the jarring news, I felt tremendous sadness for Senator Knowland and his family. I also remember wishing that people who loved dogs–like he did–had spent more time with him.

Senator William F. Knowland posed in his private office for me, Oakland Tribune building, August 13, 1973

12

Thanks for the Memory

When I served in Congress, Bob Hope told people I represented him even though I think his North Hollywood home was just outside my district. No matter; he wanted to claim a Republican congressman, so I assumed the honor gladly.

During my youth, there were few people on the planet more universally recognizable than the great comedian. In a career spanning some eighty years, Hope achieved fame on Broadway, in vaudeville, on the radio, on television, and in motion pictures. However, it was his entertaining the troops through four wars on overseas USO tours that endeared him to America.

Like most people in my generation, I grew up loving Bob Hope, so as a teen I jumped at the chance to meet him when he came to San Francisco to promote his latest book, *The Last Christmas Show*, which chronicled his decades of performing for the military. San Francisco's Emporium (a famous department store that operated on Market Street for ninety-nine years) proclaimed "Bob Hope Day," and featured a free showing of his films before he appeared in person to autograph copies of his book.

My brother, Pat, and I arrived at the Emporium two hours before Hope's scheduled event and saw an unhappy sight: hundreds of people formed a line starting at the sixth floor auditorium; it wrapped up the stairs and around the entire roof of the store. We took our place at the end of the line. After a three-hour wait, we made it inside the auditorium, where the one line branched off into two: the "buyer" line (for book purchasers), and the "looker" line (nonbuyers wanting a glimpse of Hope). Since I'd bought a book, I got in the preferred line.

"Thanks for the Memory!" Bob Hope inscribed his signature song line on this January 10, 1944, *Life* magazine cover for me on January 10, 1975.

Hope sat at a table, greeting his fans, who appeared quite diverse. Scores of parents brought young children to meet him, while World War II, Korean War, and Vietnam vets brought faded snapshots of him entertaining them in the field decades earlier. He studied each photograph and shared recollections with the aging photographers.

When my turn came, a store clerk opened my book to the title page and handed it to Hope, who scrawled his name on it. As he did with everyone in front of me, Hope thanked me for coming and shook my hand. He not only signed nearly a thousand books that day, but when he finished, he remained for another

hour and signed autographs for everyone who couldn't (or didn't) buy a book.

No wonder people loved Bob Hope for so long. By my observations, he loved them right back.

. . .

I saw Hope a few months later in a venue where he shined: the concert hall. He made a rare live appearance at the Concord Pavilion (now

Comedian Bob Hope, the Emporium, San Francisco, February 21, 1975

the Sleep Train Pavilion), a beautiful outdoor theater in Concord, California. Even in his seventies, Bob Hope packed the twelve-thousand-seat arena.

After the orchestra played a medley of tunes from Hope's best-loved movies, he walked onstage to a standing ovation. He wasted no time in his monologue, launching into an hour-long, rapid-fire series of songs and gags. He joked far faster than I could write, but I managed to memorialize a few; the first ones came at the expense of his longtime costar in the classic *Road* movies, singer Bing Crosby:

> During World War II Bing and I had to room together while we were entertaining the troops overseas. The man snores terribly! I finally found a way to cure him of it. One night while he was snoring, I walked over to his bed, bent down, and kissed him on the lips. Not only did that cure his snoring, but he stayed awake all night watching me sleep!
>
> Once Bing and I were out in the jungle, taking a jeep ride. We parked and took a walk; a coiled snake sprang and bit Bing in the crotch. I told Bing to lie down and rest while I rushed back to get medical advice about how to save him from the poisonous bite. The doctor told me to suck the venom out

of the wound. I returned to where Bing was resting. He asked what the doctor said; I told him, "He says you're gonna die!"

A young fellow walked down the streets of Belfast late at night. A hand in the shadows reached out, grabbed him, and put a knife to his throat. A sinister voice asked, "Are you a Protestant or a Catholic?" The terrified young man didn't know what to say, thinking he would be killed if he gave the wrong answer. Finally, the young man decided to play it safe. "I'm a Jew," he responded. The voice said, "I must be the luckiest damn Arab in Ireland tonight!"

I took a plane flight to Oakland from LAX to come up here for the show. A little guy was sitting next to a big monster that was sound asleep. After we were airborne the little guy, who was terrified of flying, heaved up his Waldorf salad all over the sleeping man. When we were landing, the big guy woke up and found the mess all over him. The little guy leaned over and asked, "Are you feeling better now?"

A man was doing poorly at golf one day. Suddenly a genie appeared. The man told the genie he would do anything to hit a hole in one. The genie said the man must give up five years of his sex life. The man thought it over, agreed, and then made a hole in one. The genie said he could make a birdie if he gave up ten years of sex. The man again agreed and made a birdie. The genie asked the man's name. The man replied, "Father O'Toole."

A hunter sent his dog to retrieve a quail. The dog walked on top of the water to fetch it. The hunter's friend said, "There's something wrong with your dog." "I know," the hunter replied. "He can't swim."

A gorilla at the zoo grabbed a woman. He began to hug and caress her. "What should I do?" the woman cried. Her husband said, "Do what you always do–tell him you have a headache."

A woman told the psychiatrist that her husband keeps climbing into the bathtub and goes fishing in the toilet. The shrink asked her, "Are you sure you aren't the one who needs to see a psychiatrist?" "I don't have time," the woman said. "I'm too busy cleaning fish."

A man called his seven children together and asked which one of them pushed the outhouse in the lake. When none of the children confessed, the father said, "George Washington never told a lie when his father asked him who chopped down the cherry tree, and he grew up to be president." Finally, one of the kids confessed. The father slapped the hell out of him. The bewildered kid said, "I thought you said George Washington didn't lie, and he became president." "That's right," the father said, "but Washington's old man wasn't sitting in the tree when he chopped it down!"

During the show a woman in the third row heckled Hope repeatedly for his prior support of President Nixon and the Vietnam War. Theater ushers tried to silence her, but with no success. Hope remained unperturbed; finally, security arrived. As they scooped her from her seat, she threw a coin onto the stage and yelled, "Here's a nickel, Hope. That's all your show is worth."

Hope stopped his monologue. Without saying anything, he bent down, picked it up, looked at the coin, and then slid it into his pants pocket. The crowd roared with laughter.

By the time the orchestra played Hope's theme song, "Thanks for the Memory," the audience suffered from laughter exhaustion. He bowed and walked offstage to lengthy applause. The audience begged for an encore; he reappeared to another standing ovation. After firing off a dozen more jokes, he sang his signature song, blew a final kiss, and said good night.

For those of us present for his live concert, Bob Hope was half-right: he should have said "great night."

Bob Hope in concert, the Concord Pavilion, September 6, 1975

. . .

During my last few weeks as a student at UCLA Law School, Hope came to my campus to tape his Thanksgiving television special for NBC, "Bob Hope Goes to College," with comedy skits taped at various colleges across the country. The network scheduled the UCLA segment for outdoor filming on the Janss Steps, but on the day of taping, a steady rain fell. One hour before showtime, the director ordered the production moved to the Women's Gym steps (which offered the entertainers some covering from the elements). Unfortunately, the venue provided no similar protection for the audience: those of us waiting to watch the show had to do so in a downpour. Although I arrived for the taping only twenty minutes early, I still got a front row seat. The heavy rainfall discouraged the otherwise expected crowd from coming.

As the engineers concluded their sound and equipment check, a man behind me patted my shoulder and said, "You kids sure are brave to be here in this rain. Thanks a lot for coming out." I turned and saw that the man talking to me was Bob Hope, dressed casually in a necktie, sports jacket with patches on the elbows, and a badge on his lapel with the letters USC and a red slash through them. Hope then walked onto the makeshift stage; the couple hundred students enduring the weather didn't recognize the eighty-year-old comedian immediately, but soon an enthusiastic cheer engulfed the area.

"You know, you kids are just marvelous," Hope said as he looked out at the students huddled under ponchos and umbrellas. "I didn't think anyone would show up today because of the rain, but this is going to be great."

Hope's show lasted two hours; he read his monologue and gags off huge cue cards held aloft behind me. When he flubbed a line, he simply reshot the scene, suggesting to the audience, "When you hear the punch line again, do me a favor–laugh as if it was the first time."

During a break in the taping, Hope complained about getting wet. A student in the audience ran onstage and offered him his blue UCLA baseball cap. Hope liked the gesture so much that he returned the cap to the student and asked him to repeat the gesture for the cameras. He then donned the hat and wore it throughout the rest of the show.

Bob Hope's cue-card man enjoying his job during the comedian's monologue, UCLA taping, November 11, 1983

I managed a spontaneous contribution to the entertainment. As Hope set up a joke about the networks cancelling television programs, he asked, "How do you know anymore when your show's been canceled?" But before he could deliver the punch line, an electrical short from the rain caused all of the lights and power to go out momentarily.

"That's how you can tell, Bob!" I yelled from my seat. Hope and the audience laughed. When the lights came back on, he resumed taping.

After Hope finished the UCLA segment, he again thanked the students for turning out to greet him. He asked if there was anything he could do for us. I called

Bob Hope, UCLA taping, November 11, 1983

out a request to sing his theme song, "Thanks for the Memory." "I'll do the best I can," Hope said, "but in the last fifty years, I've sung so many parodied versions that I forget the true lyrics." He then warbled several verses of the tune and received a standing ovation.

With the taping over, the UCLA homecoming king and queen presented Hope with gifts, along with a certificate from the chancellor naming him an Honorary Freshman, with this added sentiment: "We hope you never graduate."

. . .

A few years later, when I was a young lawyer, I came to know Hope's longtime publicist, Ward Grant. I mentioned to Grant that I'd seen Hope in person several times over the years, but lamented that I never got the chance to meet him. Grant gave me Hope's private mailing address and told me to drop him a note, reference our discussion, and he said Hope would be delighted to set up something. I sent the note; a couple of weeks later I received this reply:

October 6, 1986

Dear Jim:

I would be happy to see you. The only problem is when. If you're ever around my way, drop by and see if I'm home. Either that, or come to NBC Studios on December 6 or 7 when I'm taping. You can tell the usher you have an appointment with me (either that or yell out at me from the audience). And if you get arrested I'll try and fix it. Anyway, there must be a way. Maybe I'll come by your house.

Regards,

Bob Hope

Despite the brashness I often demonstrated as a youth, I didn't want to barge over to Bob Hope's house and start banging on the gate, so I opted for the second suggestion. His secretary forwarded four tickets for Hope's annual Christmas show at NBC Studios in Burbank.

With my old friend Bob Wyatt and our dates along, I arrived at NBC Studios for the 6:00 p.m. taping; we took our places in the long line for his show, which wrapped around the complex. About an hour before the doors opened, I spotted Hope as he exited a back door of NBC. He was dressed casually in slacks and a silver auto racing-style jacket bearing American flag patches on the sleeves; only a few people in line recognized the comedian as he and a couple of friends climbed into a car and pulled out of the driveway. "We're going for some quick dinner," he called out to a surprised fan. "We'll be back!"

At 6:00 p.m. the audience began filing inside the studio. Since we had special tickets, our group was brought to the front of the line. My letter from Hope also granted me special dispensation to bring a camera inside NBC, which is otherwise forbidden during a taping. We settled into seats on the steep bleachers inside the soundstage and waited for the show to begin.

At 7:30 p.m. Hope walked out and received a standing ovation. Dressed in a black tuxedo, he bantered with the audience and crew while the technicians prepared to begin shooting. When the show started, he again read his monologue from large cue cards held underneath the main camera. The audience laughed along, even when a joke was old, corny, and predictable. After all, it was Bob Hope telling it, and that fact alone made the gag funnier.

When Hope left the stage for a costume change, the director played on a large monitor the segment shot a day earlier to gauge audience reaction. Hope reappeared a few minutes later, wearing Australian bush clothes and carrying a large rubber alligator. He then did a comedy segment spun off from the recent hit film *Crocodile Dundee*.

It was almost 10 p.m. when the skit ended. Hope invited the audience back for the final taping the following morning; he said good night, took a final bow, and left, to another standing ovation.

An NBC page asked our group to remain in the bleachers until the rest of the audience had left the studio. He then escorted us across the soundstage, down the corridor, and into Hope's private dressing room.

Still in his "Crocodile Dundee" costume and heavy television makeup, Hope waved us inside with a hearty welcome. After he saw our two dates huddled outside the door (too shy to crash inside), he went and got them: "Hiya, dolls. Come on in and join us." We took pictures with Hope, who then asked us detailed questions about the various skits and gags from his show. He joked that since we were keeping an old man up past his bedtime, the least we could do is critique, from an audience perspective, which jokes worked and which didn't.

"Glad I'm Dressed Formal": Comedian Bob Hope (still in his "Crocodile Dundee" costume) and me, NBC Studios, Burbank, December 7, 1986

As we thanked him again for the chance to visit, he asked if we planned to come back tomorrow to see the rest of the taping. I told him I had a court appearance in the morning and couldn't make it. "Can't make it, eh? Then give me back the picture!" With that, he snarled and pretended to lunge for my camera.

On the way home that evening, Bob Wyatt's date told me how impressed she was that I'd got us into Hope's dressing room for a private meeting. "Oh, that's nothing," I said, feigning indifference. "Hope actually wanted to come over to my house, but I turned him down. If he wants to see me, he has to entertain me …."

. . .

In 1993, America prepared to celebrate Hope's ninetieth birthday, which fell on May 29. Pre-birthday celebrations in anticipation of the event began early: the city of Burbank renamed the main street near NBC "Bob Hope Drive"; at the same network, a two-hour birthday special aired that Hope's daughter Linda produced.

My friend Ward Grant (Hope's longtime publicist) offered several times to set up a photo with Hope and my family. With age ninety rolling up, I thought I'd better take him up on it before it proved too late. Before long Hope's secretary called and invited my family over to his house on May 26, three days before his birthday.

We drove to Hope's longtime home at 10346 Moorpark in Toluca Lake (the Hopes moved there in 1939 and remained there for sixty-three years). The house rested on a quiet, tree-lined street; tall hedges hid most of the property from public view. A secretary greeted us at the large, black iron gates emblazoned with an *H* and ordered them opened; we pulled into the driveway and parked behind the bungalow. His house was a large, two-story, white brick building with manicured gardens. Next to it were small, white cabanas; a pool in the rear; a golfing area; and a massive yard, where workers set up tents for yet another upcoming television show taping. All of Hope's secretaries and staff came out to greet us and look at our twin babies, irresistibly darling in their red, white, and blue sailor dresses and white bonnets. Claire was alert, smiling and laughing at the attention; Dana (just awakened from her afternoon nap) was more circumspect and studied everyone intently.

Hope's assistant said her boss was concluding an interview and would join us in a few minutes. While waiting, we admired the photographs adorning the walls, depicting Hope with notables such as Cary Grant, Jackie Gleason, President Eisenhower, and General George Patton. There was a golfing print signed by the artist and President Gerald Ford, a pencil sketch of Hope with Bing Crosby, a plaque inducting him into the Golf Hall of Fame, and several sketches and paintings portraying him during various phases of his career.

A few minutes later I looked out the door toward the house and saw Hope approaching. The spring in the old comedian's step now was replaced by a hunched shuffle as he negotiated the couple of stairs into the bungalow. He had aged significantly since I last saw him a few years earlier: his hair was mostly gone; white whisker stubble dotted his chin and neck area, and a small skin cancer marked the side of his famous ski-nose. Most notably, the energy I remembered appeared depleting: now he moved like an old man. Still, Hope didn't let the infirmities of age dampen his spirit. As he approached, he sang an old Bing Crosby song, "San Antonio Rose."

When Hope entered and saw me holding Dana, he let loose a high-pitched cackle: "Well, hello, baby! Hello, baby!" he said as he waved playfully at my daughter. "My God, you're beautiful. What's your name?" Just then he noticed my wife, Christine, holding Claire, and he laughed even louder: "Oh, God, look at them! Twins! They're beautiful!" Turning to his secretary, he called out, "Go get Dolores [Mrs. Hope] and tell her to get over here! She needs to see these babies!"

A few minutes later, Dolores Hope (his wife of fifty-nine years) joined us. She fawned over the twins at length, and she and Hope took turns holding their hands, kissing their cheeks, and talking to them. Claire took it all with a good nature, laughing and smiling at the attention. Dana studied Hope as he wiggled his finger before her. "Be careful, Bob," I said, "She's cutting teeth and may think that finger is lunch." Sure enough, she leaned forward and took a nip on it. Hope howled and pretended she'd bit off his finger at the knuckle.

Dolores asked if Christine had a rough delivery when the girls were born. "Actually," Christine smiled, "it was a perfect delivery!" She shared the story of our adopting the girls. Hope listened intently, and then told us the story of how he and Dolores also adopted their children.

Hope talked about his ninetieth birthday, now only three days away.

"Ninety years old—can you believe it!" he exclaimed, and then he looked at Dana in my arms. "I remember as if it were yesterday picking my daughter Linda up from her bassinet in that Chicago hospital after we adopted her, and holding her in my arms like you're holding Dana," he said with a smile. "Now she's my producer. I'm very proud of her."

Hope drafted a maintenance worker as a photographer. We all lined up inside the bungalow; Dolores tried to beg out of the photograph ("Oh, look at me—I'm a mess"), but we insisted she stay. Just as the picture was about to be taken, I had to stop the cameraman and excuse myself for a moment: Dana had thrown up all over my tie! After a quick wipe-up, we posed again. Hope's attention was turned to Dana, who suddenly came to life. He laughed and leaned forward as she playfully grabbed at his nose and face, pinching his cheek and chin with her tiny fingers.

When it was time for us to get the girls home, we wished Bob a very happy birthday and thanked him and Dolores for letting us bring them by. Hope kissed both girls good-bye, saying "Bye-bye babies! Bye-bye babies!" Dolores told us they were the most adorable little girls she had ever seen, and made me promise to send her copies of the pictures.

Dana Rogan, tickling her favorite comedian's chin (from left): Dolores Hope, Christine and Claire Rogan, Bob Hope, Dana Rogan, and me, 10346 Moorpark, Toluca Lake, California, May 26, 1993. In the photograph, you can see Christine's arm draped behind her back. Look carefully and you will see she is hiding the diaper she used to mop up Dana after she puked on my necktie!

I escorted Bob back to the house, taking his arm to steady him as he climbed down the steps. As Hope headed for the door, he looked up at the sky and then turned and told me, "I still need to get in some golf before the day gets away from me!"

Bob Hope might have been 90 years old, but he still played with a twelve handicap.

. . .

In later years, during my service in both Sacramento and Washington, I saw Bob Hope several more times. Sadly, this time with Bob on the eve of his 90th birthday was the last time we spent together while he still enjoyed reasonably good vigor (considering his age). It was sad to see his health deteriorate. Perhaps one day I'll impart more memories and photographs of him in these later years. In any event, and despite his advancing old age, Bob Hope remained a trooper who loved and gave his all to fans.

On July 27, 2003, in the same Toluca Lake house where we visited, Bob Hope died at age one hundred. A comedian to the end, when Dolores asked him on his deathbed where he wanted to be buried, Bob replied: "Surprise me."

Dolores Hope died at age 102 of natural causes on September 19, 2011. Like her husband, she passed away in their Toluca Lake home.

13

President of What?

When an unknown, one-term governor of Georgia told his mother in December 1974 he'd decided to run for president, she asked, "President of what?" Jimmy Carter labored in obscurity through most of his twenty-month lead-up to the 1976 Democratic National Convention; once he started winning the early primaries, however, he became a rapid favorite for the nomination.

Carter brought his campaign to San Francisco in May 1976, a few weeks before reaching the delegate count needed to secure the presidential nod. Since I had read much about Carter by then but had never met him, I went to the event and (eschewing my childhood habits) actually bought a twenty-five-dollar ticket. That was a lot of money for an eighteen-year-old: I had to spin pizzas next to a 525-degree oven at my fast-food job for about ten hours to earn it.

When Carter arrived at the Hilton for his reception, I photographed him as he greeted supporters (many of whom wore "Damn Yankees for Carter" campaign buttons). Carter didn't look very presidential: a short man in a polyester suit, he had wide, almost cartoonish lips encasing a mouthful of long teeth. Yet, he worked the room like a seasoned campaigner as he flashed his famously large grin to all.

Hoping to meet Carter, I saw my chance during the later banquet. Carter skipped eating and instead walked around the room, shaking hands. During a lull, Carter stood alone against the rear wall, with nobody around except a lone Secret Service agent. I introduced myself to Carter, and he treated me to the same friendly, toothy grin everyone else got. However, when I told him

Former Georgia governor Jimmy Carter, San Francisco Hilton Hotel, May 26, 1976

about my political memorabilia collection and asked if he would sign a picture for me, the big smile disappeared quickly.

"No, I'm not signing any autographs," Carter snapped. "If I sign one for you, then everybody will want one."

His refusal didn't upset me; I knew that sometimes such requests are not convenient or welcome. What caught me off guard was Carter's personality change at my polite request—he went from smiley to surly in a heartbeat. As I told Carter I understood his position and thanked him anyway, I couldn't help but chuckle slightly. He asked why I thought the refusal was funny. With due respect, I explained that as a kid I had snuck into countless events to meet political leaders to get an autograph. Now, at the first event where I actually bought a ticket, the candidate turned me down.

"Bring the picture over to my table later and I'll sign it," Carter said coolly, and then turned and walked away.

A short time later, with Carter seated at his table and again unoccupied by admirers, I took up his invitation and walked over to him with my photograph. As soon as Carter saw me approaching, he made a hand signal to the Secret Service agent who earlier had stood with Carter when he told me to bring the photo to his table. The agent stopped me and said Carter would not be signing anything. I reminded the agent of Carter's earlier promise. "No, he didn't tell you that," the agent replied. "He told you to send it to his home in Plains, Georgia." Carter watched with an approving eye as the agent shooed me away.

After Carter's speech that evening, and just before he exited the ballroom, he climbed on a chair and raised his arms in the air as if to embrace the cheering crowd. "Good night, everybody!" he shouted. "I love you all!"

Sorry, but I felt the only thing Jimmy Carter loved about me that night was the twenty-five bucks he'd grinned out of my wallet.

· · ·

I saw Jimmy Carter a few more times during his 1976 presidential campaign. One appearance he made late in the race leaves me with an unsettled memory, but the reason has nothing to do with him.

Three weeks before the election, on October 6, 1976, Carter debated his general election opponent, President Gerald Ford, in San Francisco. Carter's campaign scheduled a postdebate rally with Carter and local Democratic candidates at the Civic Auditorium, only a few minutes from the debate location.

Carter partisans at the rally site watched the debate on Jumbotron screens. Shortly after the debate ended, the auditorium's rear doors opened and the band played "Happy Days Are Here Again." Accompanied by a large entourage that included his wife, Rosalynn; California governor Jerry Brown; and Democrat National Committee chairman Robert Strauss, Carter entered the auditorium and walked down the center aisle, shaking hands. A standing ovation greeted him when he reached the stage.

"Anybody here want to debate me?" Carter joked before delivering a brief campaign speech pledging to lead the Democrats to victory in November. After introducing his wife, Rosalynn, he thanked everyone for attending and waved good-bye. Security whisked the Carters from the auditorium to the Fairmont for a fund-raising dinner.

"What's so bizarre about that?" you may wonder.

One of the main organizers of this rally was Jim Jones, founder of the local Peoples Temple. The following year, Jones moved twelve hundred members of his cult from San Francisco to the tiny nation of Guyana to establish an agricultural colony. Later reports surfaced that Jones used beatings and extortion against cult members to enslave them. In November 1978, congressman Leo Ryan led a congressional delegation to Guyana to investigate. During the visit, Jones ordered the murder of Ryan and his party. As the executions took place at the nearby airstrip, Jones instructed his entire flock to commit suicide; his thugs murdered those who refused to drink the poisoned Kool-Aid potion they'd concocted. Almost one thousand people died in Guyana that afternoon; very few Temple members survived the grisly horror in Guyana.

I remember seeing many of Jones's glaze-eyed followers at the Carter rally–cheering wildly on cues from Jones. Later, when I studied my fuzzy photographs taken that night, I saw Congressman Ryan on the same stage with Carter. Ironically, Ryan also shared the stage that night with his murderer. In these same photographs, San Francisco mayor George Moscone is standing next to Leo Ryan. Only a week after Ryan's assassination, San Francisco supervisor Dan White murdered both Moscone and fellow supervisor Harvey Milk in their city hall offices.

14

A Night of Heroes

Every two years, the living recipients of the Congressional Medal of Honor reunite for a weekend of reminiscences, drinks, laughs, and tears shed for fallen comrades. The 1977 biennial celebration, held in San Jose, was a two-day jubilee featuring receptions and parades before the banquet finale. The 167 decorated veterans who journeyed west for the event covered every twentieth-century military conflict to date: Vietnam, Korea, World Wars I and II, and even the 1900 Chinese Boxer Rebellion. Their theaters of battle may have differed, but they shared in common blue ribbons around their necks, acknowledging America's tribute to their valor.

My college radio station press credentials garnered me two tickets to the Congressional Medal of Honor Society reception and dinner; I brought my classmate and longtime pal Bob Wyatt. We arrived at the San Jose Civic Auditorium that evening and picked up our passes in the media center. Taking advantage of a momentary lapse in security, we walked into the private (no press admitted) cocktail reception for the banquet speakers and honorees. Since my credentials didn't permit access to this event, I kept a low profile.

Legendary movie star James Stewart stood in a corner, chatting with guests and signing autographs. Stewart's accomplishments went beyond the silver screen: at the outbreak of World War II, Stewart enlisted as a private in the Army Air Corps: he flew twenty bombing missions over Germany, earned the Distinguished Flying Cross, and retired from the Reserves as a general. Bob and I introduced ourselves to Stewart, who was very down-to-earth. He told us the Society had given him their "Patriot Award," and he felt a tremendous honor in receiving it.

Stewart also talked about his Hollywood career. I told him how much I enjoyed his classic films, such as *The Philadelphia Story*, *Harvey*, and *It's a Wonderful Life*. "Boy, we sure made good pictures in those days," he said, and then shook his head in disgust. "But they sure don't make them like we did anymore." After mentioning that I saw another of my favorite films recently, *Mr. Smith Goes to Washington*, I asked Stewart if they filmed the congressional scenes inside the actual US Senate chamber. "No," he explained, "they wouldn't let us shoot in there. Frank Capra [the director] did everything he could to talk them into it, but the answer was no. So the studio spent over a million dollars to build an exact re-creation of the Senate." Stewart laughed as he asked me, "After they spent that million, do you know what they did with that set when we finished the picture? They chopped the whole thing up into firewood!"

Later, as Bob and I stood in the rear of the room, we noticed an elderly lady alone in a corner, sipping her drink and shifting in and out of her shoes as if her feet hurt. Bob brought her a chair; she thanked him for the courtesy and introduced herself as Josephine ("Call me Joe!"). We struck up a conversation with her; she said she was glad to meet two young men with manners and that she wanted to introduce us to her husband. "He's around here someplace," Joe said as she scouted the room. Then she spotted a short, bald, smiling old man and called him over. "Oh, Jimmy!" she shouted as she beckoned him to join us.

Actor James Stewart, unidentified woman, and me, San Jose, November 12, 1977

Like many of the tuxedoed men at the banquet, "Jimmy" wore the Medal hanging from a blue ribbon around his neck. He beamed as he greeted us, while Joe made the introductions: Bob and I almost fell over when we realized "Jimmy" was General James H. Doolittle, a living legend and one of America's great heroes from World War II. Doolittle had gained fame originally in the 1920s as a test and stunt pilot, winning many national races and flying cross-country when aviation was still in its infancy. He had pioneered the concept of "flying blind," meaning the pilot relies on instruments only for takeoffs and landings. But it was after the outbreak of World War II that Doolittle had earned his lasting fame. Commanding a squadron of planes taking off from the USS *Hornet*, Doolittle had led the daring bombing raid over Tokyo and other Japanese cities. Every plane in Doolittle's mission was shot down or forced to crash-land, with Japanese soldiers capturing and executing some of Doolittle's crew. For his gallantry, President Roosevelt had awarded Doolittle the Medal of Honor.

General and Mrs. James Doolittle and me, San Jose, November 12, 1977

Doolittle showed great interest in my current studies at the University of California in Berkeley because Cal was his alma mater too. Doolittle said he'd enrolled there in 1916 to study mining engineering, but dropped out the following year to enlist in the military. After World War I, he had returned to Cal and obtained his degree in 1922. Joe, also a Cal alumnus, shook my hand and said, "We Cal folks need to stick together!"

Doolittle showed us his Medal of Honor: on the reverse was an engraved account of his exploits for which he received the commendation. Then Joe reached into her purse, retrieved her wallet, and produced a faded snapshot of Franklin Roosevelt presenting Doolittle's award to him. "I remember that night so well," she said. "I got a call late at night from [General Henry] 'Hap' Arnold, who said to come to the White House right away. He didn't give me any other information, and I had no idea what the visit was all about. When I got there, I saw Jimmy for the first time in many months. He looked thin, pale, and near-dead. We went into the Oval Office and met the president, who gave Jimmy the Medal. Nobody told me anything ahead of time!"

. . .

At the banquet, when the Society presented James Stewart its Patriot Award, he choked up as he called the honor "the proudest moment of my life." Noticing tears in his wife, Gloria's, eyes as well, he pointed to her and said, "My wife seems to be crying!"

"Oh, shut up!" she called out to him, evoking great laughter.

Near the end of the evening, Joe Doolittle spied Bob and me near the rear of the ballroom at the press table. She insisted we come and join her table. As we walked to the front of the room, she told us about her husband's current activities: "These days he serves on the board of directors for Mutual of Omaha," she said. "It's the only real business venture he's ever been involved in." She said at eighty-one he still keeps active. "We're flying home tomorrow, and then he leaves on a pheasant-hunting trip."

Throughout the evening, whenever I asked any Medal winners I met what they did to earn their decoration, most replied with something like, "I was in the wrong place at the wrong time," or "I acted before I thought about it." That humility and storytelling reluctance at the beginning of the dinner relaxed as the evening progressed (and liquor flowed). General Doolittle was no exception: when we joined his table, he was discussing the raid on Tokyo with another Medal winner. After Bob and I showed obvious interest in his firsthand account, he pushed all the plates and flatware aside, took out his pen, and sketched for us the epic battle maneuvers on the tablecloth. (I returned later to salvage the tablecloth for posterity, but a waiter had already consigned the relic to the laundry chute.) During this incredible first-hand history lesson,

Doolittle interrupted his narrative and introduced us to the man with whom he was so engrossed in conversation when we joined them: retired Marine colonel Gregory "Pappy" Boyington.

Boyington was every bit as legendary as his tablecloth-defacing companion. As leader of World War II's famous "Black Sheep" squadron, Boyington had shot down twenty-eight Japanese planes, winning both the Navy Cross and the Medal of Honor. Boyington's exploits later became the basis for a network television drama in the 1970s *Baa Baa Black Sheep*. Boyington didn't look like the rest of his decorated colleagues: he eschewed a black tuxedo and showed up in a blue blazer and ruffled shirt. His wardrobe, coupled with his bangs combed down his forehead, made him look more like a lounge singer than a combat hero.

Boyington introduced us to his other tablemates, Thomas A. Pope and Phillip C. Katz. Showing modest reserve, Pope just said that he earned his Medal in 1918 while fighting in France; later I looked him up and learned he'd charged a German machine gun nest to keep their soldiers from firing on his platoon. After hand-to-hand combat, his platoon captured more than one hundred German prisoners. Pope became one of ninety-five Medal of Honor winners from World War I.

Another one of those ninety-five men was Phil Katz, then ninety. When I asked Katz how he earned his Medal, he grinned and said, "Oh, it was just something I did." Jimmy Doolittle filled in the rest: Katz had climbed out of a trench near Eclise Fountaine, France, during World War I and ran through German machine-gun fire to rescue a wounded friend, Phil Page. When Page begged Katz to leave him there and save himself, Katz replied, "Go to hell." Dragging Page to safety through more machine-gun fire, he earned both his Medal and a lifelong friend. Years later, Page managed Katz's successful campaign for the San Francisco Board of Supervisors.

. . .

In 1990, Joseph L. Galloway wrote this about the significance of the Congressional Medal of Honor:

The Medal itself is modest, a gilt bronze star suspended from a pale blue ribbon with 13 tiny white stars. It was born during the dark, early days of the Civil War, created to inspire the reluctant citizen soldiers who filled Union ranks. Before then, the young Republic resolutely spurned military baubles, which seemed a decadent European habit with no place in the New World. From that modest beginning, the Medal of Honor came to represent the highest honor a grateful nation could bestow on its warriors. In [its history] 3,416 men and one woman have earned the nation's highest decoration for valor, about 65 percent of them posthumously. Rarely worn, seldom seen, to today's soldiers it is "the Blue Max," and most serve to retirement without ever meeting even one of the 214 living men entitled to wear it. When they do, they rise automatically to show respect for the man, the Medal, the deed.[1]

As Galloway noted, most people never meet a holder of the Congressional Medal of Honor. As a young college kid, I was privileged one night long ago to share an evening with more than a hundred of them. I came away from that evening with the understanding that the Medal, by itself, means little. But when it is worn around the neck of a recipient, it means liberty, sacrifice, freedom.

It means everything.

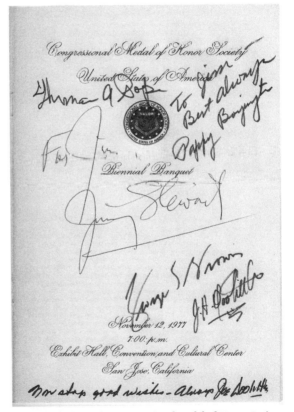

My program from the Congressional Medal of Honor Society banquet, November 12, 1977: autographed by General and Mrs. James Doolittle, actor James Stewart, Colonel Gregory "Pappy" Boyington, General George S. Brown (chairman of the Joint Chiefs of Staff); and Thomas A. Pope

---

1   "Medal of Honor: Profiles in Courage," *US News & World Report*, September 10, 1990.

The Doolittles and I corresponded frequently over the next few years. Age didn't slow down either of them: the letters I received from Joe and the general came postmarked from adventures such as elk hunting in Idaho, fishing in Washington, antelope hunting in Wyoming, cattle ranching in Oregon, Bohemian Grove encampments; postcards came from vacations in London, Honolulu, and many other cities.

In 1979, after Bob and I moved to Los Angeles to attend UCLA, Joe and her "master" (as she called him) moved from Santa Monica to Carmel, California. When Joe flew to Los Angeles to see her eye doctor, she'd call us to say she was in town. One day after she moved north, we picked her up at Los Angeles International Airport and drove her to her medical appointment. Later we spent a delightful afternoon with her, dining at the Doolittles' favorite restaurant (Stern's Barbecue in Culver City), and then touring her favorite haunts in Santa Monica, including her former home at 233 Marguerita Street. During our visit she shared recollections of their old military friends: General "Georgie" Patton ("a great historian and egotist who only wanted to lead a battle"); General "Doug" MacArthur ("Jimmy says he was as good a general as he thought about himself, but my, how he desperately wanted to be president"); "Ike and Mamie" Eisenhower ("During the war, Mamie liked to play mahjong; she was disappointed when I stopped playing with her"); and General Mark Clark ("He calls

General James Doolittle (wearing the Congressional Medal of Honor), San Jose, California, November 12, 1977

Jimmy 'Junior,' since Jimmy is three months younger").

Once I wrote Joe and asked if the general had any of his World War II military patches left. She wrote back an apologetic note, saying all his memorabilia had been donated years ago to the Smithsonian. However, a few weeks

later, I received another note from Joe. She said that while cleaning out a trunk, she found Jimmy's old Eighth Army Air Force Command flight jacket (from 1943); she removed its embroidered patch and sent it to me.

To this day, the general's patch is a prized treasure in my memorabilia collection.

General James Doolittle's jacket patch from his 1943 Eighth Army Air Force Command

. . .

Academy Award–winning actor James Stewart died of a heart attack at age eighty-nine on July 2, 1997. His wife, Gloria, had died of cancer three years before, on February 17, 1994.

General James Doolittle died peacefully at his home in Carmel at age ninety-six on September 27, 1993. His wife, Josephine, had died five years earlier, on Christmas Eve 1988 (their seventy-first wedding anniversary).

Colonel Gregory "Pappy" Boyington died of cancer at age seventy-five on January 11, 1988.

Thomas A. Pope became the last surviving World War I Congressional Medal of Honor winner. He died at age ninety-four on June 14, 1989.

Phil Katz was America's oldest surviving Medal of Honor winner when he died one month before his one-hundredth birthday on October 29, 1987. A few years before he died, the California State Legislature awarded Katz and the state's thirty-five other Medal of Honor recipients a special "Congressional Medal of Honor" license plate. As the oldest of the Medal winners, they issued to Katz plate number one.

15

Memphis

Midway through Jimmy Carter's presidency, the Democratic National Committee (DNC) convened a three-day "midterm" party convention in Memphis. Carter hoped to use the forum to solidify his base and quell those liberal dissidents hoping to convince Senator Edward Kennedy to challenge Carter's 1980 renomination bid. Although Kennedy stated he "expected" to support Carter, he criticized the administration's social policies frequently. These potshots fueled the Carter campaign's concern over both Kennedy's steady lead in the polls and the feverish media preoccupation with the senator's intentions. From the White House's perspective, Ted Kennedy was an irritant, not a soul mate.

The Carter loyalists in control of the DNC's midterm convention couldn't silence Kennedy, but they could sequester him. They scheduled Carter for the primetime keynote address on the opening night (with his speech preceded by a pro-Carter documentary film); the DNC relegated Kennedy to a fifteen-minute afternoon speech at an off-site workshop on health care, where he would share the forum with ten other panelists.

I attended the Memphis conference as a delegate from Alameda County, California. As my diary notes show from our first delegation meeting, my dissatisfaction with the party of my youth was growing apparent even then:

December 7, 1978

Today I attended the caucus of the California delegation in our Memphis hotel. Mary Warren, chair of our delegation, issued our convention credentials and presided over the election of a vice chair. A representative from every conceivable group nominated one of their own for the position, urging us to vote for their favored candidate based solely on "qualifications" such as race, gender, union membership, sexual proclivities, and similar factors. Not one nomination speech urged the selection of a vice chair based on ability, merit, or party service. It was a quota free-for-all, with each group trying to "out-victim" the other. The spectacle distressed me; I walked out without casting a vote.

When I entered the Cook Convention Center, it became clear that the White House dominated the agenda: Jimmy Carter's face adorned the convention program, the official convention schedule, and even the DNC magazine tucked in every participant's "Welcome to Memphis" bag. As delegates entered the hall, people checking their credentials issued them a green-and-white campaign button reading, "Carter Mondale 1980."

I wandered around, taking pictures, before the opening gavel. Near the Arkansas delegation the news photographers trained their lenses on the president's son, Chip Carter, as he chatted

Here I am as a delegate to the 1978 Democratic National Midterm Convention, Memphis, December 7, 1978

with a shaggy-haired, thirty-one-year-old state politician wearing a tweed coat with wide lapels and shank buttons on the pockets. This unknown, young Southerner's moment in the convention sun would come the following afternoon when he served as moderator for the much-anticipated panel discussion featuring Senator Kennedy. But right now, on the convention floor, all cameras were trained on the presidential offspring, not on his conversation mate.

The convention opened a half hour late, and disruptions from various state delegations delayed the program further. To make up the lost time, handlers started scrubbing scheduled speakers: among the casualties were Democratic National Committee chairman John C. White and Speaker of the US House of Representatives Thomas P. "Tip" O'Neill, Jr. By the time the lights dimmed for the Carter propaganda film, the convention ran almost two hours behind schedule.

At the film's conclusion, White introduced the president; the Memphis State Marching Band played "Hail to the Chief" as Jimmy and Rosalynn Carter appeared from behind the curtains and greeted Vice President and Mrs. Walter Mondale at the podium. Carter and Mondale joined arms and waved to the delegates; when the surprisingly brief ovation ended, Carter began his remarks by joking that the film preceding his speech was "the best network news program I've seen since I became president!"

Following Carter's lackluster speech, Mrs. Carter and the Mondales joined him onstage. The audience applauded politely, but Carter's uninspiring speech struck no emotional chord with the delegates. *Newsweek* magazine later described Carter's missed opportunity:

> [The midterm conference] seemed like the perfect setting for Jimmy Carter. ... [Yet] when he pronounced his grand theme, no one clapped. One delegate from New York munched a ham sandwich; one woman from Texas fixed her makeup. When the band played "Happy Days Are Here Again," it looked as though nobody believed it. "It showed both his problems and his potential," said a delegate from Illinois. "How do you bring a crowd to its feet by talking about inflation?" ... Even many of Carter's supporters seemed lukewarm. "He creates no great enthusiasm and he creates no great hostility," sighed Rep. Paul Simon of Illinois. "There's simply no verve of any kind."[1]

---

1   *Newsweek*, December 18, 1978.

If Carter came to Memphis to do oratorical battle with Ted Kennedy, then his mission failed—even before Kennedy uttered a word.

The "exclusive" invitation I received to a private reception for the Carters and the Mondales (following the president's address) from North Carolina governor Jim Hunt was anything but that: when I learned the "exclusive" guest list included every delegate and alternate to the convention, I decided to skip it. During the benediction, I slipped out of the hall and headed in the opposite direction of the presidential soirée, hoping to avoid the maddening crush of delegates flocking to Carter's event. As I made my way through the almost-empty lobby of the convention center, I stopped to put away my camera. Someone from behind tapped me on the shoulder; I turned and faced a ramrod-straight military officer with close-cropped hair and a large presidential emblem on his chest. "Excuse me," the officer said, "but the president would like to greet you." As he spoke, he placed both hands on my shoulders and spun me gently ninety degrees until I looked directly into the blue eyes of Jimmy Carter. I was so taken off guard by the encounter that it took a moment before I recognized him. Carter shook my hand: "It's nice to meet you," he said. "How did you like my speech?"

Mercifully, I didn't need to answer. Someone shouted excitedly, "Hey, there's the president!" From out of nowhere, hordes of people converged on Carter. "Thank you," Carter said as he gave my hand a quick pump and tossed me over to Mrs. Carter, Vice President and Mrs. Mondale, and Governor Hunt (whose "pump-and-go" handshake marked the end of the reception).

. . .

The next day, the convention held twenty-four domestic and international policy workshops for delegates, with administration officials plugging Carter's programs at each one. Two competing workshops promised to attract the most attention: one with President Carter and the other with Senator Kennedy.

At Carter's workshop, delegate attendance inside Conference Room N proved sparse enough for me to find a center seat in the front row. The panelists filed in and took their places: US senator John Culver (D-IA), two Carter administration officials (David Aaron, national security adviser to the president; William Perry, under secretary of defense), and the moderator, South Carolina governor-elect Richard Riley. One seat remained empty at the table. Riley introduced Aaron and Perry, each of whom promoted the Carter administration's goals of increased defense spending while seeking arms reductions with the Soviet Union. Liberals in the audience cheered Culver, who dissented and urged cutbacks in the military to help fund more social programs.

President Jimmy Carter speaking at a defense policy workshop, Memphis, December 9, 1978

As Culver spoke, Riley interrupted: "Senator Culver," Riley said, "I apologize, but it is time for me to introduce our mystery guest. Ladies and gentlemen, the president of the United States." Surrounded by Secret Service agents, Carter shook hands as he made his way to the table.

During the workshop, Carter defended his military spending goals to the dismay of the heavily liberal audience. After Culver spoke for them and challenged the administration's priorities, Carter delivered a stern rebuke: "As long as I am in the White House, I will keep a strong defense."

A few hours later, I squeezed into Dixon-Meyer Hall for the health care workshop, which drew national media attention because of Kennedy's attendance. Earlier that morning, only three hundred people had shown up for Carter's symposium; more than twenty-five hundred people packed the hall for Kennedy, leaving standing room only. The young, Southern politician I had seen talking to Chip Carter the previous night now served as the forum moderator.

When Kennedy arrived and joined the other ten panelists, the audience went wild. His brief speech calling for implementing guaranteed national health insurance and a greater commitment to spending programs drew repeated standing ovations. In a direct slap to Carter's earlier remarks at the defense workshop, Kennedy thundered: "We cannot accept policies that cut spending to the bone in areas like jobs and health, but allows billions of dollars in wasteful spending for defense . . . The party that tore itself apart over Vietnam in the 1960s cannot afford to tear itself apart today over budget cuts in basic social programs." As the crowd cheered and chanted his name, Kennedy vowed to continue speaking out "as long as I have a voice in the US Senate."

Kennedy left the room after completing his remarks; when he departed, the spectators filed out of the hall with him. Only a handful remained to hear the other panelists; two hours after Kennedy left, the speakers still hadn't finished their opening statements to the almost-empty auditorium. The smiling young moderator apologized for the program falling behind schedule; he allowed only two delegates to ask questions before he adjourned the session (well past the dinner hour).

Nobody—except me—paid attention to the moderator as he collected his papers and prepared to leave. I had recognized him the night before because I'd read a previous news story about his rapid political rise: two years earlier, at age thirty (and only three years out of law school), voters back home had elected him state attorney general.

I introduced myself to the moderator and said I hoped to follow his lead into law school and, later, politics. We chatted for maybe fifteen minutes about the opportunities that open up from a legal education. He encouraged me to study law, continue my interest in government, and told me to keep him posted on my progress. I thought he was a great guy to take so much time for someone who couldn't vote for him and didn't live in his home state of Arkansas.

Although the young moderator circulated in Memphis anonymously that week, in later years he played on a profoundly larger stage.

His name was Bill Clinton.

. . .

During his Memphis speech, President Carter chided Democrats who complained that the price tag for the midterm conference paid out of party coffers was a waste of money. Although Carter later proclaimed the conference a success, I suspect he came to regret the expense. The midterm convention gave anti-Carter forces a national platform from which to showcase their organized hostility. The seeds of belligerence planted in Memphis in 1978 grew into a divisive and bitter struggle between the Carter and Kennedy forces for the Democratic presidential nomination in 1980. When the internecine warfare ended, Carter emerged the winner, but the victory was Pyrrhic. Ronald Reagan's juggernaut swamped Carter and his party in the general election, and the Democratic National Committee never again held a midterm convention.

As for the young moderator at Senator Kennedy's health care conference, it was twenty years after our pleasant meeting in Memphis—not only to the day, but almost to the very hour—that I sat as a member of the House Judiciary Committee and cast my vote to impeach President Bill Clinton. As the clerk called the roll on that tense, rancorous evening, a river of thoughts ran through my mind as I voted on the historic question.

But mostly, I thought about Memphis.

16

Something to Tell Your Grandkids

On the eve of the 1980 presidential election, every poll suggested the race between President Jimmy Carter and former California governor Ronald Reagan was too close to call. On Election Day, November 4, 1980, I took the night off work from my Sunset Strip bartending job to watch the returns. In preparation for an anticipated late-night vigil, I had a clipboard, charts, and pens spread out on the coffee table to help me track races and trends.

Since the networks began broadcasting live election coverage on the West Coast too early for any meaningful returns, I laced up my running shoes for a quick afternoon jog before anything significant happened. When I returned less than an hour later, it was over: NBC's map had America colored almost solidly red for Reagan. News anchorman John Chancellor appeared stunned that modern polls could have been so wrong: returns now showed a Reagan landslide. Just as surprising, Carter delivered his concession speech almost three hours before polls closed on the West Coast (many incumbent Democrats later blamed their loss on Carter's premature surrender).

Although still a registered Democrat, I voted for Reagan in 1980 because I came to believe in his platform of economic growth through lower taxes, peace through strength, and eliminating bureaucratic strangulation. Reagan's common-sense petition to individual responsibility appealed to me greatly. Still, I felt like a traitor entering the voting booth that morning: after glancing over my shoulder to see if anybody watched, I marked my ballot for the straight Republican ticket. As it turned out, millions of Democrats around the country did the very same thing–and for the very same reason.

When my boyhood friend Frank Ambrose dropped by, we watched the live news coverage of Reagan leaving his Pacific Palisades home in the late afternoon to dine with friends before proceeding to his nineteenth-floor suite at the Century Plaza Hotel to await the final returns. Frank agreed to my impulsive suggestion that we drive to the Century Plaza and try to see Reagan's victory speech in person later that evening.

As dusk settled, reporters, camera crews, satellite dishes, and delirious crowds packed the inside and outside of Reagan's hotel. Frank and I tried to enter the Grand Ballroom for Reagan's appearance, but the Secret Service had by then blocked all entrances and exits onto the lower floor, where the ballroom was located. From the lobby, we heard the walls shake when a thundering ovation greeted Reagan and his family as he stepped onstage to claim victory. The deafening chant of "We want Reagan! We want Reagan!" could be heard in every part of the huge hotel.

Undaunted by the lockout, I looked for an unsecured means of entry. I grabbed Frank's arm and told him, "Hey, follow me." I opened a side door, and we wended our way through a maze of hallways, corridors, and pantries, looking for an unguarded ballroom entrance. I saw a door ajar and opened it quietly: by accident we stumbled into the Secret Service observation booth above the ballroom! The agents stood with their backs toward us and watched Reagan and the ballroom crowd below through binoculars, maintaining communication with other agents through radios. I exhaled only when I realized they didn't notice our accidental discovery.

Frank panicked: "Holy shit!" he whispered. "Let's get the hell out of here!" Frank didn't wait for my acquiescence; he turned and dashed back down the hall, trying to retrace his steps frantically. Since I expected the Secret Service to arrest me anyway, I remained by the doorway to watch Reagan as he introduced his family, and then promised to work to unify the nation: "I consider the trust you have placed in me sacred, and I give you my oath that I will do my utmost to justify your faith." After Reagan finished his momentous appearance, I slipped out of the room and closed the door behind me; the Secret Service never knew I'd intruded.

When I returned to the mezzanine, I found a very agitated Frank pacing back and forth and looking for me. He wasted no time in giving me an earful: "You stupid bastard!" he growled at me. "Are you crazy with your 'Hey, follow me'? We could've been shot! Besides, I've got a warrant out for my arrest–and I've got weed in my pocket! Don't you *ever* do that to me again!"

"Frank," I reminded him gently, "you'll be able to tell your grandkids someday that you saw Ronald Reagan the night he was elected president of the United States. Isn't it worth going to jail for something like that?" Frank stared hard at me, and then he stopped yelling.

Rare campaign badge from the private reception held with Ronald Reagan and his longtime friends on the night he won the presidency, Century Plaza Hotel, Los Angeles, November 4, 1980

Later, a coterie of Reagan's earliest supporters and closest friends exited from one of the small ballrooms after a private meeting with the new president-elect. All wore orange buttons captioned, "November 4, 1980–President-elect Ronald Reagan," which were distributed to them exclusively inside this historic reception. While I bartered with attendees, trying to get one for my political memorabilia collection (I succeeded eventually), Frank slipped away and disappeared.

While looking for Frank, I passed Lyn Nofziger, Reagan's campaign press secretary. Nofziger may well have been the only person in the entire hotel not dressed for the event: his hair stood on end, his Mickey Mouse tie was askew, and his suit looked like he'd slept in it for a week (given the frantic pace of the campaign's closing days, he probably had).

I found Frank in an unlikely tableau: uncouth and unemployed Frank sat on a marble table in a busy corridor; seated next to him and engaged deeply in conversation with Frank was the legendary comic from radio, television, and movie fame, Red Skelton. Frank and Skelton laughed and joked as if they were long-lost brothers–all while puffing on expensive cigars from Skelton's private stock. The star didn't seem to mind Frank's earthy expression of appreciation for his talent (I've cleaned up the language so you wouldn't think Frank's vocabulary was dominated by a single four-letter word): "Red! You're a funny dude, Red! Hey, thanks for the stogie, babe! Yeah, Red, you're a funny dude..." Then Frank saw me approach: "Hey, Jimmy, come over here. Red, here's my friend, Jimmy. Give him a cigar too, Red."

I shook hands and accepted a cigar from Skelton, but I was still too dumb-founded by the weird scene to make sense of it. Skelton whispered something to Frank; they shared another hearty laugh, Skelton patted him on the back, and then he left. I looked at Frank in amazement. "What the hell was that all about?" I asked.

Frank just smiled and shrugged: "What can I say?" Frank chuckled. "I'm a man of the people."

A few minutes later, a sudden commotion erupted in the hallway. Red Skelton ran by, shouting, "Somebody took my briefcase! Where's my brief-case? Call hotel security!" I looked at Frank (known to have more than a bit of larceny in his veins).

"I swear to you!" Frank whispered as he raised his hand in oath-like fashion.

"Relax, Frank," I said. "You might swipe a case of beer from a delivery truck, but I know you'd have no use for Red Skelton's briefcase. Grab your cigar and let's go."

By now security had reopened the Grand Ballroom; although the Reagans had left the hotel, the jubilee remained in full swing. The band played while happy celebrants danced and sang, toasting their victory from one of several open bars in the festively decorated room. Reporters and camera crews scoured the floor, interviewing local and state Republican Party leaders. My hopes of finding additional campaign memorabilia for my collection were dashed: nobody wanted to part with mementos of a very historic night.

In that ballroom, only minutes earlier, the Reagan Revolution had begun.

. . .

Frank never did explain how he ended up seated on that table, smoking cigars with Red Skelton, nor did he offer any explanation about the missing briefcase. The last time I asked him about it, he told me, "There are some things that you just don't need to know—and ain't going in your book."

. . .

In later years I was privileged to become friends with Lyn Nofziger; I'll share some of his Reagan memories later. He died of cancer at age eighty-one on March 27, 2006.

Comedian Red Skelton died of pneumonia at age eighty-four on September 17, 1997.

17

What Case Is He On?

The American Film Institute named Cary Grant one of the "Greatest Male Stars of All Time." With the rich legacy of motion picture roles he left behind, few question the ranking. Twice nominated for the Academy Award for Best Actor, Grant starred in such classic movies as *The Awful Truth*, *Bringing Up Baby*, *Gunga Din*, *The Philadelphia Story*, *His Girl Friday*, *Arsenic and Old Lace*, *The Bishop's Wife*, *An Affair to Remember*, and Hitchcock's *North by Northwest*.

In 1986, when I was a young prosecutor in the Los Angeles County district attorney's office, I had a friend who worked for the legendary actor. Knowing I'm an old film buff, my friend gave me Grant's private post office box and suggested I drop him a note. "Tell him who you are, that you know me, and that you'd like to meet him," he said. "He might say yes, and then you can talk with him about his film career. What have you got to lose?" I took the advice and wrote the note to Grant. I forgot about the letter almost as quickly as I mailed it.

A few weeks went by. On November 21, after a long morning in court, the judge recessed our trial for lunch. I was leaving the DA's office with my boss, Walt Lewis, when the receptionist paged me to the phone. I picked up an extension line and heard a woman with a British accent say, "Good afternoon, Mr. Rogan. This is Mr. Grant's secretary. Please hold for Mr. Grant."

"What case is he on?" I asked, assuming that some lawyer named Grant wanted to talk about a matter I was prosecuting.

"I beg your pardon?" the secretary replied.

"Do you know what case this is about so I can get the file before I talk with him?" I asked.

"Please hold for Mr. Cary Grant."

Oh.

Within moments an unmistakable voice–imitated by thousands of impersonators over the decades–boomed over the receiver: "Hello, Mr. Rogan. This is Cary Grant." I stood gape-mouthed as he continued:

"I received your note, and I want you to know how very flattered I was to get it. I was touched by the kind words you expressed in it. I would very much like to meet with you, but I can't set up anything for a couple of months. I'm traveling extensively doing shows right now, and I am leaving for a trip to Iowa. I don't get a lot of rest for a man my age–I'm eighty-two years old! But when I get back, I'll give you a call and we'll set up something."

As I listened to Grant speak, Walt started tugging on my elbow. "Come on," he griped, "I'm hungry; let's go. Who is it, anyway?"

I put my hand over the mouthpiece. "It's Cary Grant," I whispered.

Walt laughed. "Oh, sure–tell Cary hello for me! Who is it?"

"No, it's really Cary Grant!"

I told Grant I was shocked, but honored, to get his call. "Oh, don't mention it," he replied. "I always prefer to dispose of my business over the telephone. It's much easier that way for me."

I said I looked forward to meeting him when his schedule settled down, and asked if he might send me an autographed picture as a memento of our conversation. "Well, I wish I could," he said, "but I retired from motion pictures over twenty years ago, and I haven't had a picture taken since then. I'd hate to send one of me looking like an old goat!" He balked when I offered to get one and send it to him: "The problem with you mailing one to me is that my staff routinely returns or ignores those things when collectors send them in, and I'm afraid your picture will get lost in the shuffle. When we get together you can bring one and I'll be happy to sign it. That's a promise."

I thanked Grant for the call, and said nobody would believe me when I told them about it–including my boss, who was at my elbow and didn't believe me right now. "You're a district attorney," Grant laughed. "Don't you have any credibility?"

"Mr. Grant, now you sound like an ex-girlfriend!" He laughed louder and said he'd get in touch with me when he returned from his trip. I wished him a successful journey and thanked him again.

"Who was that, really?" Walt asked when I hung up the receiver. I told him.

"Bullshit. Okay, let's go eat. You can buy lunch for keeping me waiting."

When it came to assessing my credibility, I guess Cary Grant was prescient.

. . .

Cary Grant and I never met.

On November 29, a week after his telephone call to me, Cary Grant arrived in Davenport to do his one-man show, *A Conversation with Cary Grant*. While getting ready to leave his suite at the Blackhawk Hotel for the theater, he suffered a stroke and died that night.

18

Pretend I Am Dead

Spiro T. Agnew's political career rose like a rocket. A local Maryland attorney, Agnew ran successfully for Baltimore county executive in 1962; four years later, he won the governorship, and in eighteen more months Republican presidential nominee Richard Nixon picked Agnew as his running mate. In 1968, the Nixon–Agnew ticket defeated the Democratic nominees narrowly; four years later, they won reelection in a landslide. However, as Nixon's presidency dissolved slowly with each new Watergate revelation, Agnew faced an unrelated crisis: in late 1973 federal prosecutors indicted him for allegedly accepting bribes of more than a hundred thousand dollars while a local, state, and federal official. On October 10, 1973, Agnew resigned the vice presidency and pleaded no contest to a single charge of failing to report income.

Unlike many former political leaders, Agnew craved anonymity. Eschewing almost all requests for interviews and public appearances after leaving Washington, he lived quietly in the Palm Springs area, pursuing his private business interests. Of course, as a student of history, I wanted to meet Agnew and discuss his years in Washington. Knowing he refused interviews, I wrote anyway and made my request, mentioning that as a member of the Young Voters for the President delegation to the 1972 Republican National Convention, I had witnessed his acceptance speech.

Once again, brazenness paid off. On January 5, 1987, I returned home from work to a voice message on my answering machine. "Mr. Rogan," the nasal voice intoned, "this is Mr. Agnew. Please call me back." When I dialed the home number he left for me, Agnew answered the phone himself. He suggested we meet at Los Angeles International Airport a few days later: "I am flying to Korea on Wednesday," he said. "Meet me in the VIP lounge of the Korean Air Lines terminal about ten forty-five in the morning. You can ask your questions then."

I thanked him for the opportunity and for his call.

Two days later, Agnew called me at work to delay our meeting by a day. The district attorney's receptionist answered the telephone.

"Is Mr. Rogan there?" the former vice president asked.

"I'm sorry," she responded. "He's in court. May I take a message?"

"This is Mr. Agnew."

"Who?" the receptionist asked, not knowing to whom she spoke.

"Mr. Agnew," he said again. "A-G-N-E-W."

She repeated back the spelling, and then she asked, "Agnew–is that spelled just like Agnew the crook?"

Later, I returned Agnew's call without mentioning my receptionist's horrible social blunder. Gratefully, he didn't mention it either.

. . .

After making an early court appearance, I drove to LAX and checked in with the clerk at the Korean Air Lines lounge. She escorted me inside a private waiting area, where a couple dozen businessmen sipped tea and read newspapers while awaiting their flights. Agnew sat alone at the far end of the room, working quietly on the *New York Times* crossword puzzle. The other travelers appeared oblivious to his identity.

I approached Agnew and introduced myself. He put down his newspaper, stood, and welcomed me. Neither the years nor his prior travails appeared to do him any long-term damage: Agnew looked tanned and fit. He invited me to join him for tea. "I'm in no hurry," he assured me. "I have almost an hour to kill before my plane arrives."

Agnew asked how long I had been a prosecutor with the Los Angeles County District Attorney's Office, and mentioned he kept following news reports on the lengthy McMartin preschool child molestation trial that dominated the local news in the 1980s. "Your boss, Ira Reiner, is doing a good job," he noted, "although I don't care much for prosecutors after what a bunch of them did to me.

Nothing personal, but I felt the prosecutors looking into my case were dishonest."

Not wanting him to dwell on his distaste for my profession, I changed the subject and handed him a few items to autograph for my collection, including his memoir, *Go Quietly ... or Else*.

"Have you read the book?" he asked.

When I told him I'd just obtained it for our meeting and hadn't perused it yet, he leaned forward and locked his eyes on mine, saying, "When you read it, you will see what I mean. It shows how the prosecutors in my case relied on perjured testimony and unreliable statements from known criminals to pursue their case. They gave them immunity for their lies and made me an open target. I was given nothing before entering my plea. I obtained my discovery documents later under the Freedom of Information Act. Had I known how terrible their case was against me, I never would have been blackmailed into pleading no contest."

Agnew inscribed the book, and then signed for me a small campaign card from his first race in 1962 for Baltimore County executive. "Where did you get this?" he asked as he studied the card. "This was from my first political campaign. I never really wanted to go into politics and didn't intend to run for office. I got started accidentally when I joined the local Kiwanis Club. Once I got started, they would not let me out."

I asked Agnew if he ever missed politics. "No," he said forcefully. "I didn't like politics and I don't miss it. The press hated me and still hates me. They were not satisfied to beat me politically–they wanted to destroy me personally. Long after I left office, they kept trying to look into my private business deals. After going broke from having to defend myself against every crank

Early Spiro Agnew campaign card from his local 1962 campaign for county executive

lawsuit filed, I tried to get a consulting business going. Eventually I set up a lucrative deal with the government of Indonesia that would help my family and me get back on our feet. The *New York Times* learned about it and began calling every government leader in Indonesia to interrogate them. The Indonesian government did not need or want all of the publicity, so they pulled out of the deal.

"As far as the press and the world are concerned," he went on, "I want them all to forget me and pretend I am dead. I try to be as anonymous as possible wherever I go. I travel alone. I take no associates with me. Whenever a reporter calls to interview me, I hang up. I don't give interviews. Ted Koppel of ABC News keeps calling and trying to get me on his show. I tell him no way."

Pausing only to take an occasional sip of tea, Agnew continued calmly: "The thing that really gets me after all these years is this: I can never really be anonymous. No matter where in the world I travel, people still recognize me and think, *There goes Agnew the crook*. Last year I was picking up my luggage at the airport in Korea, and I noticed a few Americans standing across the baggage carousel. They were pointing at me and whispering. I knew what they were saying: 'There's Agnew the crook.' The stares really get to you."

Remembering my receptionist's faux pas, I tried again to direct the conversation to more neutral topics: "Mr. Vice President," I asked, "what was it like for you to stand on the steps of the Capitol and raise your hand to be sworn in as vice president? What thoughts went through your mind as you took the oath of office?" I expected Agnew to offer some soul-stirring memories, but I was mistaken.

"It was no big deal," Agnew replied. "I was used to such ceremonies. I went through the same thing when I was sworn in as governor of Maryland. The one big advantage to being vice president was the logistical support one gets when traveling. The Secret Service coordinated all my travel. I never drove a car in over six years while I was running for and serving as vice president."

When I asked Agnew if he ever spoke with former president Nixon, the man who'd picked the obscure Maryland governor as his running mate in 1968, Agnew shook his head in dismay: "I haven't seen him or spoken with him since the day I resigned, and I have no desire to see him or speak with him. I was very bitter over the way he treated me. He tried to use my legal troubles as a way to avoid the bad publicity he was receiving because of the breaking Watergate scandal. He treated me terribly. I have heard from friends who remain in touch with Nixon that he is now sorry for the way he treated me during those years, but he only expresses such sorrow through intermediaries. He has never expressed it to me. The only person who treated me worse than Nixon was his chief of staff, Alexander Haig, who is a terrible man."

For all the apparent hard feelings, I found Agnew to be unemotional and matter-of-fact when discussing such unpleasantries; his forthright answers proved surprising, especially since he shared them with a stranger.

Former vice president Spiro T. Agnew and me, Los Angeles International Airport, January 9, 1987

Agnew's tone softened noticeably when he discussed his current activities, saying his business travels take him to Korea at least six times a year. "Mrs. Agnew travels with me once or twice a year," he said, "I've made fifty-six trips to Korea since resigning the vice presidency. It's a thirteen-hour flight each way, so when I go, I stay for two or three weeks to get in as much business as possible. I've piled up my frequent-flier miles; they owe me five free flights."

As we took a picture shaking hands, the photographer asked if he ever felt like a beauty queen when posing for photos. "Oh, I've done this a lot of times over the years," he replied. "I remember one day when I posed with 435 members of Congress for individual photographs. Even the Democrats were excited about having a picture taken with me. But that was a long time ago . . ." His voice dropped off.

It was time for Agnew to board his plane. I thanked him for the invitation and for taking the time to visit. As we finished our tea, I asked him one last question: given everything he had achieved and then endured, was his time in political life worth it?

Agnew paused for a moment, and then grinned. "If I had to do it all over," he said, "I still would have joined the Kiwanis Club–but nothing else!"

. . .

On September 17, 1996, Agnew became ill suddenly and was admitted to a local Maryland hospital. Tests run that day revealed advanced-stage leukemia, which had gone undiagnosed. He died only a few hours after the diagnosis at age seventy-seven.

19

In the Shadows

U nder other circumstances, history might remember Mack Robinson as one of America's great athletes. An Olympic medalist, Mack set records in NCAA, AAU, and Pacific Coast Conference track meets. He is enshrined in the Oregon Sports Hall of Fame and the University of Oregon Hall of Fame. Yet few remember Mack today because he lived under two mighty shadows.

As one of America's first black Olympic track stars, Mack represented the United States at the 1936 Berlin games presided over by Adolf Hitler. In the historic two hundred–meter race, Mack (who had no running coach) wore the same beat-up track shoes he'd used in college competitions. By the time he got to Berlin, those shoes were disintegrating on his feet as he ran a close second in that race– and Jesse Owens went on to immortality by nosing out Mack for the gold medal by 0.4 seconds. Then, a decade later, Mack's athletic legacy again was overshadowed by America's fixation on the accomplishment of his younger brother Jackie, who smashed through the segregation line of Major League Baseball.

My encounter with Mack Robinson was not under pleasant circumstances. In 1987 I was a Los Angeles County deputy district attorney prosecuting the murder case of *People v. Hamilton*; the defendant's girlfriend at the time of the killings was Mack Robinson's daughter Kathy–and she proved a very reluctant witness for the prosecution. My cocounsel, Bill Holliman, and I wanted to make sure Kathy hadn't given police less-than-complete information about her boyfriend's whereabouts on the night of the killings, so we set up an interview with her parents to measure the credibility of her statements.

Along with homicide detective Janet Stewart, Bill and I arrived at the Robinson family home in Pasadena. Del Robinson (Mack's wife) greeted us at the door and escorted us inside. When I apologized for coming so early, Del waved off my concern. "I've been up since five this morning giving Mack his insulin shots," she explained. "He's a diabetic."

Once inside, Mack Robinson leaned heavily on his cane as he rose to welcome us. Now in his seventies, the man bore no resemblance to the lean, young runner in a nearby framed photograph. His gray hair sat atop thick, mutton-chop sideburns and a mustache; his portly stomach hid under a snug T-shirt. On the walls hung framed sports mementos—mostly related to his younger brother. Photographs that did depict Mack showed him at various celebrations for Jackie: Mack alongside a Jackie Robinson statue, Mack christening Jackie Robinson Park, Mack holding the official Jackie Robinson postage stamp. The only relics I saw from Mack's career was an old photograph of Mack running, which hung on a wall near the kitchen alongside a certificate captioned "XL Olympiade Berlin 1936."

Our questioning of the Robinsons produced only the vaguest recollections, and provided only marginal help. The only personal, revealing comment Mack made was when he shared his grief knowing that his daughter might have dated a guy involved in a double murder. "I don't know," he said glumly. "Kids don't listen. They never do. That boyfriend of hers never even worked—Kathy worked. I don't know . . ." His eyes filled with tears.

Hoping to change the mood to a more positive tone, I pivoted from investigation-related questions and asked Mack to tell us about his 1936 Berlin experience. That didn't have the desired result: his demeanor went from glum to resentful. "Hitler was in the stands when I ran in that race with Jesse Owens," he said. "But I wasn't watching Hitler. I was too busy running. Besides, those Nazis in Germany didn't treat us any worse than America did after the Olympic Games. Ten out of the eleven blacks on our Olympic team won medals in Berlin, but our own country ignored us when we came home. I used to sweep streets here in Pasadena wearing my Olympic jacket. The City of Pasadena has yet to honor me. They have never had a 'Mack Robinson Day,' and they never will. Nobody remembers me and nobody cares. I'm ignored and forgotten. Jesse Owens won the race by an eyelash, and he is the one now in the history books.

People remember Jesse Owens and Jackie Robinson, but they don't give a damn about Mack Robinson."

Del looked down at her shoes, saying nothing. Clearly, she'd heard this before. I told Mack he was very wrong: "Listen, Mack, here we are–fifty years after you ran in Berlin," I said, "and I don't want to leave without getting your autograph." Bill and Jan chided me for asking, but when Del dug through a box and found a few old pictures of Mack from Berlin, they almost trampled over me to get theirs first. Mack's demeanor softened at the appreciation we showed for his career. He smiled, put on his glasses, and signed each snapshot for us.

When it was time to go, the Robinsons walked us to our car. Mack appeared oblivious to the bitterly cold weather as he stood at the gate in a T-shirt and talked about his daughter. "I used to wait here for Kathy to come home at night," he said. "We tried to raise her right. That boyfriend never worked. I don't know . . ."

Mack said good-bye; shaking his head, he turned and walked slowly back inside.

Photograph of 1936 Olympian Mack Robinson autographed for me, December 30, 1987

. . .

After four separate murder trials ended in hung juries (with one jury hanging 11–1 for guilty, and another jury hanging–on the same evidence–10–2 for not guilty), the judge dismissed murder charges against Harles Hamilton.

Many years later, I was Mack and Del Robinson's congressman when he died of complications from diabetes, kidney failure, and pneumonia in Pasadena at the age of eighty-five on March 12, 2000. Had he lived a few months longer, he would have seen Congress pass and President Clinton sign into law my legislation naming the federal building in Pasadena after him.

By the way, that building is down the street from what is now the Jackie and Mack Robinson Memorial Park. A large sculpted bust of Mack sits on the street he used to sweep while wearing his Olympic jacket.

20

Finch on Nixon
(and a Few Others)

Robert H. Finch owned a historic footnote not widely known but confirmed by Richard Nixon in his presidential memoir: when Nixon won the 1968 Republican nomination, he asked Finch to be his running mate. Because of Finch's one-word answer to that question, when I met him in 1988 he was a solo-practicing lawyer in a small Pasadena office. Had Finch given a different answer, today there would be a Robert H. Finch Presidential Library, and Gerald Ford would be the name of an obscure former Michigan congressman. (By the way, in later years Finch hosted a fundraising lunch for me when I ran for the state legislature. After he introduced me, I told this story, and then made this astute observation: "If Bob had said yes instead of no, today he'd be the former president of the United States–and I could have charged all of you a hell of a lot more than the lousy fifty bucks you paid to get in here!")

Finch's Republican roots dated back to Wendell Willkie's 1940 presidential campaign. A few years later he befriended a young World War II returning veteran–Richard Nixon, who won election to Congress in 1946. After Nixon became Eisenhower's vice president in 1953, Finch joined Nixon's Washington staff; in 1960, he managed Nixon's national presidential campaign against John F. Kennedy. In 1966, Finch was elected California's lieutenant governor and outpolled the winner of the governorship–Ronald Reagan. In 1969 he resigned his statewide office to join now-president Nixon's first cabinet. My relationship with Finch began that same year: when I was eleven and in the seventh grade, I wrote Finch and asked him to send me an autographed picture for my fledgling political memorabilia collection. A month later he responded with a gracious letter, enclosing signed pictures of both Nixon and himself.

Two decades later, I worked as a prosecutor at the Pasadena courthouse in the DA's office. While reading the morning newspaper, I spotted a "Where Are They Now?" article about Finch. Although his own political career ended in 1976 with a failed US Senate race, he remained a powerful behind-the-scenes presence in California Republican politics. I grew particularly interested in the article when I read that Finch's law office was just down the street from mine on Colorado Boulevard. I sent Finch a copy of his 1969 letter and invited him to lunch. A couple of weeks later, he called, and that started a friendship that lasted until his death.

Bob and I got together socially on occasion. During one conversation over lunch, I jotted down some recollections of his years with Nixon, of whom he spoke more as an older brother than as a boss:

My association with Richard Nixon dates back to 1946, when Nixon first ran for Congress against incumbent Jerry Voorhis. Nobody thought Nixon had a chance to win, but he upset Voorhis on Election Day. Because we became close friends, I went from being a local Republican county chairman to a member of his inner circle.

When Nixon became vice president in 1953 under Dwight Eisenhower, he asked me to run his office. In 1960, when he ran against John F. Kennedy, Nixon appointed me chairman of his national campaign committee. One of the worst mistakes Nixon made that year was picking Ambassador Henry Cabot Lodge as his vice presidential running mate. The idea of picking Cabot Lodge for VP was pushed by Ike, who, for some reason, really liked Lodge. But Lodge proved to be a disaster as a candidate. He was lazy and would only do one or two speeches a day. He needed to take frequent naps throughout the day. His candidacy embarrassed us and hurt Nixon. Nixon needed a fighter on his team. Lodge was a joke.

It's true that when Nixon won the 1968 Republican presidential nomination, he asked me if I would be his running mate. After discussing the option with my friends and family, I turned him down. You can read about it in Teddy White's book, *The Making of the President 1968*. I felt being a lieutenant governor did not give me sufficient national exposure to bring strength to his ticket. After I refused, he turned to Spiro Agnew, who of course accepted and went on to become vice president. After Nixon won, he gave me my choice of whether I wanted to be attorney general; secretary of commerce; or secretary of health, education and welfare. I chose HEW because that was the department where I was most interested.

At the mention of Agnew's name, Bob grimaced and showed little regard for the man who later resigned the vice presidency:

I never had a good relationship with Agnew: he resented me because I was Nixon's first choice for the vice presidency. Agnew was Nixon's fourth or fifth choice. That ate at him. Agnew was never in the president's inner circle. He was a whiner who always complained to me that he didn't have enough access to Nixon or enough things to do. I explained to him that this was the role of a vice president: Nixon went through it with Eisenhower, so now it was his turn in the barrel. Nixon also grew tired of Agnew's whining—to the point that Nixon once sent me over to the Old Executive Office Building to meet with Agnew to tell him how good he had it. Nixon wanted Agnew to know that Eisenhower treated Nixon pretty badly when Nixon was vice president. Agnew was living like a king compared to the way Nixon was treated. When Nixon was vice president, Eisenhower didn't even give him an office in the White House.

As to two other future presidents with whom he worked, Bob shared these thoughts:

In 1966, I ran for lieutenant governor the same year Ronald Reagan ran for governor. Although both Reagan and I won in 1966, I received more votes than he did. In fact, I was the top vote-getter across the nation in those elections. This made Nancy Reagan mad that I had outdistanced her husband. Two years later, when Reagan ran against Nixon for the 1968 Republican presidential nomination, I deepened Nancy's resentment when I endorsed Nixon. Truthfully, Reagan was not "running" for president—his staff ran him. Reagan knew Nixon and I were close, and when I told Reagan I would support Nixon, Reagan said it was okay and he understood. He never held it against me. But my support for Nixon sent a chill between our respective staffs, and Nancy never forgave me for it.

George Bush and I became pretty good friends. He was a middle-level official in the Nixon administration who was competent and bright, but nobody ever thought of him as presidential material. Maybe as a future secretary of state, because he had a good résumé, but never president.

Following Nixon's resignation, Bob returned to California to run for the US Senate in 1976. His voice grew tense as he explained how Nixon's Watergate scandal and later resignation doomed his own return to elective office:

> I always wanted to be a senator, and I felt that is where I could have served with the most effectiveness. In 1976 I expected to win that Senate race. All the polls showed I was ahead and winning until the last couple of weeks. But my association with Nixon was made an issue suddenly, and the Watergate scandal tainted everyone around Nixon, even those of us who had nothing to do with it. My relationship to Nixon was well-known, and it hurt, and my Republican opponents capitalized on it.

. . .

As the years went by, Bob Finch became more than a friend. He became a mentor (despite the fact that I was a Reagan conservative and Bob helped lead the more moderate wing of the GOP), a valued consultant, and an immeasurable political resource. He held my hand through my change in political parties, administered my oath of office when I became a judge, and hosted one of my first fund-raisers when I ran for the State Assembly. In 1995, as I contemplated a run for Congress the next year, Bob was the first person I called for advice, and the first person who urged me to do it. Around this time, Bob told me he'd decided to start work on a political memoir, paying special attention to his longstanding relationship with Nixon. When he showed me his outline for the book over lunch, I told him, "Only you can tell many of these inside stories from the Nixon years. Make sure you don't take them with you to the grave."

A week later I was in full congressional campaign mode when Bob celebrated his seventieth birthday on October 9, 1995. A scheduled speech precluded me from joining his staff for a surprise party at his office. That afternoon I took a break to call Bob and wish him a happy birthday. I caught him just as he was leaving; he turned the conversation immediately to my congressional race and matters of strategy and tactics: "I guess I won't be able to call you Jim anymore after you win this race next year," he chuckled. "You'll be 'Congressman' then." Our conversation that day grew so engrossed in election details that, after I hung up, I realized I'd forgotten to wish him a happy birthday. I started to call him back, and then remembered he told me he was walking out the door. *I'll call him back tomorrow and give him belated greetings*, I thought, and then rushed off to my next event.

That night, Bob Finch died of a heart attack.

A few days later, at his funeral, California governor Pete Wilson and Herbert Klein (Nixon's former communications director dating back to RN's first congressional race) delivered the main eulogies. Wilson described his friendship with Finch starting when Wilson was fresh out of law school and worked as an advance man in Nixon's 1962 gubernatorial campaign:

> Bob was a man who could have succeeded Ronald Reagan as governor had he chosen to remain in California; he could have been elected to the United States Senate in 1970 if he had been willing to push aside his old friend George Murphy. He declined the vice presidential nomination from Nixon in 1968 to protect his friend against the charge of cronyism. After Nixon was elected, Bob chose the less glamorous position of HEW secretary because it was where he could make a difference in people's lives. He was a thoughtful and unselfish patriot who fought for the betterment of his country. California and the nation lost a man who wanted the best for all of us.

Klein recalled first meeting Finch in 1952:

> I was traveling on a bus with then senator Richard Nixon, who had just been named as Eisenhower's running mate. Nixon's campaign bus was traveling to Redondo Beach. He told me that when we arrived at our destination, he wanted me to meet a fellow named Bob Finch. "Bob is running for Congress against an incumbent," Nixon said, "and he is probably going to lose. But he will go on from the loss to do great things for California and the nation." And Nixon was right.
>
> I well remember the 1968 Nixon presidential campaign against Vice President Hubert Humphrey. When President Lyndon Johnson decided to halt the bombing of Hanoi just before Election Day, we felt it would hurt our effort, and we decided to attack LBJ's decision as sheer opportunism. None of us wanted to take on Johnson ourselves, so we called Bob Finch and asked him to do it. Bob dutifully came through, and at a press conference, he really laid into LBJ. He must have done a great job, because a short time later Johnson personally called Nixon about Bob's attack.
>
> "Dick," Johnson demanded, "you need to get rid of that guy 'Fink' on your

staff, or we will have some real problems." Nixon looked at us and winked as Johnson complained about "that guy Fink," grousing that "I don't want to hear from that Fink no more!" From that day, Bob had a new nickname among his campaign colleagues–Bob Fink!

. . .

My wife Christine and I with Robert H. Finch, at a Rogan for State Assembly fund-raiser, Burbank, California, 1994

When I think about Bob Finch–and some others like him in this book–I think about him taking the time to write an eleven-year-old interested in politics. To me, that embodies the Bob Finch I knew: a man who had time for people he didn't know, and managed to help inspire them along the way. If someone says that about me after I'm gone, it will mean that my time in public life was worth it. It will mean that I made a difference.

It will mean that I was a little bit like Bob Finch.

21

Curses–Foiled Again

In 1988, Bob Finch invited me to join his family and attend former president Richard Nixon's speech to the Orange County World Affairs Council. I looked forward to seeing Nixon with great anticipation, since the last time (sixteen years earlier) was at the 1972 Republican Convention in Miami, when I missed narrowly the chance to meet him. Knowing of my long-ago unfulfilled opportunity, Finch planned to introduce me at this event to his former boss and longtime friend.

At the last minute, business commitments forced Finch to skip the luncheon, so I went with his wife, Carol, and my pals Priscilla (Bob's daughter) and Chris Gooch (his secretary) for the drive to the Disneyland Hotel. During the trip, Priscilla Finch shared stories of growing up with a father in the center of White House power and told me her favorite Nixon story:

> I was at a party in New York a couple of years ago and was surprised to find Nixon there. I introduced myself to him and he was very charming, asking how my mom and dad were doing. His ease surprised me because he always struck me as a man who was uncomfortable meeting people. I knew he was a family man, so to make conversation I mentioned to him that my sister had recently had a baby, and that her friend Julie Nixon Eisenhower [Nixon's eldest daughter] sent the baby a stuffed bunny rabbit. When I told him that, Nixon howled with laughter unexpectedly: "She would send a bunny!" He then explained why that amused him: when he ran for the US Senate in 1950, he and his family did a live television campaign commercial. When Nixon finished his speech, he was supposed to step backward and his two young

girls were to sing their father's campaign theme song. Throughout the commercial Julie Nixon was clutching her favorite stuffed animal, a bunny rabbit, and refused to put it down.

So here I was at this party, surrounded by famous people and standing with President Nixon, when Nixon himself began singing the words to their 1950 campaign song that his daughters performed that night: *"Here we go on to Washington, to Washington, to Washington; Here we go on to Washington–vote for Nixon."*

He said that as the girls were about to sing the last line, Julie held up the doll and instead of singing "Vote for Nixon," she sang, "Vote for bunny!" as the camera faded out. For the first time in all the times I met Nixon, he looked relaxed–and human.

. . .

Our group arrived at the Disneyland Hotel, where more than a thousand people jammed inside the ballroom for the luncheon. My tablemate was Maurice Stans, Nixon's former secretary of commerce, who also worked as his chief fund-raiser during the 1968 and 1972 presidential campaigns. During Watergate, a grand jury indicted Stans, but he won an acquittal. When he learned I was a deputy DA, the courtly Stans smiled: "You won't have any trouble from me!" he said.

I spoke with Stans about his career while we waited for the program to begin. A farm boy from Minnesota, Stans became an accountant in the 1920s and worked as a CPA until Washington beckoned:

> I joined the Eisenhower administration in the 1950s as an assistant postmaster general, and then later became director of the Bureau of the Budget. I took that job on one condition: I told Eisenhower I would need to meet with him for an hour or so to go over his budgetary priorities. Eisenhower agreed, and we met privately. I told him I could give him a balanced budget his last year in office if he would give me the necessary support to back up the tough decisions I would need to make. Eisenhower agreed, and I went to work. Eisenhower called a meeting of his Cabinet and senior staff and said I was acting with his authority. Later I made the necessary cuts, and Eisenhower backed me to the hilt. We presented the American people a balanced budget in 1960–it was the last time America had one. Ike was a wonderfully charming man who was very bright and very quick-minded.

As to his future boss, Stans told me:

I didn't know Richard Nixon that well back in the old days. I got to know him during the Eisenhower years when he was vice president and I was working on the budget. When Nixon ran for president in 1968, he asked me to be his national campaign treasurer and I agreed. I essentially did all the fund-raising for that campaign.

After Nixon won, John Mitchell [Nixon's first attorney general] called and said Nixon wanted me to be his postmaster general. I said I didn't want the job: Congress runs the Post Office Department, and I had a taste of it under Eisenhower. Mitchell ran down some other options to me, but I had no interest in becoming secretary of agriculture or secretary of Housing and Urban Development. I told Mitchell I could handle either treasury or commerce. Two weeks later, Mitchell called and said, "It's commerce."

Stans said he stepped down from the cabinet at Nixon's request to become his 1972 reelection finance chairman. Once again Stans found himself as Nixon's chief fund-raiser: "During the '72 campaign I read a story in the *Wall Street Journal*: a wealthy businessman was quoted as saying if George McGovern won the election over Richard Nixon, the businessman would commit suicide. I called him on the telephone and told him I was planning to save his life. We met a short time later on his yacht, and I told him we needed a check to the Nixon campaign for $250,000. He wrote it on the spot."

Stans's government service came to an abrupt halt with the Watergate scandal. "It ruined everything and everyone it touched," Stans lamented. "Federal prosecutors went after everyone connected to Nixon. They never understood that we kept finance and politics separate. I went on trial in New York with John Mitchell. I was charged with ten felony counts. The jury found me not guilty on nine counts, and the judge dismissed one count. I felt like another former Cabinet member who said after going through the same experience, 'Where do I go now to get back my good name?'"

Stans said these days he spends time raising money for the Nixon Library, and took pride that it would be the only presidential library built without taxpayer assistance.

A sudden burst of applause and cheers interrupted my conversation with

Stans: former President Nixon had entered the room and walked to his place at the head table. After giving a stiff-arm wave to the cheering crowd, he took his seat, and then waiters served lunch.

During the meal service, I watched Nixon as he sat greeting and signing autographs for people at the head table who approached him. Because of the stage setup, the only way to reach Nixon would be to get atop the stage and walk its length to where he sat (one couldn't approach from the audience level). Having waited almost twenty years to meet him, I didn't want to let this opportunity go by without trying. Suddenly, I saw my chance: a small stairway at the far end of the stage led up to the head table–and no security guard monitored it (Nixon was the only former president to give up his Secret Service protection). *What the hell?* I thought.

With a copy of Nixon's recent book in hand to have him sign, I approached the stairs, climbed them, and crossed the stage, heading toward Nixon's seat. When I reached my target, I knelt beside Nixon and waited while he'd finished signing an autograph for his seatmate. Just as Nixon started turning in his chair to acknowledge me, a very agitated man in a three-piece suit with a radio receiver in his ear squeezed my arm and demanded I leave the stage–now. I stood and followed him back down the stairs with my tail between my legs.

"Just who the hell do you think you are?" he growled as we walked away. "You have a lot of nerve walking up to Nixon like that!" As he continued upbraiding me, I noticed he wore pinned to his vest under his coat lapel an oval plastic Disneyland employee name tag–the same kind worn at the Magic Kingdom by all the popcorn sellers and the guy who runs the Dumbo ride.

"Hey, you're not part of Nixon's security detail," I challenged him. "You're just some damned Disneyland employee!"

"Nixon doesn't have security," the man said as his face reddened, "so I'm guarding him today."

"You're guarding him? Are you kidding me?"

I was furious: after almost two decades of waiting, I missed my chance to meet Nixon–again. I shook off the glorified ticket-taker and was about to resume my mission when the program began. Reluctantly, I abandoned the effort and returned to my seat while fuming over my lost opportunity.

After the emcee introduced the numerous former presidents of the Council, he welcomed Nixon home, reminding the audience that Orange County is the place from where Nixon hailed and began his political career. Nixon rose to a sustained standing ovation. "Mr. President," Nixon began, and then pointed to the assemblage of ex-club leaders, adding, "and my fellow former presidents." The audience laughed and applauded.

Nixon stood at the microphone and folded his hands in front of him; he moved them rarely from that position during his forty-five-minute speech. He spoke without notes on world affairs, traversing the

Former president Richard Nixon addressing the Orange County World Affairs Council, Disneyland Hotel, Anaheim, California, May 4, 1988

globe mentally while discussing policy challenges that would confront the next president. Nixon focused his remarks primarily on the Soviet Union and its leader, Mikhail Gorbachev.

"Gorbachev is a charming man," Nixon stated, "but to be a good prime minister, as Gladstone noted, one must be a good butcher. Gorbachev is unlike any other Soviet leader I have known: he is cool. Khrushchev was more like Lyndon Johnson—he liked to grab people by the lapel and arm. I remember Brezhnev standing next to Khrushchev during our 'Kitchen Debate,' and then he later deposed Khrushchev. Gorbachev will not allow that to happen. What we will need in the next president is a man who can deal with Gorbachev."

When Nixon finished his speech, he acknowledged the applause, and then answered written questions read to him by the emcee. Here he shined: during his formal speech, Nixon appeared somewhat rigid and tense; during the Q&A, Nixon smiled, looked relaxed, and handled each question deftly.

Although some queries touched on foreign policy, most focused on the upcoming election. Nixon felt the two presumptive nominees (Republican George Bush and Democrat Michael Dukakis) would run a close race, with Bush winning by a whisker. He refused to suggest who might be the strongest running mate for Bush, and named a list of the most oft-mentioned possibilities. Then, with a smile, Nixon pointed to the battery of television cameras in the rear of the ballroom: "To my friends in the media," Nixon quipped, "if I forgot to mention someone, would you please list their names in your newspaper columns for me!" Even the reporters joined in the laughter.

"Dukakis," Nixon added, "may be too cerebral for the Democrats. He's tough and a good debater, but not very warm. Democratic candidates need to be like Hubert Humphrey and love the people, and really mean it." As he spoke these words, Nixon reached out his arms and wrapped them in an imaginary hug. "I don't see this quality in Dukakis."

At the end of the questions, Nixon received another standing ovation. Guests began filing on the stage to greet Nixon and get his autograph. Another chance! I started to get in line to meet him, but Mrs. Finch (my ride home) foiled that plan: she needed to leave.

Meeting Richard Nixon must again wait for another day.

. . .

Maurice Stans died of a heart attack at age ninety on April 14, 1998.

22

Plains

When I was twelve, I joined the American Political Items Collectors (APIC), a national organization of campaign memorabilia aficionados. During the summer of 1988, a subset of APIC held their first "CPIC" (Carter Political Items Collectors) meeting in Plains, Georgia, the hometown of former President Jimmy Carter. During the weekend meet, Carter and his wife planned to join the festivities. It sounded like my kind of event.

Bob Wyatt and I flew a discount airline to Atlanta and then drove a rental car down Highway 280 to Plains. Upon arrival, I found it difficult to grasp that in this modern era a peanut grower from this small, remote town could reach the White House. In Plains (population 700), things like movie theaters, fast-food establishments, and department stores didn't exist; the nearest ones were miles away, in Americus. In such a small, isolated town, one could drive past Plains in the blink of an eye without taking notice—except that a former president of the United States lived there.

Main Street consisted of a water tower and about eight small, side-by-side, brick-and-wood buildings. These structures bore historical significance in Carter's early life: at one time they housed the Carter family's peanut office, farm business, and his early county and legislative campaign offices. Now most of these buildings stood vacant; the only ones still in operation were the "Carter Worm Farm," and the antique store run by Hugh Carter (a presidential first cousin), who stocked his store with antiques and (mostly) Jimmy Carter souvenirs. One bargain from the store did well: Hugh sold hand-signed copies of Jimmy's books for the price of the book alone–$7.99. One of the locals told me later that Jimmy hated signing cartons of books for Hugh's store, but he felt obliged to help his cousin remain in business. A sign taped to the store window read, "President Jimmy Carter will teach the Sunday school lesson this Sunday at Maranatha Baptist Church. You are invited. 10:00 a.m." This would be an added bonus to our Plains trip.

A couple of blocks away stood Jimmy Carter's home on Woodland Drive. Trees, shrubs, and a large wrought-iron fence surrounded the single-story house. A television camera, security kiosk, and automatic guardrail blocked access; a sign ordered passing tourists to "keep moving."

· · ·

The next morning, two dozen Carter collectors gathered under the wooden awning on Main Street and set up their "bourse" (displays of campaign memorabilia for sale and trade), where President and Mrs. Carter were to come by and welcome us. Unlike the bustle of the Plains I remembered from television when Carter ran for and held the White House, today no reporters, television camera crews, satellite trucks, or armies of staffers awaited Carter's arrival. When a Ford Range Rover with tinted windows pulled up, most people didn't notice when Carter, his wife Rosalynn, and three Secret Service agents climbed out.

Carter greeted CPIC president Bob Linzey, who in turn introduced me: "Jimmy, this is Jim Rogan. He's come the farthest–he's from California." Carter and I shook hands; I showed him an item from my own "Carter collection," a letter I'd sent him when I was sixteen, asking whether he'd make what was then considered a very long-shot run for the presidency (the top corner of my letter bore Carter's handwritten reply to my questions). "Mr. President," I said with a smile, "this shows I was prescient." Carter looked at the letter, smiled, handed it back, and then turned and walked away without saying a word.

Oh, thanks.

Carter ambled down the street, slowly viewing the exhibits. Several CPIC collectors requested an autograph: "Sorry," Carter told each one while nodding toward the lemonade cup he held. "I've got my hands full." He made an exception to the "full hands" excuse if people asked him to sign a prepaid copy of one of his books.

When a wide-eyed young boy approached Carter nervously and asked him to sign a card, Carter refused, using the lemonade pretext. Remembering how Carter had stiffed my own boyhood request years ago, and feeling sorry for the dejected kid, I stepped forward: "I'll hold your drink for you, Mr. President," I volunteered. "Now you can sign the kid's autograph." Carter shot me a cold, angry stare. He handed me the cup silently, scrawled his signature for the boy, then took back his cup and again walked away.

"Jimmy doesn't like to sign autographs," Bob Linzey whispered to me. "He thinks people are trying to make a buck off him. He's really funny that way. He resents people asking for his autograph. He's afraid they will turn around and sell them."

"Then he should have stayed a peanut farmer," I replied. Curiously, as time went by with the collector group, Carter's signing mood swung from cold to charming and back again. One minute he refused all autograph requests icily, and the next he was smiling and signing for everyone. I didn't understand what triggered the fluctuations.

During this presidential visit, a pale, thin man dressed in blue jeans and suspenders followed closely behind Carter. His face looked worn and tired; his graying hair hung limp and wispy. I paid no attention to him at first, but as the Carters prepared to leave, I noticed someone asking the gaunt man for his autograph. The man took the pen and signed, "Billy Carter." My heart sank: I had heard earlier that the president's infamous brother (whose outlandish redneck antics during Carter's presidency presented unending fodder for the press) now suffered from terminal cancer. The cherubic face and beer belly I remembered from the 1970s were gone; now hollow eyes betrayed the ravages of illness. A Secret Service agent gently helped Billy enter the van. Mrs. Carter (an incredibly charming lady) followed behind; before leaving she welcomed me to Plains: "I hope to see y'all in church tomorrow," she said.

After the Carters departed, I returned to the bourse. Bob Linzey introduced me to an elderly woman dressed in sweat pants and a blouse. "I want you to meet Miss Allie," Bob said as I shook hands with her. "This is Rosalynn's mama." Miss Allie Smith, mother of the former first lady, also welcomed me to Plains and chatted about life in their small town. "I used to be the postmaster here," she said, pointing to the small post office building down the street.

Former president Jimmy Carter (holding his autograph-precluding lemonade cup reviewing a display of memorabilia on Main Street); brother Billy Carter is at left in striped shirt and suspenders, Plains, July 9, 1988.

Later that morning the assembled collectors started buzzing about a local Plains resident (now running Billy Carter's former gas station) who had a fistful of rare campaign buttons from Carter's unsuccessful 1966 race for Georgia governor. Throughout the morning CPIC members went to the gas station and tried to buy or trade for one of those badges, but the owner wouldn't budge. By mid-afternoon I decided to take a look, so I sauntered over to the station. Amid glass cases stocked with Carter souvenirs for sale were several examples of the desirable Carter buttons: a sign next to them read, "For display only. Not for sale."

"Hey, how y'all doing?" called out the chuckling man behind the counter. "You here with those Carter collectors?" I introduced myself to the owner, Bobby Salter. Bobby was a happy, jovial fellow serving a joke and a story with almost every breath he took. Within minutes we became fast friends.

"Bobby," I warned as I pointed to the glass case, "I've come for one of those Carter for Governor buttons. I need one for my collection, and I'm not leaving here without one."

Bobby laughed and slapped his knee. "Nobody yet has talked me out of one! They've been coming in all day, beggin' and pleadin', offering me lots of money and great trade stuff. But those buttons are stayin' here!"

"You might as well know right now," I told him, "I sold vacuum cleaners door-to-door as a kid, and I never left a house without a sale, so I'm not leaving here without a badge!" Still laughing heartily, Bobby rocked back in his folding chair, and then called his two clerks to come join him: "Boys," he cackled, "grab yourselves a bottle of pop and come watch this Yankee boy try to talk old Bobby out of one of those Carter badges." The two men sweeping the store brought some stools, popped the cap off a Coke bottle, and joined Bobby. It took over an hour, but I left with one of the badges—and made a new friendship that lasted long after my Plains trip ended.

In between my pleading, arguing, and cajoling, Bobby shared a few anecdotes about growing up in Plains with the Carters:

The coveted 1966 Carter for Governor badge

"I was much closer to Billy growing up than I was to Jimmy, since Billy and I were in the same class. Truthfully, everyone in town always liked Billy much better. Billy will give you the shirt off his back. Jimmy's so tight that he'll squeeze a nickel until the buffalo jumps off! We all know Jimmy's holding the first dollar he ever earned.

"Funny thing about Jimmy: we're all mighty proud one of our own became president, but Jimmy Carter has never carried his own precinct in any election he has ever run in—not for school board, not for the state legislature, not for governor of Georgia, and not for president of the United States."

I asked Bobby how he'd voted when Carter ran for president. Bobby leaned forward, cupped his hand to my ear, and whispered so his clerks couldn't hear: "Confidentially, I'm a Reagan man."

. . .

The next day, CPIC members attended the Sunday school class Carter taught at Maranatha Baptist Church, a small brick building nestled in a charming wooded setting. We settled in a reception room to await the beginning of Carter's class. When two large buses carrying Japanese tourists arrived unexpectedly, Hugh Carter moved the class inside the main sanctuary. Although small, there were enough seats for everyone in the pale green chapel, where a wooden lectern without a microphone or sound system stood in the front.

At 10:00 a.m., Jimmy and Rosalynn Carter entered from the side door near the choir loft. Carter walked to the podium, while Mrs. Carter found a seat right behind me. A lone Secret Service agent sat near her.

"When I entered the regular Sunday school room it was empty," Carter said, "so I thought nobody was coming to my class today!" He noted the presence of many visitors, and went around the room asking all of us where we

Former president and Mrs. Jimmy Carter outside Maranatha Baptist Church, Plains, Georgia, July 10, 1988.

lived. Carter then put on his glasses and announced the lesson this morning would be titled "Maintaining Confidence in God," from Exodus 13:17–14:31.

"Does anyone here ever worry?" he began. "Sometimes we do more than worry; sometimes we panic. That happened to me once on a duck-hunting trip when I was lost in a swamp. It took me a while to remember to ask God for guidance. The point is this: we have someone who will sustain us if we only ask Him to do so. Just as the Israelites doubted the presence of God when the Egyptians chased them, we often doubt His presence when we are in need. But God is with us, just as He was with the Israelites. Thus, there is no need for despair if we are working to achieve Christ's purpose in our lives."

Carter read from Exodus, joking that during his presidency, "I got to know the map of the Sinai as well as I did the map of Sumter County, Georgia!" Carter then began quizzing the class on their knowledge of the selected reading, saying, "I hope you all did your homework." He asked if anyone knew what the Israelites carried with them during their trek; only Mrs. Carter knew the correct answer (the bones of Joseph).

Continuing with his lesson, Carter said, "People are afraid to be like Jesus. They fear they might be called a 'bleeding heart.' Back in the 1950s the worst epithet one could be called around these parts was a 'nigger lover.' People avoided the epithet then, and they avoid epithets now. We shouldn't avoid being like Jesus. We can't be afraid to reach out and love people. But we are held back because we lack faith in God to protect and shield us. In Bible times, death or slavery was certain for those who trusted in the God of Israel. So trust in God has always involved a risk. Even the Israelites turned against Moses because they did not want to put their faith in God."

Carter again called out a question to the audience. When nobody volunteered an answer, I broke the embarrassing silence and raised my hand. Carter called on me; unfortunately, I misunderstood his question. I thought he asked, "Who *are* we more like: Moses or the Israelites?" instead of what he actually asked: "Who *should* we be more like: Moses or the Israelites?" I answered, "The Israelites."

"No," Carter admonished me. "We should be more like Moses." People in the audience (none of whom had braved raising their hands) nodded their agreement with Carter vigorously, then looked at me while shaking their heads and heaving sighs of disdain as Carter highlighted my biblical ignorance. To make things worse, I had referred accidentally to the Israelites as the "Israelis," making people shake their heads all the more furiously as Carter pointed out that error too. My buddy Bob patted my shoulder as if to console me, but then he leaned over and whispered, "You'd better shut your mouth before you embarrass us more."

With people still grimacing at me, I tried to redeem myself (or at least make them stop questioning my salvation). When Carter paused to inhale from his ongoing correction, I raised my hand again and took another swing at the pitch: "When I said we are more like the Israelites, I meant that we constantly lack faith in God, despite many manifestations of His presence and love, whenever we are faced with a crisis. I agree we should be like Moses, but in our flesh we respond more like the Israelites. This is our great challenge as Christians."

As I spoke, I saw faces once chiseled in chagrin now relaxing their cheek muscles as heads nodded approvingly. Carter smiled and said he agreed with my assessment, thereby canceling my appointment with the Baptist Dunce Cap fitter.

At the conclusion of the class, Carter summarized his lesson: "How should we deal with our problems? We should ask what portion of our life we devote to serving God's will, even when such service is not in our own personal interest. Remember God's promise: He will not forsake us. His mighty hand may be seen in a strong east wind or in some other transformed miracle. No situation is too difficult for Him, and His command for us is to go forward."

After leading the class in a closing prayer, Carter said, "Generally, when church service is over, Rosalynn and I will pose for pictures outside if there is time. But please do not ask for autographs, because I never sign at church." Carter collected his notes and Bible, and then joined Rosalynn in the pew directly behind me.

The pastor opened the regular service by leading the congregation in the hymn "Holy, Holy, Holy." Both Carters had loud singing voices; Mrs. Carter's soprano was pleasant, but Carter's wavering baritone was simply awful–about like mine. The pastor then introduced one of the Japanese foreign exchange students, who told us she wrote her college thesis on Carter's presidency. As she spoke, Mrs. Carter whispered to her husband, "Isn't she cute?"

The service lasted an hour. At the conclusion, I followed behind the Carters as we exited church. Secret Service agents protecting Carter kept their distance; once outside, the Carters posed for pictures with attendees. During the photo op, Carter gave stage directions to each person when his or her turn came. He positioned me to his left for the shot; I saw the Bible he held, stamped with "Governor Jimmy Carter" on the cover.

Former president and Mrs. Jimmy Carter with me, Maranatha Baptist Church, Plains, Georgia, July 10, 1988 (Photo by Robert Wyatt)

When Carter thanked me for participating during his class, I told him, "I'm sorry I needed to clarify my earlier comments, but I didn't want you to think I was sleeping through your lesson!"

"You did fine," said Mrs. Carter.

. . .

r I traded with Bobby Salter for that old Carter campaign
brother, Pat, and me back to Plains for a visit. Our trip
CPIC conclave and "Plains Days," an annual weekend
ing the founding of their rural community.

here filled the small town for the festivities. I entered
town; the Carters also signed up for the run, but
te. Instead, they were on hand at the finish line

tted with Rosalynn Carter. When she saw
shirt, she asked if I was a police officer. I
ity district attorney badge. She smiled and

first lady Rosalynn Carter with my brother, Pat, (right) and
the Plains Day race, Plains, Georgia, May 19, 1990

e to tour the cemetery and Civil War
Plains deserted—strange for a town
tion. When I located Bobby Salter,
ld Plains High School for a special
the few blocks to the school Carter

eople sat in folding chairs on the

la.

d chur
a few min-
e with the
igate voter
g elections
My internal
veekend for

e no regular
of the local
Main Street
f any people
ctuary were
A man raised
er asked him
e by offering
yer.
esson came
15. He shared
illiam Carey,
st missionary,
k Carey seven
s first convert
s is the forti-
and believe in

Pat and I later
rs sang hymns

grass; Jimmy and Rosalynn Carter sat in the front row. After joining
ence in singing the school song, the Carters took the stage and shared
of their high school teacher, Miss Julia Coleman (whom Carter salu
1977 presidential inaugural address), and school principal T. Y. Sheffi
credited both educators with helping him achieve his later successe

The next day, we again attended Carter's Sunday school class a
services at Maranatha Baptist Church. Carter arrived for his lesson
utes late and apologized for his tardiness: "I was on the telephon
president of the Dominican Republic. I have been back there to inves
fraud charges in their recent election. I've spent much time watchin
on a commission for both the Dominican Republic and for Panama.
clock is still a bit off, because I just flew back home to be here this v
the Plains Days celebration."

Carter said his lesson would be brief, and that there would b
church service this morning: "In honor of Plains Days," he said, "al
churches will come together to conduct a joint outdoor service on
at 11:00 a.m. You are all invited to join us there." Carter then asked

in the small san
visiting pastors.
his hand, so Car
to start the servi
the opening pra
Carter's l
from 1 John 5:1
the story of W
the first Bapti
and how it too
years to win h
to Jesus. "Th

Former president Jimmy Carter teaching his Sunday school class,
Maranatha Baptist Church, Plains, Georgia, May 20, 1990

tude God calls us to demonstrate in the long struggle to trust
Him," Carter noted. "We should never give up."

After the lesson, the Carters greeted everyone on the patio
joined them for the outdoor service on Main Street, where cho
and pastors from each neighboring church offered prayers.

At the conclusion of the joint service, Pat and I joined Bobby and Jean Salter for lunch with their family. During this lunch, I made a significant historical discovery.

Bobby told me that when Carter's sister Gloria learned she had terminal cancer, she told Bobby she wanted to sell all of her assets

Former president and Mrs. Jimmy Carter, outdoor church services, Plains, Georgia, May 20, 1990

and give the proceeds to her church. She sold Bobby the old abandoned Carter Warehouse on Main Street (the Carter family had used the warehouse during the 1950s and early 1960s as the operations center of their peanut business).

While cleaning the attic, Bobby found two dirty boxes buried amid the dust. The cartons contained some of Jimmy Carter's old 1950s business records from his peanut farm. Apparently, when Carter had moved his enterprise to a new building in 1962, he'd abandoned these boxes. The cartons and their contents showed extensive water and insect damage throughout, yet despite the inadequate storage conditions, material of historic interest survived. The boxes contained hundreds of scraps of paper bearing Jimmy Carter's spidery scrawl on old invoices, bank checks, diagrams, and notes.

The most significant discovery was Carter's handwritten desk calendar books for the years 1954–1961 (except 1959, which was missing). These books traced Carter's daily routine after returning home to Plains from the US Navy (when his father died in 1953) to assume responsibility for the family peanut-farming business. For a presidential and historic memorabilia collector, this proved the find of a lifetime. I told Bobby the material was worth lots of money—certainly more than I could afford. When I suggested he contact an auction house to get the best price, Bobby balked: "I don't want this stuff going to some collector who turns around and resells it immediately. I want it to go to someone who will preserve it for history's sake and enjoy it. I want you to have it." He mentioned that since Gloria Carter wanted the proceeds from the sale of the property to benefit her church, he wanted to sell the boxes to give her church the money according to her wishes. He told me to make him my best offer; I did, and he shipped the boxes to my home.

I pored over Carter's personal date books, reading them alongside Hugh Carter's biography of growing up in Plains with Jimmy. For example, Hugh Carter wrote that Jimmy's first political involvement came in 1954: after returning from the Navy, Jimmy joined the Lions Club and helped raise money to build a local swimming pool. Thumbing through Jimmy's 1954 desk diary, I found entries that chronicled these Lions Club fund-raising efforts–his first steps on an unimaginable ascent to the White House. Other interesting entries memorialized Carter's sightseeing trip to Washington, DC, (January 1958); his work as an officer overseeing an upcoming local election and getting the ballots printed (July 7, 1961); and his increasing political involvement in 1961, when he started attending local board of education meetings.

Despite Carter's social enlightenment, hints of the 1950s segregated Georgia popped up in his handwritten entries. For example, Carter noted he had helped get the "colored school" piano fixed (January 7, 1960). On one diary page, he listed all the people he signed up for the Red Cross blood drive, while on the next page he listed those he signed up for the "colored" blood drive. On another page he noted drafting a letter advising customers there would be an increase in the price of peanuts; on his next day's entry, he indicated he'd drafted a similar–but different–message for his "colored" customers. Also of interest were documents relating to the Wise Sanitarium, the local hospital where Carter was born on October 1, 1924. After his father's death, Carter became secretary of the Wise Corporation and kept its records until it was dissolved in the 1950s. The original incorporation documents, stock certificate book, and other items were there. Inside the original stock issuance book was the receipt for one share of stock purchased for the future president, "James E. Carter, Jr.," when he was only two.

As I sifted through each sheet, a picture of Jimmy Carter emerged. Here was a man who, true to his engineering background, paid meticulous attention to every detail of the family business and accounted for every penny he spent. He threw nothing away: irrelevant scraps of paper bearing Carter's mathematical calculations and doodles were bundled with more important documents. He

In future president Jimmy Carter's personal handwritten daybook, January 24–25, 1960, he recorded his visit to Washington, DC. Carter noted that he stayed at the Statler Hotel; he went sightseeing for two days, saw a Sarah Vaughn concert, and then took the train to Baltimore to attend a lunch at his alma mater, United States Naval Academy. Later he left Washington for Richmond and saw the film *And God Created Woman*. Given Carter's later evangelical conversion in the 1960s, this movie appears out of character for the man America came to know a generation later. *And God Created Woman* was a French film that launched Brigitte Bardot's career as an international sex symbol. According to film historians, when distributors released the film in the United States in the late 1950s, they censored it heavily because it pushed the limits of allowable sexuality under American standards of decency.

saved notes and letters from other businesses and recycled them as scratch paper for later use. He saved insignificant receipts, whether for a five-dollar gasoline purchase at the local filling station, or for a bottle Coca-Cola. Carter or his wife, Rosalynn, docketed almost every statement received by the business. Other handwritten notes from Carter proved he showed no timidity in challenging suppliers he suspected of overcharging him.

Perhaps the most fascinating aspect of going through these records was realizing that a peanut farmer in a sparsely populated, rural Georgia town, who focused deeply on things like finding spare parts for a shelling machine; applying for an SBA loan (with his mother as cosigner); watching a 1950s sanitized version of a French soft-core porn film (by standards of that era; see photograph on page 153); or wondering whether Sears Roebuck would deliver in a timely manner the adding machine he'd ordered, would–in a generation–be negotiating nuclear disarmament accords and Middle East peace agreements. These business records represent more than a silent testimony to one man following his dream.

They are a testimony to America.

. . .

Two months after I met him in Plains, Billy Carter died of cancer at age fifty-one on September 25, 1988.

Miss Allie Smith died at age ninety-four on April 1, 2000.

23

Welcome Home

After Ronald Reagan left the White House, anyone wanting to meet the former president could go to the 11:00 a.m. Sunday service at Bel Air Presbyterian Church. If in town, Reagan usually attended and always made time to greet fans there. A friend of mine who belonged to the church invited me several times to services, and I encountered Reagan each time I went.

Bel Air Pres (as its members call it) is a lovely church nestled in the mountains above Beverly Hills. It looked like any other church on a Sunday morning, with the exception of a handful of men in suits, wearing dark glasses and discreet radio receivers in their ears when "Rawhide" (the Secret Service code name for Reagan) attended.

The first time I saw Reagan at Bel Air Pres was only a month after his presidential term ended. I recognized an agent from my time in the district attorney's office; he directed me to the corner of the church as a good place from which to take pictures: "The man always enters over here," the agent said. "Go wait nearby and you'll get some great photos." I went over to the west side of the church, where a small flight of stairs led to a pathway from the parking lot to the main entrance. Two additional agents stood nearby, but they didn't keep anyone from assembling along Reagan's pathway into the sanctuary.

A black limousine pulled into the parking lot a few minutes before the service began. Former president and Mrs. Reagan stepped from the car without fanfare or ceremony; they walked along the path, greeting everyone and signing autographs for those who asked. The agent I knew introduced Bob Wyatt and me to the Reagans, who welcomed us to their church.

When the service ended, the Reagans again greeted people outside. Mrs. Reagan moved toward the car faster than her amiable husband, who obliged each autograph collector, including the one requesting (and getting) a half dozen signatures. While she waited patiently for him near the top of the stairs, we chatted; I mentioned meeting her when I was fourteen at the 1972 Republican National Convention in Miami. She smiled, sighed, and then said, "That was so long ago. A lot of water has gone over the dam for us since then."

I held out my arms in mock surprise. "Mrs. Reagan, that was only sixteen years ago–don't you remember me? I was wearing a blue jacket that night!"

She laughed; "Oh, sure, of course! Now I remember you!"

After greeting everyone, the Reagans waved good-bye and entered their car. An older man called out, "Welcome home, Ronnie! It's good to have you back home!"

Reagan turned to the small, applauding crowd and responded: "And it's good to be home!"

Former president Ronald Reagan and me, Bel Air Presbyterian Church, February 26, 1989 (Photo by Robert Wyatt)

. . .

Bob Linzey was the longtime Jimmy Carter supporter who had organized our earlier memorabilia collectors' visit to Carter's hometown in Georgia (see my previous chapter). In 1989, Bob visited me in California and asked if I'd bring him to meet Reagan. I agreed. Reminding him of Carter's rather icy attitude when he'd introduced me in Plains to the man Reagan had vanquished, I told him teasingly, "I'll take you to meet a *real* president."

When the Reagans arrived at their church that Sunday, they mingled as usual with the small group of waiting admirers. Bob had a chance to meet them both and collect their autographs; when he admired Reagan's cowboy tie pin, Reagan treated him to a mini fashion show: he showed Bob his cuff links, each bearing a horse, and said, "These cuff links and tie pin remind me of my ranch when I'm in the big city."

Thanks to my friend Bob Finch (Reagan's former lieutenant governor), Reagan by now knew I was a young lawyer whom GOP party leaders had mentioned as a future candidate for office. Reagan invited Bob and me to join the service, so we followed him inside the church. Reagan chose his usual seat; we sat alongside him on the opposite aisle.[1] During the service, Reagan closed his eyes and dozed off repeatedly. However, when the congregation sang "America the Beautiful," "The Doxology," and "Battle Hymn of the Republic," nobody sang with heartier gusto than he.

At one point in the service, Reagan nodded off again; I watched with amusement when a beautiful young woman in a clinging red sweater, short dress, black nylons, and stiletto heels entered the sanctuary and walked slowly to her seat a few rows in front of Reagan and me. Reagan perked up suddenly: his gaze fixed on her every move, and he looked her up and down several times. He even arched his back to have a better look when the woman took her place in a forward pew. Mrs. Reagan appeared unaware of her husband's sudden wakeful moment!

---

1   Memo to Bel Air Presbyterian church historians: as one enters the sanctuary, Reagan always sat on the left side of the church, aisle seat, third row from the back (at least that's where he sat every time I saw him there).

Later that day, as Bob recounted with enthusiasm his experience, I asked him if he had changed his mind about Reagan. "Well," he replied, "I'm still a Carter man through and through. But I hate to admit it–he sure is a nice fellow. He even signed a few autographs for me."

Yes, he did. And unlike another former president I met in Plains, I didn't have to hold Ronald Reagan's lemonade cup to get him to do it.

24

He Remembered Me

Over the years I saw Ronald Reagan many times; after he left the White House in 1989, I had the chance to meet him privately in his office with my new bride, Christine. Former California lieutenant governor Bob Finch, who set up a meeting for me with Reagan, told Reagan about my party switch and his belief that I might make a good GOP candidate down the road. Finch instructed me to give Reagan a copy of my recent article on why I'd changed parties in 1988 from Democrat to Republican: "I told Reagan he needs to read it," Finch said. "Reagan's an old ex-Democrat himself, so he'll like it a lot."

On the morning of our meeting, Christine and I had a disagreement about a gift I had for the former chief executive. With his presidential library currently under construction, I wanted to donate an item to the archive from my political memorabilia collection, so I settled on a pair of Reagan slippers. Each shoe looked like a bed covered with a flag-designed comforter; poking out from under the covers and resting on a pillow was a rubber head–a smiling Reagan in a nightcap was on one slipper; his wife, Nancy, on the other. I planned to hand-carry the gift in a plain brown shopping bag.

"If you carry those hideous slippers with you, especially in that awful brown bag," Christine warned me, "I'll wait in the car. You'll embarrass yourself."

The Reagan slippers, sans the brown shopping bag I used to transport them to Ronald Reagan's office.

As a compromise, I promised not to present the gift unless Reagan's staff approved in advance. Along with the slippers in the grocery bag, I also carried large pieces of cardboard to protect the two Reagan campaign posters that I wanted him to autograph. In Christine's eyes, this added insult to injury: "You want to visit President Reagan, carrying shopping bags and cardboard?" she asked, shaking her head in dismay. "Are you trying to look homeless?"

We drove to Reagan's office in Century City and took the private elevator directly to the thirty-fourth floor for our 11:45 a.m. meeting. When the doors opened, I thought we might be in the wrong place: nothing in the bare room suggested we were in Ronald Reagan's suite. To the left was a door with a glass and wire mesh window, and a telephone on the wall; a lone receptionist was visible on the other side. The only clue to our location was the jelly bean jar I spied on her desk (Reagan's love for jelly beans made their jars standard White House desktop décor during his administration). I picked up the phone and identified myself; she buzzed us through and invited us to wait in an anteroom decorated with photographs of Reagan and various world leaders. She said the entire floor was a secure area housing the private offices of Ronald and Nancy Reagan, as well as the Ronald Reagan Library Foundation.

An aide escorted us through a second security door and invited us to wait outside Reagan's private office. Remembering my promise to Christine, I opened the brown bag and produced the slippers for approval, asking the aide if she thought it an appropriate gift. "Oh, absolutely!" she exclaimed. "He'll love them! He's seen a picture of these slippers, but he doesn't have a pair and he wants them. We were trying to find them for him." I turned to Christine and smirked.

The door to Reagan's office was cracked open; from inside we overheard Reagan talking with another man. "President Reagan's with his ghostwriter, Edmund Morris," she said. "He's dictating his memoirs; I'll let him know you are here." A few moments later, Morris left the office and nodded a greeting to us. He sat on a couch and flipped through a magazine as another aide approached us: "President Reagan will see you now."

Ever the political collector junkie, as we entered Reagan's office, I scanned the memorabilia in the room. On a coffee table sat a silver tray with an engraved replica of the Reagan presidential inauguration invitation. The bookcases behind his desk housed an assortment of Remington miniature bronze saddles, along with autographed photographs from England's Queen Elizabeth and Prince Charles, British prime minister Margaret Thatcher, and Japanese Emperor Hirohito. Family photographs crowded his credenza; an unattractive green and brown mountain landscape painting hung over his chair (the same chair he'd used in Sacramento and in the Oval Office). On his desk sat a gold eagle that once belonged to President John F. Kennedy (given to Reagan by Senator Edward Kennedy); binders, folders, calendars, and notepads cluttered the work area. I recognized a brass plaque from his Oval Office that read, "There is no end to what a man can accomplish if he does not mind who gets the credit."

Wearing a green and red plaid jacket, gray slacks, and a red necktie, Reagan rose from his desk and welcomed us. He looked tall and strong, and much younger than his seventy-eight years. The only concessions to advancing age I noticed were the touches of gray now streaking through his otherwise dark hair and a miniature hearing aid concealed in his ear.

A photographer followed behind us and suggested we take a group photograph. As she focused her lens, Reagan posed the shot: "Let's put Christine in the middle," he said. "If she is between us, it will be a prettier picture."

"If you and I get out of the picture, Mr. President," I replied, "it will be even prettier."

After the photo op, I made the presentation Christine dreaded, telling Reagan about my memorabilia collection and desire to give him a memento for his library. When I removed the slippers from the shopping bag and

President Ronald Reagan, Christine, and me, Office of President Reagan, Century City, California, August 3, 1989

handed them to him, he laughed as he studied them. "Well," he said, "these are wonderful. There is just one problem with them: I am sleeping in one slipper,

President Reagan and I share a laugh over the controversial slippers, Office of President Reagan, Century City, California, August 3, 1989

and Nancy is sleeping in the other–I don't think she will like the separation!"

I produced my two posters and asked Reagan to sign them for me; he said he would be delighted and placed them on his desk. Reagan studied the first poster, which was a color jugate from 1984, depicting him and running mate George Bush. "Shall I sign over my head?" Reagan asked. "This way, I'll leave room if you ever want to have this 'other guy' sign it," he said with a wink as he pointed to Bush's picture. Reagan inscribed the poster with slow, deliberate pen strokes. He stopped writing when he reached my last name; he began fumbling through his schedule, looking for it. I could tell he was stuck.

"Mr. President," I reminded him, "it's *Rogan*, R-O-G-A-N. Just like 'Reagan,' only with an *o*.'"

Reagan looked up and smiled. "You know," he said, "I once looked at research on the derivation of the Reagan name. It was pretty comprehensive. It told all about the Reagan heritage and where all the families hailed from, mainly from Ireland and Scotland. It also covered the history of all my close cousins–the 'Regans, the 'Ragens,' and of course, the 'Rogans.' So this one is just for you, cousin!"

Reagan said the second poster was special to him. Produced in 1980, it was perhaps the most graphically beautiful of his presidential campaign. Labeled "America: Reagan Country," it showed a color photograph of a smiling Reagan in a cowboy hat. Surrounding his image were sketches of Americana scenes. Reagan started to sign the poster on the Statue of Liberty sketch and then caught himself, saying, "I have to be very careful not to mark on this lady.

"Nancy and I were invited to the centennial celebration of the Statue of Liberty in New York in 1985," he explained. "The statue was the most beautiful sight I'd ever seen, with her all lit up and fireworks exploding over her head.

"America: Reagan Country" poster; Lady Liberty–Reagan's other love–is on the left

Later we flew over her in a helicopter, and it was an even more beautiful sight from the air. I leaned over to Nancy and told her, 'Honey, there will always be two ladies in my life.'"

Reagan told us that these days he kept busy writing his memoirs; I told him I hoped he would answer my question when his book published: "Mr. President," I said, "you are one of the few men in history called to assume the awesome duties of the presidency. I have often wondered what goes through a man's mind when he stands on the steps of the Capitol with his hand raised, taking the oath of office for that job."

"You won't have to wait for my book to learn that answer," Reagan said, smiling. "I will tell you, now, exactly what I was thinking. I was praying for guidance and wisdom. I was just praying to myself the whole time I took the oath."

"Judging from your accomplishments," I replied, "I'd say God answered your prayers."

Before leaving, I gave Reagan an envelope with a copy of my earlier article that he'd requested, which explained why I left the Democratic Party to become a Republican. "As another ex-Democrat," I said, "you might appreciate this." Reagan thanked me, put the envelope in his coat pocket, and asked me, "Do you know the story of how I first registered Republican? Few people know how it happened.

"I had always been a liberal Democrat," he went on, "but in the 1950s I began to feel my party had left me. In 1960 I headed 'Democrats for Nixon.' Although I voted for Nixon, I never changed my registration after the election.

"In 1962 I was speaking for Nixon's gubernatorial campaign in some auditorium. An old lady in the audience raised her hand to ask a question. I called on her and she yelled out, 'Have you changed your registration yet?' I confessed I had been too busy and hadn't changed. 'Well,' she said, 'I'm a voter registrar!' With that, she marched up onstage, with a form in her hand, and reregistered me on the spot! She returned to her seat to a standing ovation. When it came time to resume my speech, I forgot where I had left off. I asked the audience, 'Now, where was I?'"

We shook hands and thanked Reagan for his time; as Christine and I were leaving, I looked back before closing the door and saw Reagan sitting at his desk, opening the envelope I'd handed him a few minutes earlier.

. . .

To my surprise and delight, Reagan read my article; more significantly, he liked it. A few days after meeting Reagan, I returned home from work and found a full-page handwritten letter awaiting me. It read in part:

August 3, 1989

Dear Jim:

I haven't the words to properly describe how impressed I am with your article. Thank you for giving such an account of what has actually happened to the political parties in our land in your article. Like you, I left the Dem. Party, and like you I don't believe we changed. We still support the same beliefs we always held, but the party leadership set off on an entirely different course. It is this that you so eloquently explained. It is the best and most complete exposition I have seen of the philosophical reversal of the Dem. Party.

Your essay should be the basis for freeing up Democrats who are discontented but still not aware of how far their party leadership has turned from what they as individuals believe. After dealing with a Dem. majority in the House of Representatives for 8 yrs.—a majority they've had for 55 of the last 59 years—I can't help but think our very safety requires that your exposition be widely distributed. I want you to know that I'll be quoting from your essay on my own mashed-potato circuit lectures.

My very best to Christine and again my thanks to you.

Sincerely,
Ronald Reagan

Reagan's generous comments left me humbled. Remembering how long it took for Reagan to inscribe a poster for me, I speculated on the time expended in penning this comprehensive letter. I showed it to Christine, who read it with tears in her eyes. This caused me to puff with pride. "So," I asked her, "you like what the Gipper wrote about your old man, eh?"

"Truthfully, I wasn't paying any attention to what he wrote about you," she replied. "I'm crying because of this part here—'My very best to Christine.' He remembered me!"

. . .

Weeks later, I watched a cable news broadcast of Ronald Reagan giving a speech somewhere. My heart stopped when I heard him using language right out of my article on the fundamental differences between Democrats and Republicans. Reagan proved true to his word: he really did quote me on his own mashed-

Ronald Reagan's letter to me, August 3, 1989

potato circuit! The only thing I didn't hear as he finished his speech was any mention that the words he delivered had come from me! I didn't mind: as my story in the earlier chapter, "My Governor," related, Reagan had given me his speech at the Boundary Oak restaurant in Walnut Creek back in 1973.

It was only fair that I now give him mine.

25

Spanky and the Boss

For five generations, audiences have laughed at the antics of those irrepressible kids from producer Hal Roach's *Our Gang* comedy films made in the 1920s–'40s (later dubbed *The Little Rascals* for television syndication). Of the many child actors who came and went during the life of the classic series, perhaps the best known and most beloved was George "Spanky" McFarland, the chubby leader of the gang. Along with pals Alfalfa, Buckwheat, Darla, Butch, and others, the Gang stumbled from one hilarious childhood circumstance to another.

After a decade of making *Our Gang* comedies, Spanky became a Hollywood has-been at age fourteen in 1942. During the next fifty years, he worked in various sales jobs and made rare guest appearances on television.

I came to know Spanky before we ever met personally: I did some minor legal work for him when I was a new lawyer in the 1980s, and we kept in touch over the phone and by mail afterward. During the years I knew him, Spanky (living in semiretirement in Texas) grew increasingly bitter over the endless string of lawsuits he'd had to file around the country against people and companies using his childhood image. It galled him that his legal efforts had met with little success. When his parents executed his 1930s movie contracts, they'd signed away rights to his name and image forever. Spanky often called to update me on his litigation battles, and usually to complain about his most recent failure to prevent someone from using his persona and likeness for commercial purposes. Despite this contractual reality and the discouraging results he encountered, Spanky kept at it: "I'm damned tired of people getting rich off me and my work after all these years," he often told me in exasperation. "My name and face are mine." Sadly for Spanky, I don't think he ever found a judge or jury that agreed with him.

In March 1991, Spanky called and told me he was coming to Los Angeles the next day to shoot a television commercial for Quality Inn motels. "They have me climbing out of a damned suitcase," he complained, "but what the hell. The money's good." Spanky invited me to join him for lunch; I told him my schedule was tight because of a full caseload at court, but I could sneak away for an hour or so.

After being friends for almost a decade, I got my first in-person look at Spanky when I picked him up in front of his Hollywood hotel. Now in his sixties, he was an older version of the still-roly-poly boy remembered by his fans. We drove to the Daily Grill in Hollywood for our lunch.

Despite my curiosity, Spanky showed little inclination that day toward discussing the past; he wanted my thoughts regarding several pending lawsuits he'd initiated against more businesses that had (again) appropriated his name and likeness. When I told him I couldn't give him any legal advice (California judges are precluded from practicing law or dispensing

George "Spanky" McFarland and me, catching up over lunch in Hollywood, March 28, 1991

legal counsel), I just listened while he shared his frustration with lawyers and the legal system. He told me that litigation had become such a major part of his existence that he couldn't focus on other things, like writing a long-intended book about his Hollywood experiences.

After grabbing a quick hamburger, Spanky asked me to drop him off at a rental car agency. On the way there we drove by his former home at 1616 Queens Road in West Los Angeles. "Here is where I lived when I was a kid working on the Roach lot," Spanky said. "A studio limousine picked me up for work every day, and I would get the driver to race down these winding streets each morning." Spanky said that members of the pop-music group the Jackson 5 later bought the house, and that he had his picture taken with Michael Jackson standing on the porch.

As we drove, Spanky set aside his legal travails briefly to talk about his relationship with "Alfalfa" (Carl Switzer), another beloved character from the *Our Gang* series. According to Spanky, Alfalfa was beloved only by his movie fans.

"Alfalfa was a kid who was always in trouble," he explained. "He was such bad news that my mother wouldn't let me play with him. We weren't friends off the set. He could be a mean little bastard even when he was a kid. He used to go up on the catwalk above the set and piss down on the hot klieg lights and the crew.

"When the Gang movies ended and as we grew older," he went on, "I moved home to Texas. When Alfalfa wasn't working, he had trouble with alcohol. He was the kind of guy who would steal a truck filled with wood, then try to sell the wood door-to-door. I never saw him again until 1957 at a reunion show. That was two years before he died, when he pulled a knife on his business partner in a dispute over a fifty-dollar debt; the partner shot and killed him. He was trouble right to the end."

. . .

Producer Hal E. Roach was the founder of the *Our Gang–Little Rascals* film treasury. Nicknamed "The Boss" by the actors and crew who worked on Roach's "Lot of Fun," he began his film career in 1912, when he did extra work in silent films. Within a couple of years he started his own production company, which, in the coming decades, became the premiere comedy factory in Hollywood. Harold Lloyd, Will Rogers, Jean Harlow, and Charley Chase were just some of the actors in Roach's stable; aside from casting them, and creating the *Our Gang* comedies, he also paired and produced two of his minor contract players. This union gave the world perhaps the best-loved comedy team in film history: Stan Laurel and Oliver Hardy.

Hal Roach remained the last living witness to Hollywood's transition from fruit orchards to entertainment Mecca. In 1990 I traveled to Catalina Island for a celebration of Stan Laurel's centenary. While attending a special showing of Stan and Ollie movies at the Avalon Theatre, an elderly man seated in front of me laughed heartily at the comedy antics on-screen. At the end of the showing, the house lights came up and the emcee announced, "Ladies and gentlemen, all these films will live forever because of the vision and foresight of the movie pioneering genius Hal E. Roach, who created and produced these classic treasures. Mr. Roach will celebrate his one hundredth birthday next year, and we are honored to have him with us tonight. Please welcome Mr. Hal Roach."

The audience rose in an ovation, and the old man seated in front of me, who'd laughed throughout the films, stood and acknowledged the applause. Roach chatted with fans as he walked slowly but steadily to his waiting car.

Later that evening, Roach attended Laurel's celebratory birthday banquet

Movie producer Hal E. Roach (looking decades younger than his ninety-nine years) and me, Catalina Island, June 15, 1990

at the Carno Ballroom. He invited me to join him for coffee after the dinner; at his table he introduced me to Eddie Quillan, a character actor from the 1930s and 1940s most noted for his role in the classic film *The Grapes of Wrath*. As we spoke during dinner, Quillan looked drawn and tired–two weeks later, he was dead from a heart attack.

The birthday party remained in full swing long past dinner. When I bid Roach good night around midnight, he was still holding court at his table, smoking thin cigars, signing autographs, and greeting well-wishers. I later learned he stayed until the celebration ended, after 2:00 a.m.

. . .

In the fall of 1992, Spanky called and said he planned to visit Los Angeles to meet with his former boss Hal Roach (now almost 101). "I've only seen the old man once in fifty years," Spanky told me, "and that was when I presented him his honorary Academy Award in 1984. I've never had the chance to sit and talk to him, one-on-one, as an adult, so this could be an interesting meeting. I want you to come with me."

As it turned out, Spanky wanted to meet with Roach for reasons beyond nostalgia. He wanted Roach to sign an affidavit regarding the interpretation of a 1936 contract between Roach Studios and Spanky's parents. Spanky felt the document would help in his pending lawsuit against yet another business using his name: "Some bastards in New Jersey have opened a bar called 'Spanky McFarland's.' They're using my name and likeness, and a statement from Roach might help me in the lawsuit." Although I doubted a contemporaneous affidavit regarding a half-century old contract would have much legal heft (especially since Roach had disposed of his rights to the *Our Gang* films decades earlier), any excuse to visit Roach was good enough for me.

On the appointed day, I picked up Spanky at the Beverly Hilton Hotel, where he was staying for the weekend. We encountered about a hundred movie fans awaiting the celebrity arrivals for the American Cinema Awards that evening. Someone behind the rope line at the hotel entrance recognized Spanky and urged him to come and sign autographs. He waved them off, mumbling to me that these "autograph hounds" were going to pester him throughout his stay.

We drove through the winding roads leading to Roach's Beverly Hills home, and parked in front of the single-story ranch-style house overlooking a hilltop at 1183 Stradella Lane. Roach's nurse, Don Aho, greeted us at the front door and led us into the living room. The house was decorated unpretentiously with worn furniture; stacks of magazines and inexpensive photo albums lay in piles. In the midst of this clutter stood Roach's special Oscar, bookended by photographs of Roach with President Reagan.

A few minutes later, Aho escorted Roach into the living room. Roach leaned on his metal cane and moved slowly; he wore hearing aids in each ear. Still, when he saw Spanky, his face brightened and he moved quickly toward his portly discovery. Embracing him warmly, Roach patted Spanky's girth and chuckled, "You haven't slimmed down since you were five years old!"

"The Boss" settled into his chair, and told Aho to serve all of us drinks; a few minutes later, Aho returned with a tray of Diet Cokes. "Spike mine with some vodka," Roach instructed his nurse. Then he turned and said to me with a grin, "I'm almost 101 years old. At this age, I'll have some vodka when I want it!" Spanky said he'd like his the same way.

Spanky and "The Boss" holding Roach's honorary Academy Award, September 11, 1992

Roach said he wanted some photographs taken with his guests and produced two cameras, but one was broken and the other had no film. Fortunately, I'd brought mine to record the reunion for posterity. Roach liked my suggestion that he and Spanky pose with Roach's Academy Award; I handed the heavy Oscar to Spanky, who held it aloft as my shutter clicked.

Then Roach pointed to actor Roddy McDowall's oversized book on the coffee table, which had a compilation of celebrity photographs (coupled with tributes from other stars

Spanky McFarland, Hal Roach, and me, September 11, 1992

who knew them). Printed next to the photograph McDowall took of Roach was a testimonial provided by Spanky. Roach passed the book to Spanky and asked him to read aloud the sentiment. As Spanky recited his homage to the man "who gave me my first job when I was five years old," his voice cracked; both men then began weeping openly.

Roach talked about the old days of filmmaking, saying that people had often tried to buy or borrow his film rights. He joked about taking a trip years earlier to Germany, where a film producer had given him an envelope stuffed with cash as he requested the rights to exhibit some Roach films. Roach turned to Spanky and said, "Never sign away your likeness or film rights. They are worth a fortune now." This comment served as an introduction to the business purpose of the meeting.

Spanky told Roach about his pending New Jersey lawsuit, and then handed Roach the affidavit that Roach had agreed to sign previously. As Roach took the document from Spanky, he smiled and said, "I'll sign it without even reading it!"

Despite this comment, Roach reviewed the document carefully before scratching his signature on it. "I hope this will help you," he said as he handed back the statement.

Spanky produced several photographs of the Boss and asked Roach to sign them for his family; Roach obliged, penning his name slowly on the pictures. While he signed, he invited me to tour his trophy room and den. There I saw memorabilia and dozens of inscribed photographs framed on the wall: Bette Davis, Cary Grant, Franklin D. Roosevelt, Walt Disney, and Lucille Ball were there alongside pictures of Roach dining with Laurel and Hardy and playing polo with Will Rogers; a presidential commission signed by President Truman was displayed amid countless plaques and awards. In the midst of all was a framed poster depicting the *Our Gang* children.

Over in a corner, Aho showed me boxes on the floor filled with stacks of photographs of Roach. He invited me to select a couple of them for Roach to sign for me. When I asked Aho where all the pictures came from, he pointed to a separate four-foot-high stack of envelopes: "This is fan mail that comes in," Aho said. "The old man signs maybe two or three things a day. The rest go in this pile and are never returned. He just can't do much of this anymore."

Leaning on his cane, Roach joined me in the den and gave me a guided tour of his treasures. I pointed to an oversized photograph of a scowling, bald man in a tuxedo and with his arms folded across his chest. The photo bore a lengthy but undecipherable inscription. "Mr. Roach," I said as I pointed to the picture,

"I recognize this man, but I can't place him. Is this [pioneer film director and actor] Erich von Stroheim?"

Roach bent over and studied the photograph closely. Suddenly, his eyes welled with tears. Roach looked at me intently and said, "That was my dear friend–Mussolini! He was a very great man and a dear friend." The Italian Fascist dictator America had battled in World War II was Roach's dear friend? I was caught off guard that Roach had such warm feelings for a man whose countrymen so despised him that they hung him from his ankles in the middle of the town square and desecrated his corpse after they'd killed him.

"Mr. Roach," I said with a grin, "you are probably the only man alive today who not only can say you knew Mussolini as a friend, but *would* want to say you knew him as a friend!"

Roach shrugged off my comment and shared some insights into his relationship with "Il Duce":

During my visit to Italy in the 1930s, I was summoned to meet Mussolini. I had only seen him in the newsreels, which depicted him as a ranting tyrant who would puff himself up like a big blowfish during his speeches. When I walked into Mussolini's office, I entered a long room with only a desk and chair at the far end. Mussolini sat scowling at me as I approached. But he was full of crap and I knew it! He was acting for me, and I can always spot an actor. As I drew closer, my smile grew larger as Mussolini's scowl grew deeper. Finally we were face-to-face. I had such a huge broad smile, and he had such a mean scowl! I knew he was a faker, and he knew I knew it. So he finally smiled and shook my hand, and from then on we were friends.

One night at dinner I sat next to Mussolini's wife; Mussolini sat across from me and next to his mistress; he kept fondling and groping his mistress during dinner. Mrs. Mussolini seemed oblivious to all this and showed no concern for her husband's behavior. Finally, I leaned over and said to Mrs. Mussolini, "Look, I don't mean to pry, but doesn't it bother you that your husband is so intimate with this woman?" Mrs. Mussolini appeared confused that I would even ask such a question, and replied in great seriousness, "I am but a mere woman; he is Mussolini! How can one woman ever hope to please the great Mussolini? It is an honor just to be married to him!"

I told Roach that Mussolini obviously had trained his wife better than I had trained mine. Roach laughed and slapped his knee. (Later that night I recounted this story to Christine. Without missing a beat, she looked me up and down, and then said, "You're no Mussolini!")

Roach invited me to sit with him in the den. I took advantage of the opportunity to ask him about my favorite comedians, Laurel and Hardy. As a fan, I asked Roach when he stopped making their films. He replied blandly, "When it wasn't worth it anymore."

Trying to interpret the comment, I volunteered, "Oh, you mean their style of comedy had become passé after a while and was no longer marketable at the box office?"

Roach leaned over in his chair toward me. Puffing his slender cigar, he corrected my misinterpretation: "No, that's not what I mean at all. I mean that when those two dumb bastards decided they knew more about making comedies than I did, that's when it wasn't worth it anymore, and that's when I stopped making their pictures! Neither one of them was any great brain. All Hardy liked to do was golf, and all Laurel liked to do was fish."

By now, Spanky had joined us and asked why Laurel and Hardy's films have remained so enduring. "That one's easy," Roach chuckled. "Most producers who put together a comedy team had one funny guy and one straight man. With Laurel and Hardy, we had two comedians and no straight man. When Stan did something funny, we got a laugh. Then I had the camera cut to Babe [Hardy's nickname], and we got a laugh from his reaction. Then we cut back to Stan and got another laugh from his reaction to Babe. So you got three laughs for the price of one."

Roach told a story of taking a Catalina fishing trip with Stan on Laurel's yacht during their heyday: "This one's a little dirty," he said. "We were on the ship, and Stan introduced me to a beautiful young woman. He said, 'She's the nicest woman I ever met–I met her at 6 p.m. and we were in bed having sex by 7 p.m.' Stan later married her; Stan was married many times. Women were crazy about him for some reason. I never understood it. On screen he was such a little crybaby. Yet when Laurel and Hardy went on tour, the women went mad over him."

Switching subjects, Roach nodded toward Spanky and then asked me, "Do you know how I came up with the idea of making the *Our Gang* films?"

I didn't, so he explained:

One day I was listening to this awful audition of a little girl. She was heavily made up, and I only tolerated her because she was the daughter of a friend. When the audition was done, I told her the usual answer we gave people back then: "Don't call us; we'll call you." After she left my office, I wandered over to the window and looked out at the lumberyard across the street, where a bunch of kids were playing. Two of them were having a life-and-death argument over a scrap of wood.

Later, I looked down at my watch and realized I had been watching them for twenty minutes! I couldn't understand why I would be so interested in just watching a bunch of kids do what kids do. Then I started to think that maybe a film audience would like to watch kids just be kids. I told my employees to round up a bunch of kids and test them. We made the first film, *Our Gang*, and it was a huge success. The rest is history.

This was the same thing I did with Laurel and Hardy. People liked the *Our Gang* films because they got to watch kids being kids. They liked Laurel and Hardy because they got to watch adults be kids. It was the same formula.

"The funny thing about my career," Roach added, "is that everyone remembers me for the comedy shorts. Nobody remembers I did some serious and great feature films too, like, *Of Mice and Men*, *Topper*, *Captain Fury*, and *One Million Years BC*."

Roach's cook had a young teenage son playing basketball in the rear yard. Roach insisted I go out and shoot some baskets with the boy; Roach positioned his chair so he could watch our brief pickup game from the window.

After ten minutes, Roach called me back inside. "I'm tired today," he said, then pointed to the pool in the rear yard. "I usually swim twice a day in the pool for exercise, but not today. I'm too damned tired."

Roach's nurse, Aho, whispered to me, "The old man had been in pretty good shape until recently. He really did swim twice a day for exercise, but no more."

Our visit with Roach lasted over two hours. The conversation was fascinating, but I saw Roach's energy fading quickly now. We returned with him to the living room. Spanky kissed his old boss on the forehead as he said good-bye; they held hands and lingered for a couple of minutes, both teary-eyed at the farewell, knowing it was their last.

"To our best Judge": photo signed for me by Hal Roach during our visit, September 11, 1992

"Take care of my boy here, Judge!" Roach instructed me. He took my hand in his and patted it with the other. "It means a lot that you both came to see me."

As we walked to the door, Aho told me that although Roach's health had started slipping recently, our visit was a tonic for him.

. . .

A month later, I sent two sets of the photographs we'd taken that day to Don Aho. I asked him to give one set of pictures to the Boss, and to ask him to autograph the second set for me. A week later, Aho returned the photographs bearing Roach's shaky autograph on them. His signature had deteriorated substantially since he signed pictures for me in person during our visit. A letter from Aho accompanying the photos apologized for the poor quality of the autographs, and explained that since our visit, Roach's health had declined significantly.

Hal Roach died two weeks later, on November 2, 1992, just short of his 101st birthday. While battling pneumonia, the old man suffered a fatal heart attack at his Stradella Lane home.

The next morning, I called Spanky to offer condolences. Sounding very down, Spanky said he had been giving press interviews around the world all day. He told me how grateful he was to have had the chance we had to sit with Roach and get to know him as an adult. Spanky said he was flying out to California the next day to attend Roach's funeral and asked me to join him.

Spanky and I planned to meet at St. Paul the Apostle's Church in Westwood for Roach's service on November 4. While waiting in the parking lot for Spanky, I ran into Roach's nurse, Don Aho. He told me the old man had started slipping the very day we came over. Despite his increasing frailties, Roach told him that morning, "Clean me up and make me look alive for Spanky's visit." Aho said the visit we had with Roach was the last meeting he had with visitors.

"More important than that," he said, "those photographs you took of Roach during your visit were the last ones ever taken of the old man. He never posed for another picture. Also, the photographs he signed for you a couple weeks ago were the last autographs he ever signed. I brought them to him on his sickbed, and he insisted on signing them himself, even though he could barely write any longer. He said he didn't want the judge to hold him in contempt of court!"

The last autograph ever signed by Hal Roach on the last photograph ever taken of "The Boss," who is shown here with me at Roach's home, September 11, 1992 (photo taken by Spanky McFarland)

Aho went inside the church with Roach's family; a few minutes later, I found Spanky in the crowded parking lot. One of the priests from the church asked me to take his picture with the former child star.

Spanky and I sat together during the service. He reminisced frequently about our meeting with Roach, and his eyes kept filling with tears as he talked about the man who gave him his start in movies. He also pointed out others at the service with whom he worked in the "Our Gang" movies: former child stars Dorothy "Echo" DeBorba, Tommy "Butch" Bond, Eugene "Pineapple" Jackson, and Mary Ann Jackson. One of early television's comedy pioneers, Sid Caesar, and longtime television talk show host Mike Douglas sat in the pew in front of us. "I was on Mike's show twenty years ago with Darla Hood [another *Our Gang* alumnus]," Spanky noted. "It was the last show she did before she died of a heart attack."

After the service, Spanky gave interviews and signed autographs on the front steps of the church. A television crew from the show *Entertainment Tonight* asked Spanky to share recollections on camera. "I don't know if I should," Spanky told them. "Jim, what do you think I should do?" I told him that *Our Gang* fans would enjoy it; Spanky agreed and talked on camera about our final meeting with Roach.

Spanky continued visiting with his former child costars, all of whom seemed delighted to be reunited, but melancholy over the circumstances. At one point a balding, older man approached: "Spanky," he asked, "don't you remember me?" Spanky did not. The man broke into a big smile: "I'm Darwood Kaye—I played 'Waldo' in the Gang films with you!"

Spanky gasped: "Waldo! I haven't seen you in fifty years!" They hugged, laughed, and cried together. Waldo told Spanky that he spent his post-Hollywood decades in ministry as a Seventh-day Adventist pastor. Their animated conversation grew serious when they noted how few of their costars still lived.

After the service, Spanky and I drove into downtown Westwood for dinner at Hamburger Hamlet. Since Spanky never had the chance to have Roach sign one of the pictures we took during our meeting, I surprised him by giving him one that Roach signed for me; then I had Spanky autograph the remaining ones depicting him and The Boss for my collection.

. . .

The following Spring, Spanky came to Los Angeles to film an episode of the long-running television comedy *Cheers*. After the shooting, he drove to my home in Glendale, where we spent an entire day catching up. Spanky said he was having fun filming his cameo for the show: "They are treating me well at the studio," he said. "I've enjoyed being back before the cameras so much that I would like to pick up more studio work." He hoped that word of mouth around Hollywood might let people know he was available, but he rejected my suggestion he get an agent: "They're all crooks," he snorted.

Christine and I sent him home to Texas with a suitcase filled with fresh avocados from our backyard tree.

Weeks later, Spanky was dead. He suffered a massive heart attack at his home on June 30, 1993.

A final visit: Spanky McFarland and me at my home, Glendale, California. Spanky signed this photograph for me one week before his sudden death in 1993 (Photo by Christine Rogan)

26

Kennedy's Lincoln

In 1991, I brought Christine to Washington, DC, for her first visit to our nation's capital. Five years later, we moved there when I won a seat in Congress, but on this trip, we remained tourists. Despite the vacation nature of our visit, the tug of history proved irresistible, and we enjoyed a memorable evening steeped in it.

On the twenty-eighth anniversary of President John F. Kennedy's assassination, I scheduled dinner that night with Evelyn Lincoln, who served as Kennedy's personal secretary for twelve years. She joined Kennedy's congressional staff when he ran for the US Senate in 1952, and remained with him until his death in 1963. When I was a kid, I began corresponding with Evelyn, and we struck up a friendship. She always remembered to send cards and gifts on birthdays and anniversaries, but we never met. When Christine and I planned our trip, I called Evelyn and invited her and her husband, Harold ("Abe"), to join us for dinner. To my delight, they accepted.

When Christine and I arrived at Duke Zeibert's restaurant, Evelyn and Abe awaited us in a corner booth, enjoying their cocktails. She wore her dyed jet-black hair in the same bobbed style of her early 1960s White House days; Abe wore his steel-gray hair long in the back and with bangs over his eyes. They both looked a bit eccentric for a couple in their eighties, but we hit it off immediately. Our conversation became so animated that the waiter tried unsuccessfully for over an hour to take our order.

Evelyn and Abe spoke of their early years in Washington before she joined Kennedy's staff. Her father (a Nebraska congressman) was a very good friend of William Jennings Bryan, the three-time Democratic presidential nominee. She and Abe married in Nebraska sixty-one years earlier, and shortly afterward moved to Washington for his patronage job: running an elevator in the Capitol. "The fellow running the elevator next to me was a Texas kid named Lyndon B. Johnson," Abe said with a smirk. "He was a phony then, and he died a phony." Abe said his other patronage job was as a Capitol guard: he got a gun, a uniform, and $135 a week. "It was one of the best-paying jobs in the world during the Depression," Abe said. "My only duty was to open each office of the Longworth House Office Building every night to make sure the windows were closed. Many times I caught a member of Congress having sex with his secretary, but I never revealed any of their names."

During this job Abe befriended James Roosevelt, Franklin D. Roosevelt's eldest son. James once invited Abe backstage to watch one of his father's speeches: "Roosevelt was a cripple. He arrived for the speech in a wheelchair and wore leg braces. His son lifted him out of the chair with great difficulty. Once the curtain lifted and the crowd cheered, Roosevelt's face lit up instantly with such brilliance! It was amazing. He was like a superman. Yet the minute the speech ended, the curtain dropped, and Roosevelt was backstage, the smile was instantly gone. His face and body withdrew, and suddenly he looked like a shriveled old man that had aged twenty years in a matter of seconds. It was almost frightening to watch the transformation."

Evelyn needed little prodding to share memories of her many years working for JFK:

> I first went to work for Kennedy by doing a research memo for him during his 1952 Senate campaign. I did it for free, hoping he would like my work and ask me to join his staff. He never thanked me for the memo after I turned it in. After Kennedy won the Senate race, he called and offered me a job. I went up to the Senate gallery to watch him being sworn in. He looked so scrawny that day on the Senate floor; he never did learn how to properly tie his necktie. There he stood, with the back portion of his necktie hanging lower than the front portion. He looked more like the elevator operator than a senator!
>
> Years later, on Inauguration Day 1961, we walked into the Oval Office for the first time together. He looked at me and made a strange request: "For as long as I am president," he said, "you must never take a drink of alcohol."

He was afraid I might inadvertently say something meant to be confidential. I promised him I would not drink, and I never did.

Kennedy's staff worked eighteen-hour days every day. He was a perfectionist. If you did something that was not his way, he would fire you just like that [snapping her finger]. But Kennedy never really "fired" anybody—he just wanted them gone. He would always have someone find you another job with better pay. He just didn't want the person around him anymore and it was our job to dispatch them.

I had a premonition Kennedy would die young. There was never any rest with him. Everything was done in such a hurry. He would read a book while he was shaving in the morning. He could never relax. Even when we would "vacation" in Palm Beach, when we would sit by the pool, Kennedy would dive in and swim a lap, then tell me, "Call Governor So-and-So." He would swim another lap, then dictate a letter. He would go like this for a long time: lap, dictate; lap, telephone call; lap, dictate. It never stopped. In all my years with Kennedy, I never took a vacation. We never stopped working. But if he were alive today, he would say this is a damned lie, because he took me everywhere with him. But travel with him did not mean vacation. We never stopped working. Never.

As our waiter served dinner, Evelyn said that a major publishing house contacted her that morning to write a tell-all book on the Kennedy years. "They offered me a $2 million advance if I will write about the scandalous stuff," she said. "They want to know about Marilyn Monroe, the stories of Kennedy's womanizing, and so forth. I told them to forget it. They can keep their money. Some things will go with me to my grave."

During our dinner, Evelyn remained true to her word and never betrayed any secrets about Kennedy's promiscuity. However, as the evening wore on (and the cocktails accumulated), it became clear that Evelyn wasn't taking every secret with her into eternity—starting with her dislike for President Lyndon Johnson. At each mention of Johnson's name, Evelyn's face grimaced and tightened: "That man!" she'd mutter in a voice dripping with disdain. Evelyn recounted the behind-the-scenes maneuvering leading Kennedy to choose Johnson as his running mate in 1960. "You won't read this in the history books," she said. "All of the people present in Kennedy's hotel suite from that day are dead—except me." She continued:

When Kennedy was a senator, Johnson was Senate leader. To Johnson, Kennedy was a nonentity, and he treated Kennedy like a kid. Johnson never dreamed Kennedy would beat him for the Democratic presidential nomination in 1960. Johnson thought he had a lock on it. After Kennedy won, he followed the practice of being conciliatory to his defeated opponent. Kennedy asked me to call Johnson so he could congratulate him on running a tough race and to ask for his support in the coming election. I rang up LBJ's room and was told Johnson had gone to bed and was not to be disturbed.

Kennedy asked my husband, Abe, to bring a note down to Johnson's room. The note told Johnson that Kennedy wanted to meet with him the next morning. Meanwhile, *Washington Post* publisher Phil Graham learned Kennedy had sent a note to Johnson asking to meet, so the *Post* wrote an article saying Kennedy planned to pick Johnson as his running mate. The word spread like wildfire throughout the convention.

The next morning, when Kennedy read the article, he became frantic at the thought of having Johnson as his running mate. He huddled with Bobby Kennedy for over an hour in their hotel room over what he should do. Bobby was adamant that Johnson must not be the vice presidential nominee. Bobby couldn't stand Johnson, and insisted that Johnson should not be invited to be the nominee, even if the offer was nothing more than a courtesy. But events got out of hand. By the end of the meeting, Kennedy felt he would have to offer the position to Johnson if he was to hold Texas and not offend the delegates. Just before Kennedy headed out of the room to meet with Johnson, Kennedy privately told me not to worry. He was sure Johnson would not accept.

Kennedy never, never intended to ask Johnson to be his running mate. His initial attempt to contact Johnson was just to mend fences. The man Kennedy really wanted as his running mate was Missouri senator Stuart Symington. In fact, Kennedy had already told Symington he wanted him. Kennedy didn't believe Johnson would ever accept. But Johnson did accept, and Kennedy was stuck with him. Kennedy was forced to call Symington and explain the situation. Symington understood, and as far as I know, never told anyone how close he came to the vice presidency.

After becoming president, Kennedy confided to me–often–that he was going to dump Johnson in 1964. Kennedy personally preferred North Carolina governor Terry Sanford for the vice presidency in his second term.

If Evelyn still revered Kennedy's memory, she didn't grant the same degree of admiration to Kennedy's widow, Jacqueline:

There was no love between John Kennedy and Jackie. It was a loveless marriage. Old Joe Kennedy [JFK's domineering father] hand-picked Jackie to be his bride because of her breeding and family background. Joe recognized her for what she was–a woman who would make an excellent First Lady. Kennedy dutifully went along with what his father told him to do. It was like watching the son of an ancient Chinese mandarin having his wife chosen for him–Kennedy was a son who let his patriarch pick a wife. Kennedy never loved her, but he knew he had to get married. He was afraid if he remained a bachelor for too long, people might think he was a homosexual or a playboy.

During the White House years, Jackie was having an affair with Aristotle Onassis, and we all knew it. Kennedy knew it, too, but he didn't care. In fact, once he even sent Jackie down to Greece to stay with Onassis. Kennedy asked Franklin Roosevelt Jr. to go with Jackie so the press wouldn't think anything about it. But Kennedy knew full well what was going on. Onassis and Jackie loved each other even then, and Kennedy didn't care. Kennedy told me privately several times that he intended to divorce Jackie after the 1964 election.

Abe agreed with his wife's assessment of the Kennedy marriage, but admitted he still fell under the spell of Jackie's charm. "Despite all her faults," he said, "Jackie was so attractive. Jackie wasn't beautiful, but she was just so very *attractive.*" Abe imitated how Jackie dropped her voice when she spoke to men: "She'd purse her lips into an O shape, leaned forward, and in a sultry, breathy, exaggerated tone, said something like, [imitating her] '*Governor, how do you do?*'"

"Of course," Evelyn added, "that deep voice of hers was all for show. She was not like that at all behind the scenes . . . That breathy voice of hers was all a put-on. Behind the scenes, Jackie was a shrew. She constantly harped on Kennedy and harped about his family to him. She mocked his sisters for not knowing which fork to use at dinner. She kept calling his family 'shanty Irish.' She would screech at him, 'You're shanty Irish! You and your family are just shanty Irish!' There was no question but that he was going to divorce her after the 1964 elections."

Evelyn's cool feelings toward Jacqueline Kennedy didn't end with the young widow's stoic performance after his death in Dallas:

After the shots rang out, we all rode over to Parkland Hospital. They were working on Kennedy in the emergency room, but we got the word early that there was no hope. After they declared him dead, I saw Jackie sitting in a waiting area of the hospital. She sat alone; I went over and hugged her. She gave me no response. She just sat there without emotion.

After Kennedy's death, Jackie tried to evoke this phony "Camelot" myth. "Camelot" is a farce: there is no truth to it. If Kennedy were alive today and listening to all this "Camelot" silliness, he would laugh. Kennedy was flesh and bone; he was not a god or an idol the way Jackie and the family have tried to portray him since his death. Camelot was a creation of Jackie, along with historian Theodore White.

Another public figure that evoked contempt from Evelyn was Kennedy's vanquished opponent in the 1960 election, Richard Nixon:

When Kennedy was in the Senate, Nixon's vice presidential office was near ours. I was always friendly with Rose Mary Woods, Nixon's personal secretary. When Kennedy was a senator, he had back surgery and was so ill that he was near death. The hospital priest administered the last rites of the Catholic Church to him. A Kennedy family member told me that he was going to die, and probably would not last through the night. I went to the office to be there to answer the calls that would come once we got the word he was dead. Nixon strolled into our office that afternoon and said to me in a nonchalant fashion, "I hear your senator is going to die." I became very angry with him. "No, he isn't," I told him. I was very offended by Nixon's callous attitude.[1]

Evelyn said she always liked former vice president Hubert Humphrey, who Kennedy defeated for the 1960 nomination. Later, she felt sorry for him after Humphrey became Johnson's vice president in 1964:

LBJ had his spies in government report on Humphrey. One of them told LBJ that Humphrey had privately commented that he disfavored Johnson's war policies in Vietnam. Johnson called Humphrey into the Oval Office. When Humphrey entered the room, Johnson ran up to Humphrey and screamed profanities at him. Incredibly, Johnson put his hands around Humphrey's throat, and in a mad frenzy began to choke Humphrey physically. Johnson

---

1   Author and syndicated columnist Chris Matthews, who wrote the book *Kennedy & Nixon*, disputed Mrs. Lincoln's account. He claimed Nixon was deeply distraught over the death of Kennedy, with whom he developed an early friendship since their 1946 freshman entry into the House of Representatives.

screamed that if Humphrey didn't toe the line on Vietnam, Johnson would break Humphrey's career. Humphrey left the office in shock, but stopped criticizing Johnson.

I mentioned that Christine and I visited Kennedy's grave earlier in the day; apparently, we barely missed seeing Evelyn there. "Today was my fifty-sixth visit to his grave," she noted sadly. "I go every year on his birthday and on November 22." Evelyn spoke with a halting voice of that fateful day in Dallas, saying she rode a few cars behind Kennedy in the motorcade when he was assassinated. "As his car pulled out of Love Field for the ride through downtown Dallas, I saw him sitting in the backseat. He was waving his hand. . . ." Her voice cracked, and she elaborated no further. "After all these years, it's still too painful to discuss," she said.

"We have a dearth of leaders in America," Evelyn noted. "We need another Kennedy today. You would have liked him, Jim, and I know he would have liked you. If I'd known you back then, I could have brought you to the Oval Office to meet him any time you wanted. I'm sorry the opportunity never arose," she said wistfully.

So was I.

Christine and me dining with Evelyn and Abe Lincoln at Duke Zeibert's restaurant, Washington, DC, November 22, 1991

. . .

Evelyn Lincoln and I continued our friendship in the ensuing years.

Shortly after Bill Clinton won the presidency in 1992, I mentioned to her that I heard Clinton say in an interview that his teenage handshake with President Kennedy in the Rose Garden motivated him to public service. I thought it would please her that a new Democratic president credited her former boss with his ascent. Evelyn bristled at my assumption, telling me that although she was a lifelong Democrat, she voted for independent candidate Ross Perot in 1992 and refused to cast a ballot for Clinton: "As for Clinton being impressed after shaking hands with JFK," she said, "hundreds of young people did that and they were all impressed. But if Clinton was so impressed, why didn't he follow Kennedy's example of being honest, sincere, and straightforward with the people? It looks as though the Clinton inauguration will be like a circus, with all of the clowns riding into town on a bus."

Oh. Sorry I mentioned it.

. . .

Evelyn Lincoln died of cancer at age eighty-five on May 11, 1995. Her husband, Abe, died one month later.

27

Das Kapitalist

In 1992 I received an invitation from Lodwrick Cook, chairman of ARCO, to a luncheon at the Ronald Reagan Presidential Library honoring Reagan and Mikhail Gorbachev, the last leader of the now-defunct Soviet Union—for *only* five thousand dollars! The invitation to dine with Reagan and Gorbachev was enticing but prohibitive. I thanked Cook for thinking of me, but declined respectfully: "Living on a government salary," I told him. "If my wife found out I spent five thousand dollars to have lunch with anyone, I'd need to move to the Reagan Library, because I'd no longer have a family or home!"

A few days later, Cook's secretary surprised me with a phone call: "The Reagan event is sold out anyway," she said, "but Chairman Cook wants to invite you to a private lunch for Gorbachev at ARCO Towers in Los Angeles. He is having the lunch and reception so some of our executives and local government officials can meet Gorbachev during his visit to California." She advised me to get there an hour early because the Secret Service planned to secure the building.

I arrived for the event at ARCO Towers and found the surrounding streets swarming with activity. Police closed the traffic lanes closest to the building; security agents hovered everywhere. Hundreds of ARCO employees stood behind an outdoor barricade to get a glimpse of Gorbachev when his motorcade arrived.

A Secret Service agent escorted me to a private elevator to the thirty-seventh floor; another agent brought me into a large reception room, where Los Angeles mayor Tom Bradley and other local officials awaited the Gorbachev party.

At 12:15 p.m., spontaneous applause spread through the room. Gorbachev, accompanied by his wife, Raisa, and their daughter, Irina, entered with broad smiles. Gorbachev mingled freely during the reception as he chatted with guests through a simultaneous translator, working the room like a seasoned politician on the campaign trail. Photographers jostled for the best camera angle; one grumbled, "Lod Cook nixed a receiving line because Gorby doesn't like to pose."

When Cook introduced me to the honored guests, Mrs. Gorbachev extended her hand and greeted me in her best English: "e-e-e-t e-e-z-e n-i-z-e to meet you!" Then former President Gor-

Former Soviet President Mikhail Gorbachev, Los Angeles, May 5, 1992

bachev gripped my hand tightly and pumped it vigorously. As we talked,

"Accomplished!" Former Soviet president Mikhail Gorbachev and me, Los Angeles, May 5, 1992

I got the impression he was in no hurry to move on because (unlike everyone else), I didn't speak "at him" through the interpreter, meaning I didn't look at the interpreter and say things like, "Tell Mr. Gorbachev that. . . ." When communicating with Gorbachev, I looked at and spoke to him directly, and he did the same with me. Later, he said that I was the only person he met during his California trip thus far who did this. I told him I had an unfair advantage over others: as a trial court judge in Los Angeles County, I was used to dealing with criminal defendants through simultaneous translators, so the skill came naturally to me. Gorbachev laughed and joked, "I hope that is the end of the comparison!"

After Gorbachev signed a photograph for me, he handed it back, gripped my hand, and pronounced, "Accomplished!"

Ushers invited the guests into the main dining room; I found myself seated at the table right next to the honorees, with Raisa Gorbachev sitting behind me. During the luncheon, members of county and local government took turns presenting the Gorbachevs with gifts, certificates, and plaques. Gorbachev acknowledged each memento with a smile and a bow before turning over the booty to an aide. Between presentations, he continued to greet guests and sign autographs. Even my seatmate Tom Plate, editorial page editor for the *Los Angeles Times*, was not immune to the temptation. "It's not very chic for reporters to ask for autographs," Plate grumbled. I suggested this might be a once-in-a-lifetime opportunity to obtain a great memento for his grandchildren. Plate swallowed hard, and then approached the former Soviet leader with a pen and menu in hand. Gorbachev inscribed it in Russian, "To a great news editor."

Following the luncheon, Cook began the program by mentioning that Mrs. Gorbachev had a distinguished background as an educator, and that Gorbachev loves the ballet and opera. "And," Cook noted, "he can recite the works of [Russian author Alexander] Pushkin!" Gorbachev chuckled when he heard the translated claim, then called out a response from his seat: "I can't do too much of that anymore!" Cook then presented the Gorbachevs with a handmade quilt from an Amish village in Pennsylvania. While Gorbachev admired the quilt, Mrs. Gorbachev climbed on top of her chair, pointed to the quilt, and said (in Russian), "That quilt is meant for me, and not for my husband!" The audience joined in the laughter.

Gorbachev received a standing ovation when Cook introduced him. He embraced his American host, and then waved the room to silence. Speaking without notes (and with his interpreter at his side), Gorbachev promised a brief, impromptu speech. Noting that Los Angeles had been rocked by riots the previous week, he praised local officials for their handling of the crisis. He said there had been speculation as to whether the unrest would force him to cancel his Los Angeles visit: "I had no intention of canceling," he said, earning a rousing cheer.

The heart of Gorbachev's speech focused on one issue: expanding markets in the former Soviet Union. He encouraged the gathering of business leaders to invest and bring commerce to Russia. "Your investments will help to make a free-market economy work there," the former head of the Communist Party implored the gathering of capitalists.

It was ironic to hear the man given unprecedented power to hold together his dying communist regime now preaching the gospel of free markets. Yet Gorbachev showed no hint of discomfort at his new role; he expressed his hope repeatedly that Russia and the United States would work together to help modernize his nation through pro-growth policies and economic development.

. . .

More than twenty years have passed since I sat in ARCO Towers and listened to the former president of the Soviet Union preach to an American audience the failures of socialism, and the benefits of capitalism over a command economy.

Perhaps we should invite him back for another speech.

28

Mr. Television

In 1948, only one in 150 Americans owned a television set. Then a brash comedian named Milton Berle became host of a new program called *The Texaco Star Theater*. Within a year, TV sales soared, largely because of viewer addiction to his outlandish antics. Berle so dominated the airwaves (the Nielsen ratings showed 80 percent of every US household with a TV tuned in to him) that movie theaters and restaurants closed their doors on Tuesday nights, knowing they couldn't compete with the man dubbed "Mr. Television" and "Uncle Miltie." Years later, Berle related in his autobiography that a study showed Detroit's water reservoir levels sank on Tuesday nights between 9:00 and 9:05: "It turned out that everyone waited until the end of the *Texaco Star Theater* before going to the bathroom," he wrote.

Berle's star power appeared so enduring that in 1951 Texaco signed him to an unprecedented thirty-year television contract. However, with the new medium's exploding popularity, the comedy competition grew more potent. His popularity dropped as new programs challenged his supremacy, and by 1953, Texaco canceled his show. Still, Berle remained a successful fixture in television over the years, and also remained a draw in feature films, on Broadway, and in nightclubs.

When I met Berle, he was decades removed from commanding the number-one rated television program, but he remained very much a star and showed no signs of slowing down (the *Guinness Book of World Records* claimed he performed the greatest number of charity benefit performances of anyone in show business history). It was at one of these benefits that I met "Mr. Television." In 1992 I attended a Kiwanis Club luncheon to raise money for youth programs, where Berle entertained at the event.

When he entered the ballroom, the large audience rose and cheered for the eighty-four-year-old comic legend. Chomping on his cigar, Berle quipped as he passed by the microphone on the way to his seat, "Who am I, Ross Perot?" (At the time, Perot was a third-party presidential candidate.)

Once introduced, Berle launched into a rapid-fire Borscht Belt routine filled with ethnic humor for which modern standards require frowns of disapproval; for Berle, all such political correctness gave way.

"Hey," Berle asked the howling crowd as he pointed to the Hispanic waiter serving coffee at a front table, "How did that Mexican kid know I was a Hebrew? Each time he waited on me, he kept asking [imitating a Spanish accent], '*Jew* want more chicken? *Jew* want more water?'" Berle then pushed his fist to his stomach, feigning indigestion: "I've got so much gas that I'm being chased by Arabs."

Other Berle gems:

I'm so unlucky. I loaned my friend $30,000 to have plastic surgery. Now I can't find the son of a bitch!

Anytime someone goes into a deli and orders pastrami on white bread, somewhere a Jew dies.

At my age, I feel like Zsa Zsa Gabor's sixth husband. I know what I'm supposed to do, but I don't know how to make it interesting.

I recently married a woman who's thirty years younger than I. Three months ago, we made love for one hour and three minutes. Of course, that was the night they turned the clocks back.

We owe a lot to Thomas Edison: if it wasn't for him, we'd be watching TV by candlelight.

The Los Angeles Dodgers have had a tough year. Manager Tommy Lasorda went on a Slimfast diet and lost seventy-three games.

Experience is what you get after you've forgotten her name.

And on it went: thirty minutes of one-liners from an old vaudevillian who did the show without a note before him. When it was over, Berle received another standing ovation.

As people filed out of the banquet hall, the event producer, Norman Mamey, invited me back to meet Berle, who now tried wolfing down his untouched lunch before the waiters cleared the table. Maybe it was a bad time to chat: Berle talked with a mouthful of food, and pieces of broccoli kept dropping onto his coat during our conversation. What the hell—when someone's eighty-four, he deserves a little slack cut on his table etiquette. That minor distraction aside, he was delightful.

Comedian Milton Berle and me, Castaways Restaurant, Burbank, California, June 25, 1992

I gave Berle an old movie still from a film he made more than fifty years earlier; Berle thanked me as he studied the picture: "Now just one question," he asked: "Who the hell are these people in it with me?"

When Mamey told Berle I was a great public speaker, Berle's eyes lit up.

"If you speak in public a lot," he told me, "then you need to buy my book, *Milton Berle's Private Joke File*. There are over ten thousand jokes in it, and it will be a valuable reference for you. It's only twenty dollars."

Remembering that Berle had a reputation throughout his career for comedians suing him, claiming he stole their material, I chided him: "I'll buy your book if nobody will sue me for using your jokes!"

"Buy my book and I'll give you a waiver!" he promised.

Before leaving, a photographer snapped a picture of Berle and me. Moments later, as Berle shook my hand and said good-bye, he took a step back; his foot slipped, and he began falling off the riser. I grabbed his arm and caught him as he reeled backward. Berle was unharmed, but the experience left him shaken. I helped him to his chair until he felt ready to stand. After regaining his composure, he said somberly, "Thanks for saving me. That's how Bing Crosby died. Crosby fell backward off a stage, and it led to him having a heart attack a few months later."

That instant was the only time during his appearance in Burbank that Berle–and everyone else–didn't have a smile on his face.

. . .

Milton Berle died of cancer at age ninety-three on March 27, 2002.

29

Dream Team

As noted earlier, on the last night of the 1972 Republican National Convention in Miami, I waited in line to shake hands with President Richard Nixon, but my turn never came. In 1988, I got within a second of meeting him, but a faux Disneyland "guard" foiled my opportunity. Twenty years after Miami, my chance came finally. However, when I did meet Nixon, it wasn't over politics–it was over baseball.

In 1972, lifelong baseball fan Nixon, along with son-in-law David Eisenhower (grandson of President Eisenhower) collaborated in selecting their ideal all-star "dream team." In 1992, Nixon and Eisenhower renewed their selections and named those they considered the best players of all time. They planned to unveil their updated picks at a special luncheon honoring Baseball Hall of Fame players at the Nixon Library. Tickets for the luncheon were two hundred dollars each; five-hundred-dollar donors received a special "Dugout Club" pass entitling the bearer to attend a private reception with Nixon and his retired baseball star guests. After waiting decades to meet Nixon, I refused to let the opportunity pass. Despite the steep price, for the first (and last) time in my life, I bought a five-hundred-dollar ticket to something.

Once at the Nixon Library, I found a private schedule left behind by an errant staffer. In flipping through it, I learned more details about Nixon's attendance. He planned to depart Santa Barbara by helicopter at 9:30 a.m. and fly to Yorba Linda Middle School, where a car would pick him up and drive him to the "Eureka Entrance" of the Nixon Library. He would be escorted to the Marriott Room for makeup and rest before doing an interview. Whoever prepared the memo anticipated Nixon's comfort: handlers were directed to have Diet Pepsi, ice, yellow legal pads, and pens available for the former president while he awaited the start of the program.

After checking in and obtaining my ticket, I went to the lower-level Olin Room for the Dugout Club reception. As I was about to enter the private gathering, I heard a familiar voice to my left. I turned and saw Nixon entering the Marriott Room with library director John Taylor and several private security guards in tow. Amazingly, none of the arriving guests recognized Nixon as he lingered in the doorway, receiving a last-minute event briefing by Taylor.

A few minutes later, Nixon entered the Olin Room with David Eisenhower and addressed the Dugout Club guests briefly, saying he preferred to save his remarks for the upcoming luncheon. He thanked everyone for coming, and then took his place in the receiving line. I was one of the first people to move through Nixon's photo op. When my turn came–finally!–to shake hands with the former president, Taylor introduced me as "Judge Rogan."

"Nice to meet you, Judge," Nixon said as he gripped my hand. Then, looking at me closely, Nixon said, "Are you really a judge? You look too young!"

"Bless you for that, Mr. President," I said, smiling, and then the photographer memorialized the moment for me.

While welcoming guests, Nixon often wiped beads of perspiration from his brow and upper lip. Despite the uncomfortably warm temperature in the room, Nixon smiled and greeted everyone, and made a point to chat with each of the many children passing through the line with their parents. He never hesitated or complained about signing, despite the "no autograph" rule printed on the reception bulletin. Nixon inked his name to dozens of cards, baseballs, scraps of paper, and photographs (irrespective of staff attempts to fend off the requests). One child later complained to his father that Nixon signed his baseball "RN" instead of penning a full signature. "That's the way he signs his name," the father growled, "so shut your ungrateful mouth and be glad you got it!"

After greeting the last guest, security and library officials escorted Nixon from the room to the dining area, where ticketed guests gathered under a huge outdoor tent erected near the parking lot for the luncheon. In entering, we filed passed a rope line behind which stood dozens of young boys in Little League uniforms, and hundreds of additional spectators and fans waiting to

Finally! Twenty years and $500 later, former president Richard Nixon and me, Nixon Library, July 15, 1992

catch a glimpse of Nixon and the players as they entered. Large library medallions and American flags decorated the red, white, and blue stage; a banner reading, "Nixon–Eisenhower All Time Baseball Greats" revealed the names of their special team picks. Each table had a box of Cracker Jack as the centerpiece, with baseball cards strewn around it. The organist for the Los Angeles Dodgers entertained with baseball-themed musical selections.

The luncheon began shortly after noon, with library director John Taylor welcoming each current and former baseball player: Johnny Bench, Bob Feller, Brooks Robinson, Harmon Killebrew, Johnny Mize, George Kell, Rollie Fingers, Maury Wills, Buck Rodgers, Tony LaRussa–even Babe Ruth's daughter, Julia Ruth Stevens. While the honored guests took their seats, Nixon stood at the tent entrance, awaiting his cue. When Taylor introduced him, Nixon entered to a standing ovation while the USC marching band played a medley of tunes, including "You're a Grand Old Flag" and "Yankee Doodle." Nixon smiled and shook hands as he walked to his table. Adding to the atmosphere, Roger Owens, the "Peanut Man" famous for throwing bags of roasted peanuts with deadly accuracy to customers at the Los Angeles Dodgers Stadium, arrived in his uniform and tossed bags to people seated throughout the tent. The press lined up a shot where Owens threw a bag to Nixon from half a tent away; Nixon caught it on the first toss.

During lunch, a small ring of private security guards kept a watchful eye on Nixon as he chatted with his tablemates. After a few people approached him to request an autograph and the guards did nothing to dissuade their presence, I walked over and asked him to sign a rare item from my political memorabilia collection: a campaign brochure from his 1950 US Senate race against Helen Gahagan Douglas. It bore the caption, "Let's elect Congressman Richard Nixon United States Senator–The man who broke the Hiss-Chambers espionage case."

"Where on earth did you get this?" Nixon asked as he studied the vintage flyer. He

1950 "Nixon for Senator" flyer autographed for me by the former president at his library, July 15, 1992

pointed to the young picture of himself on the cover and looked at it for several seconds. When I asked jokingly if he'd used his high school yearbook picture for the brochure, Nixon laughed, nodded, and penned his signature to it. "That pamphlet takes me back a long, long time," Nixon said reflectively.

Within minutes, the line of people wanting autographs grew from a few to a few dozen. Nixon didn't enjoy another bite of food; he signed throughout the luncheon, and never turned down a request. With Nixon now setting the example, the baseball stars got into the act and signed too. Only Johnny Bench did so grudgingly, griping to fans about them breaking the no-autograph rule.

After lunch, David Eisenhower began the program by announcing the Nixon–Eisenhower picks for the greatest ball players, and explained their reasons for each selection. Eisenhower then invited each visiting player to join him onstage for commentary. Johnny Bench remembered playing one game in 1968 and seeing Eisenhower and his fiancée (later wife), Julie Nixon, in the stands. "I only had eyes for Julie that day," Bench quipped. Other players also shared brief insights: Bob Feller described his lost playing time because of his military service in World War II ("At least we won that one!"); Rollie Fingers compared modern pitchers to those in his heyday; Tony LaRussa shared his philosophy of what it takes to keep a great team together; George Kell talked about his years as a third baseman for the New York Yankees; and Harmon Killebrew reminisced about meeting President Dwight D. Eisenhower at a baseball game in 1959: turning to David Eisenhower, Killebrew said, "Your grandfather asked me to sign a ball for you that day. I asked him to sign one for me. We traded autographed balls, and I still have his."

"And I still have yours!" Eisenhower replied.

Maury Wills told of driving with friends down to Tijuana after Nixon resigned the presidency. As a joke (and after a few drinks), he stopped at Nixon's San Clemente home and rang the bell. "Let's see if 'Dick' is home," he kidded his friends. Wills had no expectation of seeing Nixon, and was shocked when the gates opened and they were ushered into Nixon's study. "Mr. President," Wills noted, "you were bigger than life then, and you still are." Eisenhower asked Wills what it takes to win a baseball game. Nixon could not resist: he walked to the stage with Wills and answered the question for him: "Steal!" Nixon thundered.

When Nixon rose to speak, the seventy-nine-year-old former president received another standing ovation. Two aides removed the podium that the previous speakers used and replaced it with a stand-alone microphone. (In later years, Nixon eschewed notes and made a practice of speaking extemporaneously.) Nixon mentioned the presence of Anaheim Angels manager Buck Rodgers, injured recently in a team bus traffic collision. "Now you know why I am opposed to busing," Nixon quipped. "And I want you to know I always root for the home team. I want the Angels to win the World Series while [owner and former cowboy star] Gene Autry is still around."

For almost thirty minutes, Nixon reminisced about his love for baseball and sports. He said he attended his first baseball game in 1925, and had been addicted ever since. His love of baseball even affected his thinking on signing autographs.

"You know, I signed lots of autographs today," he said. "I try never to refuse a request, and I will tell you why. Back in 1942, I was eating dinner with my wife, Pat, in a restaurant in New York. Seated across the room from us was the legendary baseball star Babe Ruth. Pat went over to Ruth and asked him for his autograph for my little brother Eddie. As busy and as famous as the Babe was, he took the time to sign that autograph. When I came to a position in my life where people wanted my autograph, I have always tried to remember that if Babe Ruth had time to sign an autograph, then so do I."

Nixon said the first home run he ever saw hit in a baseball game was in the 1940s, when Joe DiMaggio smashed one out near the stands where Nixon sat. "But the greatest player I ever saw," Nixon added, "was Jackie Robinson. In fact, Jackie was the greatest all-around athlete ever. He could have played professional football, basketball, or been an Olympic athlete. One of my fond memories was in attending a UCLA–Oregon game with Jackie."

Nixon recalled another baseball memory of attending a game with the legendary New York Yankees manager Casey Stengel. "Had Casey lived," Nixon joked, "I might have made him secretary of state. The first rule of politics is to confound the opposition. When Casey spoke, nobody could understand him! Only he could understand himself."

He then noted that in 1992, all the major presidential candidates (Republican George Bush, Democrat Bill Clinton, and Independent Ross Perot) were left-handed. "So it is settled," Nixon concluded, "Our next president will be a southpaw":

"Any baseball man will tell you that left-handers tend to be a little wild," he went on. "Our next president will be a left-hander, but we hope he isn't wild and that he will emulate one of baseball's best left handers and hit home runs for America the way Babe Ruth hit them for the New York Yankees!"

Nixon returned to his seat to another ovation. Jo Lasorda, wife of Los Angeles Dodgers manager Tommy Lasorda, presented Nixon with one of her husband's jerseys. As the luncheon adjourned, Nixon joined the players onstage for a group photograph; meanwhile, guests swamped Nixon, who remained for another twenty minutes, shaking hands and signing for them.

As the baseball stars boarded a special bus for the return trip to their hotel, I went inside the library to see a special exhibit of baseball-related presidential memorabilia. While looking at treasures such as George Bush's first baseman's mitt from Yale and Jimmy Carter's softball gear, Nixon appeared suddenly and was followed by photographers as he entered the side door of the small theater for a library docent reception. When I ran into him again before leaving the library, Nixon gripped my hand: "I still say you look too young to be a judge!" he teased me with a big smile.

"Mr. President," I replied, "it's that sort of narrow thinking that kept you from becoming governor of California!"

Nixon laughed heartily, patted my shoulder, and then signed an engraved White House vignette for my collection with his "RN" initials. Unlike the little boy earlier in the day, I was not disappointed to receive the abbreviated version of his autograph—the in-person signature I waited twenty years to collect.

. . .

Baseball Hall of Famer Bob Feller played from 1936 to 1956. He died of leukemia at age ninety-two on December 15, 2010.

Hall of Famer Harmon Killebrew played from 1954 to 1975. He died at age seventy-five on May 17, 2011.

Hall of Famer Johnny Mize, the four-time National League home run champion, played from 1936 to 1953. He died at age eighty on June 2, 1993.

Hall of Famer George Kell, the 1949 American League batting champion, played from 1943 to 1957. He died at age eighty-six on March 24, 2009.

30

Pat

Edmund G. "Pat" Brown became governor of California shortly after my birth. Serving two terms (1958–1966), he had the unique distinction of running for governor against two future presidents of the United States. In 1962 he won reelection by beating former vice president Richard Nixon handily; four years later, he lost just as handily to political newcomer Ronald Reagan. Brown's legacy continued decades after he left Sacramento: his son Jerry succeeded him as California's thirty-fourth governor (1974–1982); twenty-eight years later, Jerry recaptured the governor's chair in 2010.

I first met Pat Brown in 1974 when his son ran for governor. Although I saw him a few more times at political gatherings over the years, we became acquainted when I was a deputy district attorney and I introduced him as a guest speaker at a local function. He called me out of the blue a few days later. After schmoozing with me about politics, he came to the point: the police had arrested for drunk driving the son of a major client of his law firm. "Jim," he asked, "can you do a favor for your old governor and make this go away for me?"

"Sorry, Governor," I told him. "Those days are long gone. You'll have to take care of this the old-fashioned way: plead him guilty or go to trial."

Brown chuckled. "Well, I thought you'd say that," he replied. "I'll plead him guilty, and then you and I can go to lunch and talk politics."

I liked Pat Brown—a lot. He was a friendly, backslapping pol from the old school. He never held it against me that I cut his client no slack (or that I was a Reagan Republican). I never could bring myself to call him Pat, at least to his face, although almost everyone else did. The nickname fit the man: breezy, casual, and affable.

In late 1992 Pat invited me to join him for lunch near his office. He had a modest storefront suite across from the Century Plaza Hotel in Los Angeles. As a collector, I was mildly disappointed at the dearth of memorabilia on his wall: all I saw was an autographed photograph of 1952 Democratic presidential nominee Adlai Stevenson and a picture of Pat with President Lyndon Johnson in the Oval Office.

Pat complained that his weight had dropped from 185 pounds to 145, and that his right leg was troubling him. "It's hell growing old," he muttered. "I'm eighty-seven now. I'm having trouble sleeping at night, and then get very tired during the day. I'm also having lots of trouble walking because of my leg. My muscles feel very stiff."

Reminding him that I had newborn twin girls at home, I said, "Come on over and change Dana's and Claire's diapers for an afternoon, Governor—that'll loosen you up!"

In truth, Pat did not look well. He appeared thin and haggard; small clumps of white whiskers protruded from parts of his face and neck (he said that as his eyes grew weaker, it made shaving more difficult). Yet, despite his infirmities, he said he still enjoyed golf, although he hadn't played in two weeks. "My leg is too stiff and sore to play," he said.

Pat suggested we dine at an outdoor bistro above his office. He took my arm and gripped it tightly as we negotiated the stairs. He wanted to sit at an outside table so we could enjoy the beautiful day. During our luncheon many people walked by and greeted him, and he enjoyed the recognition.

As we dined, Pat recounted his early years in the law:

I was admitted to the bar sometime in the 1920s—I don't even remember what year it was anymore. I first worked for a blind attorney who gave me what he called the best advice in the world: stay out of politics! I didn't listen, of course, and ran for my first office shortly after law school. I don't even remember what that was for. I had a real dilemma in the early years. My father-in-law was chief of police in San Francisco, and my dad ran a gambling operation. I lived in constant mortal fear that my father-in-law would arrest my father! Anyway, as you know, I later ran for district attorney of San Francisco, attorney general, and governor.

When I mentioned there were more than nine hundred deputy district attorneys in the Los Angeles County DA's office, he shook his head in disbelief: "When I was district attorney of San Francisco," he said, "there were twenty-seven deputy prosecutors working under me. I knew every one of them, I knew their wives and kids, and I had been to each of their homes for dinner."

During lunch, Pat shared these brief impressions of some leaders he knew during his career in politics:

HARRY S TRUMAN: "A great president that I was proud to nominate at the 1948 Democratic National Convention."

ADLAI E. STEVENSON: "A wonderful man that I knew very well. He was witty, funny, and brilliant."

JOHN F. KENNEDY: "He was quite a fellow. In public, he was very urbane and polished. In private, he was very down-to-earth."

RICHARD NIXON: "He was pretty stiff and cold as a person. Still, over the years, Nixon and I have become friends and have remained in contact."

Pat reminisced about his campaign against Nixon for governor in 1962. With Nixon having been a US senator from California, a two-term vice president, and coming within a whisker of defeating John F. Kennedy for the presidency (Nixon carried California that year), I asked if Pat feared Nixon would defeat him in 1962. "There was little doubt in my mind that I would lose," he said. "I thought Nixon would beat me for all those reasons."

"In fact," he continued, "Nixon's popularity coincided with a steady decline in my own. I had made some tough decisions that angered many people, such as giving Caryl Chessman a sixty-day reprieve on Death Row.[1] I would go to speak at public functions and would be introduced as "the governor of the great state of California" to a loud chorus of boos. So I thought Nixon would beat me. We debated several times that year; Nixon was a fine debater but very stiff as a

---

1   California's infamous "Red Light Bandit" executed in San Quentin's gas chamber during the Brown administration.

person. But in the end, I won. That was a very gratifying moment in my life."

I asked what he attributed as the key factor to his upset victory that year. Pat smiled and said, "I guess I just overcame Nixon with the sheer force of my personality and charm!"

Next he talked about Ronald Reagan: "You can't help but like Reagan," he said. "He is one of the most charming men I ever met." Pat said that four years after he beat Nixon, he knew Reagan would be a difficult candidate to beat: "Many of the leaders of the Democratic Party felt Reagan would be a pushover, but I knew he would be tough. I had watched him on television and was reading the early polls very carefully."

Ironically, a quarter century after they squared off for governor, the office of former president Reagan was now just a block down the street. I mentioned that to Pat, and asked if they ever got together socially. "No, we don't," he

Former California governor Pat Brown and me at lunch, Century City, California, October 20, 1992

said. Then, after taking a long sip of water, he laughed and added, "You know, Reagan has made an entire career out of having us Democrats underestimate that son-of-a-bitch!" Pat said his defeat by Reagan didn't surprise him: "It's difficult to run for a third term. You've probably accomplished all of the major goals you are going to be able to get through in two terms."

After the waiter took our photo, Pat kidded, "Jim, this picture of us together will get me reelected governor of California!"

"Governor," I teased him, "I have to run for reelection to the bench in conservative Glendale. If my voters there see me hanging out with Jerry Brown's dad, I'll be out of a job!"

Pat roared with laughter: "I guess Glendale hasn't changed much since I last ran! Don't worry, Jim. I'll make sure Kathleen makes you her first pick for the California Supreme Court!"[2]

. . .

A few weeks later, Pat came to Glendale to visit me. I was presiding over a case when Pat entered the rear of the courtroom. Relying heavily on his cane, he made his way slowly to the bench and greeted me.

Once we settled in my chambers, Pat complimented me on the decor of my office (vintage political memorabilia framed from floor to ceiling): "I love all these campaign posters–they give me a warm feeling," Pat said. Mischievously, I pointed to a large 1966 "Ronald Reagan for Governor" poster hanging in the corner. "Well, maybe not that warm!" he laughed.

At Pat's earlier request, I had brought several trays of old Democratic campaign buttons from my collection to show him. Pat took off his glasses and held the trays close to his face to study the historic artifacts. He marveled aloud while looking at the grouping, which included delegate badges and ribbons from Democratic National Conventions dating back to 1900–a 1914 "Franklin D. Roosevelt for US Senate" badge, a 1934 "Harry Truman for Senate" button, and a set of early Al Smith campaign buttons (for sheriff, board of aldermen, and governor of New York). "These are worth a fortune," he said, "but don't ever sell them. Give them to a library someday, like I have done with all of my memorabilia."

---

2   Brown's daughter, California state treasurer Kathleen Brown, won the 1994 Democratic nomination for governor. Although leading in the polls through most of the campaign, incumbent governor Pete Wilson defeated her.

Pat looked intrigued when I said I saved my favorite tray of campaign buttons to show him last, and assured him they held "the most historical significance." Then I handed him (with a straight face) a tray filled with memorabilia from Richard Nixon's unsuccessful campaign against Pat for governor of California in 1962. Pat threw back his head and laughed, then examined the Nixon items carefully: "My victory over Nixon in 1962 gave me my greatest political satisfaction," he told me again.

Finally I produced a tray of items from Pat's own election campaigns. He pointed out a 1946 campaign postcard from his race for state attorney general. "Boy, I sure looked young then," he noted. I got the biggest laugh out of him when I showed him a badge the Nixon campaign had put out in '62, proclaiming "SOB–Sweep Out Brown."

Recently Pat and his wife, Bernice, had signed for me a family photograph of them with their two children, former governor Jerry Brown and daughter Kathleen. Both Jerry and Kathleen later signed the picture; I told Pat I sent the photo to Kathleen with a note saying her father promised she would make me her first appointment to the Supreme Court: "I told your daughter my legal research had uncovered an ancient legal maxim: It is the doctrine of 'Ex Governis Promiso Patricae,' which legally binds a governor's daughter to the promises of her father," I joked. "I told Kathleen I would release her from the obligation and save her the embarrassment of having to appoint a conservative Republican if she would simply sign the photograph. The picture was returned to me shortly after that, with this inscription from Kathleen: 'Judge Rogan, The doctrine of "Ex Governis Promiso Patricae" has just been declared unconstitutional by the Republican-appointed Supreme Court–whew!'"

Pat laughed heartily at the punch line, then said earnestly, "I really think Kathleen will be the next governor of California. Then we will be the first family in history where a father, son, and daughter have all been governor of the state."

Reminding him of my Republican roots, I kidded him: "Thank God you only had two kids!"

As we walked down the hall, Pat clung tightly to my arm for support, muttering about how tough it was to grow old and not being sure-footed anymore. His frailty became evident when, in the parking lot, Pat slipped while stepping from the curb and began to fall. Fortunately, I had him by the arm and caught him.

Several of my colleagues and I took Pat to lunch at the Oakmont Country Club. The day was especially clear and brisk outside, and the drive there showed off the nearby mountain ranges. Pat remarked, "I had no idea how pretty Glendale is," he said.

Reminding him that Glendale was one of the state's most conservative cities when he ran, I joked, "You didn't know how pretty it was because this is the first time you ever came through Glendale without the cover of darkness!"

As we motored toward the club, Pat again mentioned how tired he grew these days: "At eighty-seven years old, I find myself getting sleepy during the day, and then I can't sleep at night."

"Don't get too sleepy," I warned him. "After lunch we're bringing you back to my court. There's a drunk-driving case we've saved for you to try. You're an old DA, so you can just saddle up."

Pat assured me he was ready to climb back into the arena.

When we arrived at the country club, I helped Pat out of the car. He again gripped my arm as we made our way slowly to the table reserved for us. It was a charming lunch, but we kept it brief because Pat appeared quite fatigued. Still, Pat reminisced at times about his career and family:

"My daughter Kathleen is a great kid and will make a great governor," he said confidently. "And Jerry was a good son; he was in the seminary for many years before he decided to study law and politics. He was a good governor, but did not always make good decisions. The paper recently reported he now is thinking of running for mayor of Los Angeles, but that won't happen. Jerry just says things like that because he likes to get his picture in the paper."

He went on, "In 1970 I thought about running against Reagan again and settling the score for him defeating me. But my wife told me no: she said it was Jerry's turn to make his name and I had to step aside for him. Just as I did so for Jerry, now it is Kathleen's turn to run, and Jerry will step aside for her. He won't run for mayor."

I asked Pat what thoughts went through his mind that morning in 1959 when he took the oath. He took a sip of wine, smiled, and said, "Just that I am going to be a damned good governor!"

Pat said that Republican governor Earl Warren (later chief justice of the United States) became his good friend. "In fact," Pat noted, "Earl didn't campaign for my Republican opponent when I ran for attorney general. Earl was a great big guy with a warm smile. He was not a great legal scholar, but he had great instincts."

When it was time to go, Pat thanked everyone for the lunch. "Let's do this again soon," he said cheerfully, and then added, "Jim, I almost forgot your present." He handed me an inscribed copy of his book on capital punishment, *Public Justice, Private Mercy*.

Pat took my arm, and I escorted him across the dining room toward the exit. He leaned even more heavily upon me than earlier. Suddenly, I felt Pat's arm slip off my own. My heart stopped: I thought he collapsed. As I turned quickly to grab him, I saw him returning to the restaurant area at a surprisingly fast clip. I had to rush to catch up! When I offered him my arm for support, he waved me away. Pat then entered a room where a couple dozen (mostly) elderly members of the Glendale Federated Republican Women dined.

"Good afternoon, ladies," he greeted them cheerfully as he bounded inside. "When you go home today, tell your husbands you all had lunch with the governor of California!"

"Oh my!" one of them exclaimed. "You're Pat Brown!" He shook hands and kissed each surprised and delighted lady. He signed autographs, posed for pictures, and charmed every woman in that room. "Governor," one Federated lady told him solemnly, "we are all Republican women. To be honest, we didn't care too much for Jerry–but we love you!"

Pat winked at me: "Now we can go," he whispered. He blew the ladies a kiss, gave them a little bow as they applauded, and walked jauntily (and without any assistance) away. Once we cleared their sight line, he grabbed my arm, leaned heavily on it, and re-aged the fifty years he'd shed for a few minutes when he strode into that room.

. . .

Former governor Edmund G. "Pat" Brown died of a heart attack at age ninety on February 16, 1996.

31

Sissy Picture

R and Brooks was a fixture in our local Glendale business community. For almost thirty years he owned and ran Professional Ambulance Service; many of his business friends and acquaintances never knew that this was a later-in-life career. In the 1930s, Rand started off in show business: first he worked as a trick-riding cowboy in a Wild West show where his partner threw knives at him. Later he tried his hand at acting in movies and early television, and enjoyed some success in each medium. But Rand had one role that guaranteed his place in motion picture history: he played Charles Hamilton, Scarlett O'Hara's first husband in the immortal 1939 film classic, *Gone with the Wind*.

A loyal Republican, Rand often came to political events where I spoke. We became good friends over the years, and when I ran for office, nobody was a more reliable supporter. I urged him repeatedly to write a memoir of his Hollywood experiences. "Nobody would want it," he'd say in reply. When I suggested he tape his stories, again he demurred: "I'll do it only if you are the one asking me all the questions."

I never taped an interview with Rand, but on occasion I did get him to tell stories about the old days. Once, when I expressed concern over lunch that my questions took him away from business, Rand laughed: "I'm seventy-five years old," he said, "so I'm in no hurry for anything. Besides, I don't do any work around here anymore; I just come in when I feel like it. Now, in the early days of the business, things were different: I was the dispatcher *and* the ambulance driver!"

As long as Rand wanted to talk, I wan[...]

Rand once showed me the stacks of fan[...] after making *Gone with the Wind* (or, as the [...] received twenty-five or more letters a day ask[...] Although he accommodated every request, he [...] back signed photos depicting him in western g[...] tably, that wasn't the one fans wanted, so his a[...] almost exclusively on *GWTW*. When I asked why h[...]

photos over his famous role, he said, "Because in that movie I looked like a sissy. They made me up to look like an orange-haired sissy in that damned picture, but that's the photo everyone wants. Still, I like people to know I made other movies besides that one!"

I told Rand I suspected he only pretended to dislike being remembered for *GWTW*, since his place in movie legend was forever cemented because of that one role. "I guess you're right," he sighed. "But I still hate to see how they made me up like a sissy for that part!"

The "Sissy Picture": Scarlett O'Hara (actress Vivien[...] Charles Hamilton (Rand Brooks) in *Gone with the W[...]

He continued:

I'll never forget going to that damned beauty parlor every day to be made up with curly orange hair. They did the same thing to Leslie Howard [who played "Ashley Wilkes" in the film]. We used to sit under the big hair dryers together each morning and shoot the breeze.

When we were filming, news reached our studio that the great international actress Ingrid Bergman was coming to the United States to make a [film]. Both Leslie Howard and I were dying to meet her. We kept pestering [our] producer, David O. Selznick, to bring Bergman to the studio.

One morning Leslie and I were in makeup for a full day of shooting. [We] were sitting with curlers in our hair under those damn hair dryers with [orange] dye all over our heads. Selznick walked in with a big smile on his face. ["Boys]," he said, "I have a surprise for you!" In walked Ingrid Bergman. She [looked] at Leslie and me sitting there under those hair dryers and laughed at us.

"We girls should get together some day and go shopping," Bergman said [with] a smile; then she walked away. I never forgave Selznick for that!

Rand had very fond memories of the film's star, Clark Gable: "He was a [man]'s man in every way," Rand recalled. "Gable could hunt, fish, drink, gamble, [cuss], and laugh with the best of 'em." He shared this little-known story about [G]able from the filming:

Gable absolutely didn't want to make *Gone with the Wind*. He knew there would be great expectations about his performance, and he had just been trashed by the critics for making a dog of a picture called *Parnell*. Gable was no "actor" in the traditional sense: he was just Gable playing himself. He didn't think he could do the job, and didn't want to do it.

After he signed on, he was great, but one scene threw him. It was the scene when his little daughter died, and he was supposed to cry. Gable just couldn't do it. He didn't know how to "act" out a cry, and he felt his fans would think he was a sissy. Directors and coaches spent a long time trying to get Gable to cry, but nothing worked.

Finally, the director, Victor Fleming, called a break in shooting. Fleming was like a father to Gable. He was much older, tougher, and experienced–Gable thought of him as a second father. Fleming put his arm around Gable and said, "Let's go get a drink." As they left, Fleming turned and signaled to the crew to stay put. "Nobody leaves," Fleming whispered to a cameraman. Gable and Fleming went out and for three hours got drunk. When they returned, they were laughing, singing and carrying on. They were almost falling down. Suddenly, Fleming pretended that Gable somehow offended him.

"You're no goddamned actor," Fleming growled at Gable. "You're just a no-good, goddamned pretty boy. You make me sick. Look around, King, at

some real actors.[1] You're nothing! You've held up this production, and we've all wasted our time with a worthless piece of shit named Clark Gable."

Gable was stunned and was really shaken up. Fleming persisted in his insults: "You're bringing down this whole picture, you sorry son of a bitch. Look around: Vivien Leigh, Olivia de Havilland, Thomas Mitchell, Leslie Howard–they're actors. You're a no-good, pretty boy, asshole. You can't act worth a shit, and you make me sick."

With that, Fleming shoved Gable onto the set where the crying scene was supposed to be filmed. He ordered Olivia to join him. "Come on, King, let's see you act. Let's have a good laugh at the pretty-boy King who isn't worth a shit." Fleming ordered the lights on, and then whispered to the cameraman: "Roll it." Suddenly, Fleming was no longer drunk! He was cold sober when he called out, "Action!"

Gable filmed the scene, sobbing all the way through it. He shot it in one take. It was one of the tenderest scenes in the entire film. When Gable finished, the crew gave him a standing ovation. Gable still didn't know what had hit him. Fleming threw his arm around Gable. "You are the King," he said with a smile.

As for the female leads in GWTW, Rand had fond memories of each. Vivian Leigh, he said, was "a great actress": "She was very nice, but she was also very serious. During the day she was being directed on the set by Victor Fleming, and she was intimidated by him. Fleming was a man's director. There was nothing subtle or gentle about him. So at night she would go to the home of her director-friend George Cukor, who would coach her in preparation for the next morning's shooting."

He and costar Olivia de Havilland remained friends over the decades, "although she's mad at me right now:

"Olivia knows my wife and I are good friends with Ann Rutherford [who also was in GWTW, playing the role of Scarlett's younger sister] and go out to lunch often with her," he said. "Well, I think Ann was once involved with a man married to Olivia's sister, actress Joan Fontaine. In fact, I think Olivia was once involved with the man herself. Anyway, I called Olivia in Paris a couple of weeks

---

1   In a 1930s fan magazine contest, Gable was named "King of Hollywood," and the nickname stuck.

ago and asked her for some traveling advice. She grew very haughty with me; Olivia is a sweet woman, but she still is the 'queen bee'–and she snapped at me: 'Why don't you call Ann Rutherford for advice?' I got mad at her and got off the phone. But I guess it's time for me to call her and make up."

Rand once put me in touch with Olivia de Havilland, and she and I corresponded a few times. Rand even brought it up once to my wife, telling her jokingly, "Be on your guard! Olivia's very fond of the judge. She always asks about him and says, 'James Rogan–James Rogan, that's a fine Irish name,' and she always pronounces it with a thick brogue."

On another visit, Rand reminisced about his good friend and fellow actor from their early Hollywood years, President Ronald Reagan: "I used to go on publicity shoots with Ronnie when we were both young," he recounted. "In those days, the studios would set up things for us to attend on weekends, and the photographers from the different magazines would come and take our pictures. I remember one Saturday the studio sent Ronnie and me to the opening of an ice cream shop on Sunset Boulevard. They dressed us up in turn-of-the-century clothes and had us dispensing ice cream to a young starlet for the photographers."

Nothing pleased Rand more than talking about his early days as a cowboy in the Wild West shows. He told me that for ten years he roped, rode, and stood against a wooden backdrop while his partner threw long knives at him. He once showed me a picture of him standing against the wall, with knives circling him and another blade sailing through the air toward him. "My partner was amazing," he remembered. "If he threw one knife at me, he threw twenty thousand–he never drew blood and only once pierced my shirt." When I asked him how he could stand there three shows a day and let someone throw knives at him, Rand laughed: "Because I had to feed the kiddies!" he replied.

Besides Rand's career in early Hollywood, there was another link that endeared me to him: for many years, Rand's wife was Stan Laurel's daughter Lois. As an old Laurel and Hardy fan, I delighted in listening to Rand reminisce about my favorite comedy duo:

> Babe [Oliver Hardy's nickname] gave Stan all the credit for their success. Babe always said, "Stan was a genius, and all I did was do what he told me to do."

Although Stan could be funny in private, he was basically a very serious man. He was sweet, but serious. We had a wonderful relationship.

Stan was married many times. One of his wives, Lois, was a bitch. She was cheap as well as mean. I celebrated the day she died. I was married to their daughter Lois for twenty-eight years. The first twenty years were good ones. My ex-wife, Lois, was a good lady, but her mother did everything possible to destroy our marriage.

The guy that owns the merchandising rights to Laurel and Hardy, Larry Harmon, is a crook. He stole the rights from Stan. I was going to handle all that for Stan, and Stan would have made money. Instead, Harmon did it and cheated him. Stan's attorney, Ben Shipman, was also a crook. He kept Stan broke while he lived high off the hog from Stan's money. Stan kept Shipman around because Shipman was always able to get Stan out of trouble.

Rand offered a brief insight into another Hollywood legend, his onetime costar, Marilyn Monroe: "I got a call from a guy in New York recently who wanted me to talk about Marilyn for a scandal magazine. I told him to go to hell. I made a low-budget movie with Marilyn many years ago [*Ladies of the Chorus*, 1948] when she was

Lobby card from *Ladies of the Chorus* (1948), costarring Marilyn Monroe and Rand Brooks

first getting started. There was no scandal there. Our relationship was friendly and pleasant. There was nothing sensational. Marilyn was just a sweet, naïve, and insecure girl.

. . .

Rand was a great guy and a great friend. Around the time I ran for Congress, Rand sold his ambulance company and retired to his ranch in the Santa Ynez Valley to breed horses. He died of cancer at age eighty-four on September 1, 2003.

32

Woooo–Hoooo

Our family friend Peggy Grande worked as former president Ronald Reagan's assistant chief of staff in his Los Angeles office for many years. Some months after our twin daughters were born in 1992, Peggy offered to set up a meeting with President Reagan so they could have their picture taken with the great man.

After we arrived at the Fox Plaza Building, Peggy introduced us to each member of the staff before leading us to Reagan's private office for our 11:00 a.m. appointment. She stepped inside and announced our arrival; Reagan came from behind his desk to welcome us. He wore small hearing aids in each ear and moved a bit slower than I remembered, but he still stood arrow-straight for an eighty-two-year-old man. Besides, there was nothing elderly in his firm handshake.

His private office had changed little since we last visited. Reagan's desk was framed with cases filled with books, photographs, and political mementos. The desk set I saw in 1989 (a gift from his secretary of defense) was now replaced by a large, swiveling block with "Yes," "No," and "Maybe" carved on it. His bronze saddle collection had been moved to the Reagan Library; now on the corner bookcase rested a pair of binoculars near the window overlooking a westerly view of the Los Angeles skyline. The sofa had a pillow with the Reagan brand stitched on it.

As Reagan greeted Dana and Claire with a "finger" handshake, the girls appeared captivated by the grandfatherly statesman. Peggy, with camera in hand, suggested we pose for a group photograph. Reagan initially began to put Christine in the center, but I asked him to be in the middle so the girls would be next to him in the picture. I held Dana in my arms while Peggy readied her camera; Reagan looked into Dana's transfixed eyes and leaned in closer, telling her she was a beautiful girl. In a flash, Dana reached up with her right hand, grabbed Reagan's nose, and began to twist it! Reagan laughed; I tried to hide my panic as I gently pried her fingers loose from the presidential proboscis.

Just before our picture was taken, Claire began wiggling in her mother's arms and kicked off her right shoe. I bent to retrieve it; despite his advancing years, Reagan beat me to the draw. He bent down quickly, scooped up her shoe, and put it back on Claire's foot.

With Claire again fully dressed, and Reagan's nose free from groping fingers, we smiled for Peggy. She tried to click the shutter, but it didn't work: "Mr. President, I'm so sorry," she said. "There's no film in the camera! This will just take a second." While Peggy fiddled with the camera, Reagan turned to me:

"You know, Jim, from what I hear, you'll end up in politics yourself. And when you're in, you'll need to take a lot of these kinds of group pictures like we're doing here, with the politician standing in the middle of the shot," he counseled. "So I want to teach you a little trick that the actor Fredric March taught me when I was a young actor making pictures in Hollywood: when the photographer poses a group picture like this, and you're the guy standing in the middle of the photo, you get the photographer to count for you, *one . . . two . . . three*, before taking the picture . . ."

As Reagan told this story, he looked very intense–as if he wanted me to know he was imparting some serious wisdom. I listened just as intently: "Okay, Mr. President. Got it: stand in the middle; get the photographer to count one, two, three."

Reagan's eyebrows arched when he finished the advice: "Now, when the photographer is counting for you, when he gets between the numbers two and three, here is what you do": with that, Reagan got up on his tiptoes, wiggled all ten of his fingers down by his sides, and sang in a warbling falsetto voice, "*Woooo-hoooo!*"

With the demonstration completed, Reagan nodded his head vigorously to affirm the wisdom of this practice. I just stared blankly at him, thinking he was pulling my leg. When his earnest expression never wavered, I broke down.

"Mr. President, I'm sure there's a really good reason you want me to count one, two, three, and then wiggle all my fingers, get up on my tiptoes, and say,

'*Woooo-hoooo.*' But I'll be darned if I can figure it out on my own."

Still looking at me intently, he gripped my arm and said, "Because, Jim, when you wiggle your fingers, get up on your toes, and go, '*Woooo-hoooo,*' everyone will look at you like this": Reagan then made a slack-jawed, vacant expression with his face. Now I was even more baffled.

"Mr. President, why do I want people to look at me like this?" I asked, and then I mimicked the dim-witted face back at him.

Reagan beamed. "Because," he said, "when they look at you like this [he again made the dopey face], in the photo it will look like this." Reagan then opened his mouth and eyes wide, as if looking with awe and admiration.

Because I still thought he was putting me on, I said, "Mr. President, for fifty years you've been a movie star, a TV star, a governor, a four-time candidate for president, and a two-term president. You've probably taken a million group photos. Are you telling me that in all those poses, you've had the photographer give you a one-two-three count, and then you got up on your toes, wiggled your fingers, and said, "*Woooo-hoooo*"?

Reagan patted me on the shoulder paternally, leaned in, and whispered with a big grin, "Damn near!"

Woooo-Hooo! Former president Ronald Reagan with the Rogan family, Office of Ronald Reagan, March 29, 1993

When Peggy returned with a roll of film, I winked at Reagan and nodded my head toward Peggy, signaling I wanted to play a joke on her. Reagan nodded his assent silently: "Mr. President," I said, "my wife really wanted this photograph to have a homogenous look to it. So that you can match our daughters' outfits, we brought you a large, floppy, polka-dotted cap to wear, just like the one the twins are wearing!" I pretended to rifle through the diaper bag for the nonexistent hat while Reagan reached out his hands and said, "Oh, that's great–give it to me!" Reagan laughed at Peggy's shocked reaction to the anticipated loss of her boss's dignity!

By now Peggy had loaded the film. She had trouble getting everyone to look at the camera because Reagan kept kidding throughout the session. When he said that he babysat for a reasonable fee, I handed him Dana and said Christine and I were going to the movies, and we'd pick up the kids in a few hours.

"Take as long as you like!" he replied as he held Dana.

With the photo op completed, Reagan asked if we had visited his new presidential library; I said we had gone the first week it opened. He showed us his framed copy of the "five presidents" photograph taken at the dedication, telling us it was the first time in history that five chief executives came together for such an occasion. I asked if Reagan had any plans to invite newly inaugurated President Bill Clinton to a similar event and make it a six-president picture; Reagan (reportedly slighted by Clinton's failure to invite the Reagans to his inauguration) broke into a wry smile and shook his head. "No comment," he said dryly.

Reagan said he reread my 1988 article explaining why I switched from the Democratic to Republican Party. He said as an ex-Democrat himself, he became a Republican for many reasons. "But the thing that really did it for me was a radio address by Al Smith I heard in the 1930s. Smith was the 1928 Democrat nominee for president and former governor of New York, who had been a big Franklin Roosevelt supporter. Smith broke with Roosevelt and declared the Democratic Party had abandoned its leadership role during Roosevelt's term . . . ."

It was during this story that Reagan's humor and vigor disappeared momentarily: he lost his train of thought and stood in uncomfortable silence as he groped for the words to finish. Fortunately, I was up on my FDR trivia, and I helped him complete the story by filling in the details of Smith's break with Roosevelt.

We had scheduled only a brief photo op with the girls, but Reagan (as usual) prolonged our appointment with anecdotes and stories. Not wanting to impose on him further, I thanked him for making time to see our children. Christine assured him that in years to come our girls would treasure their photograph with him. Reagan thanked us for the visit, and we bid him good-bye as he escorted us out the door.

When we exited his private office, we encountered a half dozen secretaries and assistants gathered outside, awaiting our departure. Word had spread throughout the office that adorable twin babies were here, and they had waited to see the girls. The charming staffers surrounded us, each wanting a turn holding one of the girls. Reagan remained standing in his office doorway, watching amusedly the commotion Dana and Claire had caused. After passing the girls around and sharing a few "new father" stories, I chatted with Dottie Dellinger, Reagan's longtime personal secretary.

About twenty minutes later, someone handed Dana back to me as I got ready to leave. Then I noticed that Christine and Claire were nowhere to be seen. When I asked Peggy what happened to them, she said, "They're back inside with the Boss! They've been in there all this time."

I peeked inside Reagan's office and saw Christine deep in conversation with him, while Claire nestled quietly in Mom's arms. Knocking on the door, I stuck my head inside and asked, "Do I need to be jealous?"

Christine told me later that after we left the office, Claire, whom she was holding, was looking backward at Reagan. When the secretaries intercepted us as we exited, Reagan (unbeknownst to me) followed Christine out the door, wiggling his finger at Claire, and making her smile and laugh. While the secretaries took turns holding Dana as I chatted with Dottie, Reagan invited Christine and Claire back inside. During their second visit Reagan showed Christine the artwork on his office walls, including a horse and pasture scene painted by his barber's twelve-year-old daughter.

Reagan invited Dana and me to rejoin him; he then spoke at length about his beautiful ranch near Santa Barbara, saying he'd bought it many years ago and had done much of the brush clearing himself. He said he was still working on some roads, and had concern about a series of recent hill fires. Christine told him that we had recently stayed at the Alisal Ranch near Solvang, which abuts a portion of his property, and that we went on a horseback ride near his common border with the Alisal. Reagan (an avid horseman) replied that he knew almost every tree and rock on those paths, and told us the next time we were riding there to come get him and he'd join us.

Reagan told Christine he had heard from Peggy the story of how we adopted our twin daughters. He said his son Michael also was adopted and that adoption proved a great blessing: "But then," he added as he patted our twins, "you don't need me to tell you that."

Again we attempted to take our leave, thanking Reagan profusely for his generosity in giving us so much time. He told us he enjoyed the visit, and then escorted us through the office suite to the elevator.

After saying a final good-bye, Reagan headed back to his office. Peggy then invited us inside the conference room for a family photograph before we left. While snapping the pictures, she told us of a congressional candidate who came to the office for a photo with Reagan recently. While they posed in this conference room, the candidate's little boy dropped his pants and went potty on the carpet! Not only was Peggy the office photographer, but clean-up duty also fell to her.

As we boarded the elevator to leave, a young Boy Scout with a sash full of merit badges arrived and was about to be brought to Reagan's office. The young scout looked up at me and said excitedly, "I'm going to shake hands with President Reagan and get his autograph!"

Remembering my own youthful enthusiasm, I understood how he felt– perhaps better than most.

33

Nixon at Twilight

I may have only met Richard Nixon once (once and a half, if you count when that Disneyland employee yanked me away from him), but I did get to hear him speak several times in his twilight years. The next was in early 1993, when I received an invitation to attend a policy conference on US–Asian relations in the post–Cold War era, with a luncheon address by former President Nixon.

More than one thousand people crammed into the Biltmore Bowl in Los Angeles. I must have had a good seat: at the tables next to me were former secretaries of state Henry Kissinger and Lawrence Eagleburger, former treasury secretary William E. Simon, former Japanese prime minister Toshiki Kaifu, former national security advisors Robert McFarlane and Brent Scowcroft, and California governor Pete Wilson.

In introducing the former president, Wilson said he began his political career as a young assistant during Nixon's unsuccessful 1962 race for California governor; in 1966, Nixon offered him a permanent staff position as he geared up to run for the presidency. Wilson demurred, telling Nixon he wanted to run for the California legislature that year. "Pete," Nixon told him, "if that is how you feel you can best serve your country, then run." Wilson ran and won, which started a political career that spanned three decades.

When Nixon took the stage, he appeared to have aged since I saw him last: his hair looked grayer, and his voice sounded more gravelly. Still, his mind was sharp, and he joked about giving Wilson his start in politics: "Pete, I'm sorry I got you into so much trouble so long ago!"

Nixon delivered a lengthy, cogent discourse on Asian policy without a note before him. He said that if peace and stability are to continue there, the United States must remain involved in that region along with the other major players. "We are the only power that is not considered to be a potential threat to any other nation," Nixon claimed. "The unanswered question is whether the United States has the will to rise to the challenge. America responded magnificently to the threat of the Cold War when it began. The question is, with the Cold War over, can we respond to the promise of peace?"

Nixon recalled his first visit to Japan shortly after World War II, when the prime minister told him America had done his country a favor by destroying Japanese factories. "We are now building better ones to compete better," the minister told Nixon long ago. "And," Nixon added, "he was right. Japan's gross national product is one-half the size of America's, and they are gaining." Regarding China, Nixon quoted Napoleon: "China is a sleeping giant. Let him sleep. For when he wakes, his size will be felt throughout the world."

"China," Nixon added, "no longer sleeps. The Great Wall [of China] is very thick. It is difficult to be heard from the inside, but it is impossible to be heard from the outside."

Turning to Russia, Nixon urged the United States to continue sending economic support there to help maintain democracy and establish free markets. Without the United States making this investment, "the peace dividend will go down the tube." That, in turn, would force America to rearm at previous levels. Nixon praised President Clinton for supporting aid to Russia, and insisted that a market economy there would eventually strengthen the American economy and create thousands of domestic jobs. Noting that Kissinger, his former secretary of state, dissented on this point, Nixon laughed and said, "I hate to disagree with Henry on anything!"

Former president Richard Nixon, the Biltmore Hotel, Los Angeles, April 21, 1993

"It is almost cliché to say the Cold War is over and the West has won it. That is only half-true," Nixon argued. "It is true the communists have lost the Cold War, but the West has not yet won."

President Nixon was eighty when he delivered this speech at the Biltmore on April 21, 1993. He had one year and one day remaining to him.

. . .

On January 20, 1969, the day Richard Nixon took the oath as the thirty-seventh president of the United States, I was an eleven-year-old boy who cut school to watch the ceremony from start to finish on our rabbit-eared black-and-white television. Using my Christmas gift (an old reel-to-reel tape recorder), I draped the microphone over the channel knob and made an antiquated recording of the event. For months thereafter, I replayed my tape of Nixon's inauguration until I could recite it almost by heart. I never imagined that, a quarter century later, I would attend the silver anniversary of that historic event with him.

Nixon commemorated the twenty-fifth anniversary of his inaugural by hosting a reunion for his cabinet and senior administration officials at his presidential library in Southern California. The ceremony was by invitation only; through my friend Bob Finch (a former Nixon cabinet member), I obtained two tickets; I brought Walt Lewis, my former boss in the Los Angeles County district attorney's office (and a lifelong registered Democrat) as a guest. A perennial Nixon hater, I thought Walt might find the event intriguing.

The morning was beautiful, with a warm sun and light breeze blowing. Folding lawn chairs faced the reflecting pool, with American flags circling the makeshift outdoor theater. Scores of police, Secret Service agents, reporters, and guests filled the area. While other guests and I enjoyed refreshments at the garden reception, an agent tapped me on the shoulder and asked if our group might step to the side briefly so he could clear a path: I looked over and saw former president Gerald Ford (Nixon's second vice president) and his wife, Betty, stepping from a limousine and walking toward us. A few minutes later, guests were asked to take seats for the ceremony. Walt and I found chairs in the front row of the nonreserved area (the most forward seats were saved for Nixon's cabinet members).

A bell choir played "America the Beautiful" before library director John Taylor introduced the dignitaries. The roster was a "Who's Who" of Washington power brokers during the four previous Republican administrations: secretaries of state Henry Kissinger, William P. Rogers, and George Shultz; secretaries of defense Caspar Weinberger, James Schlesinger, and Donald Rumsfeld; secretary of the treasury William Simon; secretaries of housing and urban development George Romney (father of 2012 GOP presidential nominee Mitt Romney) and Samuel Pierce; budget director Roy Ash; postmaster general Winton Blount; secretaries of education Terrel H. Bell and Lamar Alexander; secretary of transportation Claude Brinegar; secretaries of labor Peter Brennan and James Hodgson; secretaries of commerce Ann McLaughlin, Maurice Stans, Barbara Franklin, and Peter Peterson; secretary of health, education, and welfare Bob Finch; secretary of the interior Walter Hickel; and ambassadors Leonard Firestone and Walter Annenberg. The biggest round of applause went to Kissinger, the final cabinet member to arrive.

While awaiting their introductions, Nixon, Ford, and Mrs. Ford stood together along the corridor from the library leading to the outdoor stage, with Nixon wiping perspiration from his brow and upper lip. When Taylor announced them, the crowd gave the trio a rousing ovation as they arrived smiling and waving, and then took their seats in the front row.

William Simon opened the program by recalling the mood in America twenty-five years earlier on that blustery Inauguration Day:

Former presidents Richard Nixon and Gerald Ford, the Nixon Library, January 20, 1994

"America was rocked by Vietnam and civil unrest. Richard Nixon challenged us to overcome these difficulties. He led America out of Vietnam, led our prisoners of war home with honor, and led the way to better relations with the Soviet Union and China. Despite the pounding he received, Richard Nixon would not let the tragedies of life or of his presidency destroy him. He was truly the last casualty of the Vietnam War."

George Shultz spoke directly to Nixon, asking, "Do you remember, when I was your secretary of labor, when we did the 'Philadelphia Plan' and the full-employment budget?" As Nixon nodded, Schultz added, "I tried to think of something nice to say about your wage and price controls! At least we showed that if a great cast of characters–John Connally, Don Rumsfeld, and I–couldn't make them work, nobody could!" When the laughter and applause subsided, Shultz threw in, "And Bill Clinton still hasn't gotten the message!"

Former secretary of state Henry Kissinger, the Nixon Library, January 20, 1994

In his remarks, Henry Kissinger referenced the faint chants heard from a small group of protesters across the street: "[In 1969] protesters believed that ending the Vietnam War was as easy as changing television channels. We knew the logistics would be a difficult, heartbreaking task. But Richard Nixon's position was one of highest morality: that those who relied on the word of his predecessors and threw in their lot with democracy would not be abandoned. The honor of the United States was an element of the peace process. By becoming the architect of peace, Richard Nixon served the children of those who protested against him."

Kissinger also directed a personal observation to Nixon: "As a refugee from totalitarianism, and speaking with a foreign accent, and having always supported your political opponents, it is a tribute to your generosity that you gave me the opportunity to serve our nation. Our country will always remember you for your policies and legacies."

William Rogers walked to the stage slowly and fumbled for his reading glasses before sharing these early impressions of his future chief:

I first met Richard Nixon during the Hiss-Chambers case.[1] He was the only member of the Congress who wanted to continue investigating Alger Hiss. Nixon's philosophy was simple: if Chambers lied when he said he knew Alger Hiss during his communist activities, then we should say so and exonerate Hiss. If Hiss was lying, then America needed to know. This determination led to the successful case against Hiss, because Richard Nixon refused to quit.

Next was the "Fund Crisis."[2] Many people on Eisenhower's campaign train wanted Richard Nixon off the ticket. But Richard Nixon refused to resign until he had the chance to address the nation. This was before the era of political damage control teams. Richard Nixon spoke without notes or a prepared text. Yet after his speech, the crowds grew bigger for him than appeared for [Democratic presidential nominee] Adlai Stevenson.

Finally, Rogers recalled the defeats and the victories:

When Richard Nixon lost the presidency to John F. Kennedy in 1960, it was the closest election in history. Many Nixon supporters demanded a recount, but Richard Nixon refused. He was too concerned about the stability of the American government. He lost again in 1962 when he ran for governor of California. But this quality of resilience led to his election to the presidency in 1968, and his huge reelection victory in 1972. It was a tribute to his leadership, and his activities over the last twenty years since he left the White House are a testimony to his determination.

It fell upon former president Gerald Ford to introduce Nixon. Speaking from three-by-five note cards, Ford remembered:

---

1   During the Truman administration, news editor Whittaker Chambers admitted having been active during his youth in the Communist Party and claimed to have known Alger Hiss—a high-ranking government official—as a member of the same communist "cell." Hiss denied the allegation and said he never met Chambers. Then congressman Nixon pressed a congressional investigation; Hiss eventually went to prison for perjury. After the publication of the Venona Papers in 1995, as noted by Ted Morgan of the Claremont Institute, Hiss's guilt became indisputable.

2   Shortly after Dwight D. Eisenhower selected Nixon as his 1952 running mate, Democrats accused Nixon of accepting a "slush fund" from wealthy businessmen to cover personal expenses. With pressure mounting for Eisenhower to dump him, Nixon appeared on live television and delivered a denial in what came to be known as his "Checkers" speech. Eisenhower kept Nixon on the ticket, and they sailed to victory in November.

When I first went to Congress in 1949, Richard Nixon had already emerged as a leader from the Alger Hiss case. He exposed the dangers of communism around the globe, and it now becomes my job to sum up Richard Nixon in five minutes!

When thinking about President Nixon and how he helped to meet and win some of our greatest public challenges of all time, and how he met and prevailed in a myriad of personal challenges as well, it comes down to two words in my opinion: resolve and resilience. The resolve to stay the course against all odds, and the resilience to outlast, and sometimes even outlive, his critics in one personal crisis after another.

The audience stood and cheered as Ford presented Nixon. Ford stepped down from the stage and waited to greet his predecessor; they embraced and waved while library assistants mounted the stage and removed the podium, replacing it with a lone microphone on a stand, signaling Nixon's plan to speak extemporaneously.

When the crowd fell silent, Nixon clasped his hands behind his back and thanked Ford for the generous introduction, and then paid tribute to his White House successor:

"I have known Jerry Ford for many years. Jerry was a football star center at the University of Michigan, and I couldn't earn a letter at Whittier College! I once asked Jerry if he made the All-American football team. He told me, 'No, I wasn't that good.' Although Jerry Ford did not

The final public speech of a long career: former president Richard Nixon, the Nixon Library, January 20, 1994

make the all-American team in football, after thirty-three years of service to his country, he sure made the team for America."

Mentioning the small group of chanting protesters across the street, Nixon chuckled and said to the audience, "I hope you haven't been distressed by some of that background noise we've had here. I remind our young people out there that I've been heckled by experts!"

Commanding the attention of the rapt crowd with a voice raspy with age, Nixon remembered his Inauguration Day of twenty-five years ago, and compared that day to the state of the world today:

During my 1969 inaugural parade, I was disappointed the Secret Service insisted we ride in a closed car from the Capitol to the White House. They told me there were too many protesters along the parade route, waiting with eggs and other overripe substances. Things are so different in the world today than they were in 1969. One hundred million people have been liberated in Eastern Europe, while communism is collapsing in China. And in America, there is a different spirit. When I last met [Chinese communist dictator] Mao Zedong shortly before his death in 1976, he asked me, "Is peace all you want?" I told him we want peace, but we want peace with justice. That simple answer would not be sufficient today.

Today America has the heritage of freedom being spread around the globe. This idea of freedom must be our focus for peace . . . Can the West provide to these searching peoples the freedoms they seek? That is the challenge of today: the challenge to peace.

As to the future, Nixon offered this prediction:

As we look into the next century, I see a very exciting prognosis. We will see a century where enormous progress will be made in health. Political freedom will be the rule rather than the exception, because the communications revolution has had the effect of making dictatorships unviable. They cannot stand having their closed societies opened up.

As we approach the day of a new millennium, I would say you could not possibly think of a day in which one would be more fortunate than to live in the United States of America on this day and in this time. The reason for that is what we can achieve in the future. In the next century, the role for the United States will be to provide leadership. If we refuse, who will do it? The United Nations? De Gaulle once said that parliaments can paralyze policy; they cannot implement it.

Looking across the courtyard to the modest house where he was born eighty-one years earlier and where his beloved wife, Pat, was laid to rest in the garden recently, Nixon ended his remarks with a simple analysis of the incredible ups and downs of almost fifty years in public life:

> Is politics worth it? I remember in 1973 when we entertained a choir from a South Central Los Angeles church at the White House. At the end of the performance, a young black man said to me, "It's a long way from Watts to the White House." Today, standing in the shadow of the simple home my father built only a few feet from here, I can tell you it was a long way from Yorba Linda to the White House, too. Politics is never going to be heaven, and sometimes it is hell. But it was worth the trip!

. . .

The celebration of Nixon's inaugural anniversary was a magnificent success. As *Los Angeles Times* reporter Gebe Martinez wrote the next day, "[I]n the eyes of his assembled friends and colleagues, Nixon . . . has transcended his time as a mere politician to become a world statesman, with the shame of Watergate receding into the past. . . . Now, almost 20 years after leaving the White House, the image of Nixon the ruthless politician may be fading into what one historian describes as 'not just our elder statesman, he's our beloved elder statesman.'"[3]

Nixon biographer Stephen E. Ambrose summed up the feelings of America about the man so despised when forced from office amid scandal: "He's back, and he's respected, and he is welcome in the White House, and people turn to him for advice. It's almost a miracle."

After hearing Nixon's speech at the library that day, on the drive back I asked my old boss Walt Lewis about his impressions. He told me:

> You know, I supported John F. Kennedy over Nixon in 1960, and grew up despising Nixon. I always supported anyone that ran against Nixon. In fact, one of the happiest days of my life was the day Nixon resigned the presidency. That's why I still can't believe I'm saying this, but when I sat listening to

---

3   Gebe Martinez, "Analysis: The Quintessential Fighter Battles Back to Statesman Status: Image: Twenty years after leaving White House in disgrace, Watergate stain fades. Nixon enjoys new respect at home, abroad," *Los Angeles Times*, January 21, 1994, http://articles.latimes.com/1994-01-21/news/mn-13913_1_nixon-white-house.

Nixon, I hung on his every word. He has a charisma that I've never seen before. Maybe it just doesn't come across on TV. I don't know how else to express it–I was drawn to him.

Not long after, Walt became a Republican.

. . .

At the end of Nixon's remarks that day, his administration alumni joined him onstage for a group photograph. When the program adjourned, Nixon stood at the side of the stage, greeting guests and signing autographs. I was in his receiving line and (yet again) just about to meet him when Bob Finch called me aside to introduce me to some of his former White House colleagues. As I stood talking with Bob, I saw Nixon's security detail lead him away. Although my habit of just missing the chance to meet Nixon was getting monotonous, today I didn't mind because Bob gave me some great news: Bob said he had talked to Nixon about me earlier, and also about my oft-frustrated desire to meet him, discuss his career in politics, and seek his advice. Bob said Nixon planned to return to the library for an intimate dinner with friends on June 16, and Nixon had personally invited me to join him. "Nixon told me to tell you that at our dinner you can ask him questions until you get bored!" Bob said.

Finally, my chance would come.

Former presidents Richard Nixon and Gerald Ford, former First Lady Betty Ford, and alumni of the Nixon Administration, the Nixon Library, January 20, 1994

. . .

I paid another visit to the Nixon Library before my scheduled June 16 private dinner with the former president: on April 22 I attended a luncheon there for former First Lady Barbara Bush. A few days earlier, Nixon had been hospitalized; although library officials that day spoke optimistically about his resilience, there was somberness in the air.

While leaving the Library that afternoon, I saw the United States and presidential flags flapping in the breeze from their masts in front of the museum.

A few hours later, a military officer lowered both to half-mast. The speech he delivered at the inaugural anniversary became Nixon's final public address.

. . .

When Richard Nixon left the stage on that twenty-fifth anniversary of his inaugural that I attended, he walked to the small nearby courtyard to visit his wife's grave before leaving. Three months later, he was laid to rest beside her.

34

I Don't Do Trash

I n early March 1994, I left the state court bench and announced my candidacy for a special election to fill a sudden vacancy in the state legislature. After winning an unexpected victory, I resigned from the bench and took office as a member of the California State Assembly on May 9. The next day, I flew back to Los Angeles to attend a fund-raiser for state attorney general Dan Lungren and his guest speaker, former secretary of defense Dick Cheney.

A popular national figure in 1994 because of his leading role in helping direct US forces during the Bush administration's Persian Gulf War, Cheney now traveled America as an undeclared candidate for the 1996 Republican presidential nomination. At a private reception, Lungren introduced me to the balding, bespectacled Cheney, who congratulated me on my victory and asked to get together with me in Sacramento soon to discuss his White House plans.

Once inside the ballroom, I found myself table-hopping: having entered politics only weeks

Former defense secretary (and future vice president) Dick Cheney with me, Century Plaza Hotel, Los Angeles, May 10, 1994

earlier, I now had donors and supporters everywhere. It seemed surreal to go from political spectator to politician so quickly.

During his introduction of Cheney, Lungren said he argued his first case before the United States Supreme Court recently: later that evening, at a cocktail party in Washington, he saw associate justice Ruth Bader Ginsberg, who said she remembered Lungren from his oral argument. "It isn't often," she told him, "that we get many tall, good-looking men arguing before our Court."

"Can you imagine," Lungren asked rhetorically, "if I had said something like that to her?"

Calling Cheney a "quiet and tough leader," Lungren introduced him to a standing ovation. Cheney's physical appearance belied his oratorical abilities: the dour-looking man had polished speaking abilities and a great sense of humor. He began his remarks with this story:

> When I was first elected to Congress in 1978, my best campaign worker was Mrs. Johnson, my high school English teacher. She would return all my campaign flyers and mailers with all the grammatical errors corrected. Mrs. Johnson liked to call me from time to time, and when I was secretary of defense she somehow managed to get the personal telephone number that rang directly on my desk in the Pentagon. In August 1991, we were in the midst of an international crisis with an attempted coup against Soviet leader Mikhail Gorbachev. I was in a high-level strategy meeting with the chairman of the Joint Chiefs of Staff, the secretary of state, and many other officials. Suddenly, my private telephone rang in the Pentagon. It was Mrs. Johnson calling from Jackson Hole, Wyoming.
>
> "Hi, Dick," she said. "How are you?"
>
> I told her I was very busy, that we were in a big meeting, and that there was a coup going on in the Soviet Union. I asked if I could call her back. "No," she said. "I've got a big problem now." I asked her what was wrong.
>
> "Dick, they're not picking up my trash."
>
> I told her, "Mrs. Johnson, right now I have generals and admirals in my office, the Soviet Union is collapsing, and we are facing a military coup against Gorbachev. I'm secretary of defense now, not a congressman. I do war and peace–I don't do trash."
>
> Mrs. Johnson said, "Dick, you were in Congress for ten years. Don't tell me you don't do trash."

I asked why she didn't call old Joe Sullivan, the city maintenance worker who lived down the street from her. "I didn't want to go that high up," she replied.

. . .

Five months later, Cheney's office called and invited me to join him at a GOP luncheon at the Quiet Cannon Restaurant in Montebello. I met privately with Cheney before the event; he asked how my reelection campaign was going (by then I was running for a full Assembly term). He again suggested coming to Sacramento to meet with my colleagues and me after November to discuss his 1996 plans. I said I'd be happy to introduce him around; he thanked me and said he'd be in touch after Thanksgiving.

During the luncheon, I sat with Andrew Goldman, a member of Cheney's staff. Goldman said Cheney had been campaigning for Republican candidates for the past eighteen months, and would announce his own presidential candidacy before Christmas. "We'll have about a month to rest after the November elections," Goldman sighed, "and then we are in for two years of hell!"

Following his introduction, Cheney began his speech by claiming that his marriage was a result of a Republican election:

"My wife and I met after the 1952 presidential campaign when I moved to Wyoming. As a result of Eisenhower's victory that year, my father moved our family out there to accept a position in the Eisenhower administration. I once told my wife that if Eisenhower had lost the election in 1952, we never would have met in Wyoming and she would have married another man. She replied, 'Yeah, and he would have become secretary of defense instead of you!'"

Cheney focused his remarks on what he saw as the likely prospect of upset Republican victories in the 1994 midterm elections. Since I always heard GOP leaders make similar predictions every cycle (only to see the claim fall flat each November), I gave this commentary little weight. After all, Democrats held uncontested control of the US House of Representatives for forty uninterrupted years. Still, Cheney saw a different horizon:

"Nineteen ninety-four can be one of the defining elections," he said, "just like 1980. In that year President Jimmy Carter endured military failure: our defense rescue helicopters crashed in the Iranian desert and he couldn't get our hostages out. Later that year America elected Ronald Reagan. After twelve years of Republican rule, nobody questioned the credibility of US military force. Our friends knew they could count on us, and our enemies knew not to cross us."

Cheney said that he has been campaigning for Republican candidates for the last a year and a half and had driven alone in his car across the country over eight thousand miles. "I wanted to reconnect with the American people," he said:

> When I was secretary of defense, I spent a lot of time on international problems and Soviet issues. Now I wanted to do like I did when I was in Congress. I hit all the truck stops and McDonalds' along the way. It reminded me that America is really all of us. There are 250 million people who get up each morning and contribute to our nation. I believe the Republican Party of 1994 is about America. People have had a belly full of government in their face. We are spending too much money and allowing government to interfere too much. The good news is that in November of 1994, we will see a new phenomenon—a national Republican victory in state and federal races.

Cheney predicted that after the 1994 elections, Republicans would hold more than two hundred House seats: "We will have the greatest number of Republicans in the House of Representatives than we have had in over forty years," he promised. "And Bill Clinton's worst nightmare will come true: waking up the Wednesday morning after the election and finding Newt Gingrich as the new Speaker of the House!"

...

In October 1994, Dick Cheney saw a tsunami coming that few others recognized or believed. He was right: that November, Republicans swamped Democrats in the midterm elections and seized control of Congress for the first time in four decades.

The one thing Cheney didn't see that day was his own change of heart: after spending two years prepping for a White House run, he backed out of the 1996 presidential contest. However, he didn't remain sidelined on the bench long: four years later, George W. Bush picked Cheney as his running mate; he went on to serve two terms as vice president of the United States before returning to private life in 2009.

35

Before the Storm

I encountered President Bill Clinton a couple of times during my state legislative tenure and before I served in Congress (where he and I crossed swords during our impeachment duel).

The first time was in December 1994, when I was in Washington to attend the American Legislative Exchange Council conference. While there I visited my friend John Emerson at his White House office, where he worked as a special assistant to the president. I first met John when I was a deputy D.A. for Los Angeles County and he worked as the chief deputy for the Los Angeles city attorney. John invited me to attend President Clinton's signing ceremony for the General Agreement on Tariffs and Trade (GATT) treaty, designed to cut global tariffs and abolish trade barriers between the signatory nations.

On the morning of the ceremony, I arrived at the Organization of American States building on Constitution Avenue and was escorted by the Secret Service into the ornate second-floor chamber. On a center-stage table rested the treaty, bordered by a neat row of a dozen bill-signing pens for Clinton's use. A podium framed by the United States and presidential flags was to the right; a staffer removed the presidential seal from a worn leather pouch and hung the emblem on the lectern.

The Marine Band played as the guests filled the hall. Dignitaries on the stage included Senate minority leader Bob Dole (two years away from becoming Clinton's 1996 GOP opponent), outgoing Speaker of the House Thomas Foley, commerce secretary Ron Brown, and treasury secretary Lloyd Bentsen (the 1988 Democratic vice presidential nominee). The audience gave an impromptu ovation to the popular Bentsen, who had announced his retirement two days earlier.

With everyone seated, the band played "Ruffles and Flourishes" and "Hail to the Chief" as Clinton and Vice President Al Gore entered the room together. Clinton smiled and nodded as the audience rose and applauded.

Gore opened the meeting with welcoming remarks, thanking those responsible for helping to pass the treaty. "But the person who helped the most," he added, "was the president of the United States." With that simple introduction, Clinton joined Gore at the podium and credited his vice president for the treaty: "If [Gore] hadn't gone on television in that national debate on NAFTA and refuted the theory of the 'giant sucking sound,' I'm not sure we would be here today."[1]

At the conclusion of his remarks, Clinton sat at the table as the dignitaries gathered behind him; he executed the treaty using each pen to write a portion of his signature and passed them out as souvenirs to those who helped secure passage. Then Clinton greeted our group briefly before heading to his waiting motorcade. It was the first time I'd seen him since our Memphis encounter almost twenty years earlier.

President Bill Clinton, GATT Treaty signing, Washington, DC, December 8, 1994. In the background are (from left) commerce secretary Ron Brown, House Speaker Tom Foley, and senator Bob Dole

Dole welcomed me to Washington and indicated he'd like to talk with some of my Assembly GOP colleagues and me about his planned presidential race; we agreed to meet in Sacramento later. While we talked, a White House aide rushed over to Dole

---

1   GATT's companion treaty was the North American Free Trade Agreement (NAFTA) that passed Congress the previous year. Prior to its passage, Gore debated former presidential candidate Ross Perot, who claimed if NAFTA passed, Americans would hear a "giant sucking sound" as we lost domestic jobs to Mexico.

and handed him one of the treaty-signing pens. "Oh, I almost forgot this," Dole said as he slid the memento into his coat pocket.

. . .

A few months later, I returned to Washington for the annual bipartisan legislative trip hosted by the speaker of the California State Assembly. For three

Senator Bob Dole, GATT Treaty signing, Washington, DC, December 8, 1994

days, administration and congressional leaders briefed us on issues of state and national interest; on our final day, we boarded a chartered bus for a meeting with President Clinton at the White House.

An aide greeted us at the North Gate and escorted us up the circular driveway to the West Wing, where a Marine sentry stood guard. Our delegation settled into the Roosevelt Room (right next to the Oval Office), so-called because on the mantel rested Theodore Roosevelt's Nobel Peace Prize, along with a sculpted bust of Eleanor Roosevelt and portraits of the presidents Roosevelt (Theodore and Franklin).

Shortly before 9:00 a.m. California Assembly speaker Willie Brown advised us that Clinton and White House chief of staff Leon Panetta were en route: "When the president gets here, I will introduce him," Brown intoned solemnly. "The president will then speak. There will be no time for questions." While Brown briefed us, the door opened and Clinton and Panetta entered. The delegation rose and applauded; Brown (in an uncharacteristic loss for words) could only come up with, "Ladies and gentlemen, the president of the United States of America, William Jefferson Clinton."

"You did that well," Clinton cracked to Brown as he stepped to the podium. Looking tanned and dapper in a dark blue suit and black onyx cuff links bearing a gold presidential seal, Clinton looked around the room at the collection of Republican and Democratic legislators (currently engaged in a protracted speakership battle after the elections left our chamber in a 40–40 tie) and joked, "Well, y'all look like you're gettin' along okay!" The legislators laughed as he added, "Maybe the press reports coming out of California are as wrong as the press reports coming out of Washington."

Clinton spoke for almost twenty minutes about federal issues related to California, but also confronted his party's recent loss of the US House of Representatives for the first time in forty years. As to new GOP Speaker Newt Gingrich's "Contract with America," upon which Republican House candidates ran and won, Clinton claimed the GOP saw it as a cure for America's problems. "I agree with some of the things in the Contract," Clinton added, "for example, prison policies and tort reform."

"I want a smaller government, but I want a more effective government," he asserted. "I want a government that is lean but not mean. We need to empower the people to make do in their own lives. We need to worry about the security of our own people on their own streets. The great debate in America now is this: first, what should government be doing, and who is going to pay for it. In the federal government, we want you to tell us what we can do to help you, so that you can do what needs to be done."

Clinton then introduced Panetta (a former California congressman), who discussed administration policies for disaster relief in California. While Panetta spoke, Clinton stood off to the side with Speaker Brown. Because of my proximity, I could hear Clinton ask Brown in a whisper which GOP member was his "nemesis" in the ongoing Speakership battle. Brown whispered in Clinton's ear, and then Clinton's eyes scanned the crowd until they locked on Assembly GOP leader Jim Brulte, seated in the rear of the room.

After taking questions, an aide signaled that Clinton needed to leave. Brown stepped to the microphone: "Just so everyone knows," he said while pointing to Clinton, "it was his idea to take questions, not mine! So staff, please don't be mad at me!"

Clinton thanked us for attending the meeting and waved good-bye. As the legislators stood and applauded, Clinton approached those of us seated in the front row and shook hands. I handed him a document signed for me by his five predecessors I'd met over the years and asked him to autograph it. "How long did it take you to get all of these on here?" Clinton asked as he inked his signature to the collection.

"Too long!" I told him, and thanked him for the favor.

. . .

When I ran for Congress in 1996, Bill Clinton came to my district that June to campaign—not for my opponent or against me, but on his own behalf. I hadn't planned to attend his speech at Glendale Community College, but the

President Bill Clinton with (from left) me, Assemblywoman (later Congresswoman) Barbara Lee, unidentified White House staffer, Assemblyman (later Los Angeles Mayor) Antonio Villaraigosa, Assemblywoman Sheila Kuehl, the White House, March 15, 1995 (official White House photograph)

Republican National Committee called the night before and asked me to go and rebut everything he said that the GOP didn't like. Of course, a lowly state legislator trying to compete with the president of the United States for press attention was something of a silly notion, but I was game for the challenge.

On the morning of his speech, ushers showed me to a reserved seat with other elected officials; as usual, Clinton ran behind schedule, so we all sweltered under a hot sun, awaiting his arrival (reporters used to say he was "running on Clinton Time"). Eventually, a formation of three Marine helicopters circled overhead; the last had emblazoned on its side the presidential seal. A few minutes later recorded music blared "Hail to the Chief," and Clinton emerged onstage amid the cheers of a very enthusiastic crowd.

After delivering a stump speech extolling what his advisor Dick Morris called "small bore" campaign issues (tax breaks for college students, more educational programming on television, mandatory school uniforms in public schools, and teenager curfews), Clinton jumped off stage, shed his coat, and dove into the crowd. While he shook hands along the rope line, I searched for reporters who might be interested in my rebuttal to the president's nanny-state remedies. When it became clear there weren't any wanting to hear my alternate vision for America, I abandoned my RNC assignment and invited my staff to join me for lunch at the Rocky Cola Café in nearby Montrose.

36

Bobby's Friend

As some of my earlier stories noted, I had mixed experiences meeting President Jimmy Carter. Truthfully, whenever I encountered him over a twenty-year period, I usually found him moody (interspersed with moments of transitory friendliness). When I was a member of the California legislature and he visited my district, I hoped the experience might be more pleasant than others; I'll let you be the judge.

By 1995, Carter (out of office almost fifteen years) had become a prolific author, with eight books to his credit since leaving the White House. Carter's newest effort, *Always a Reckoning*, was something different: a collection of his poetry. While on his book promotional tour, Carter scheduled a book signing in Glendale–the heart of my Assembly district. My staff called his office in Atlanta and asked to set up a brief photo op for my infant daughters, and also to allow me to present him with the customary resolution from the legislature. When his staffer heard I was a Republican, he denied the request summarily. When my assistant gave me the news, I told her I would take this to a higher authority–and I did: I placed a call to my pal Bobby Salter, who ran the only gas station in Plains, Georgia (Carter's hometown).

As told in an earlier chapter, Bobby grew up in Plains with the Carter family. Some years earlier, Bobby purchased the town gas station from Billy Carter, the president's brother. I knew that each week Bobby hosted a fish fry for Carter's Secret Service detail at the filling station, and always fed them well. When I called Bobby and explained my problem, he responded, "Jim, don't you worry none. I'll take care of my ol' Yankee cousin! Consider it done. You just show up to that event and tell the head of Carter's Secret Service detail that you're a friend of ol' Bobby's!"

With nothing more than Bobby's assurance in hand, I flew home from Sacramento on the appointed day and drove my family downtown to the bookstore. We arrived half an hour before the scheduled 7:00 p.m. event; Carter was inside, signing books already, while a huge crowd of people wrapped around the block waited their turns. I asked a security guard to give my card to the head of the Secret Service detail. Within minutes the agent in charge approached with an outstretched hand: "You must be Bobby Salter's friend!" he said with a big smile. Before I knew it, a swarm of agents had lined up to say hi: "Always glad to meet a friend of good old Bobby!"

The agents ushered us inside the store and made a path through the crush of bodies. I found the scene humorously ironic: that I was the elected representative for the district meant nothing, but because I knew Bobby, the welcome mat rolled out. Christine teased me: "Assemblyman Rogan can't get the time of day, but dropping the name of the guy who runs the gas station moves heaven and earth here!"

"The way to a cop's heart is through his stomach," I replied. "I guess they don't want to bite the hand that feeds them once a week!"

Carter sat at a table in the midst of all this activity, scrawling "J. Carter" in machine-gun fashion on books thrust before him. He rarely looked up from his signing task: there were too many people waiting to buy a book to allow for idle conversation.

Agents escorted Christine, Dana, Claire, and me into the stockroom at the rear of the store, now in use as a temporary Secret Service command post. Ladders, shopping carts, and scores of shipping cartons cluttered the room, along with piles of books stacked all over the floor. A small wooden table with bottled water awaited Carter; when he finished signing for customers, he was to come inside the stockroom and sign additional books for the employees and police assigned to his detail. "The president will probably keep signing for all the customers until the books are gone, or until everyone lined up around the block gets one, so it may be a while," the agent advised me.

"He doesn't like to be disturbed while he is signing," he added, "so I'm sure he won't stop to pose for a picture with your girls until he's done. Please make yourself at home in here, and when the president is through, we'll bring him in for the picture with your daughters. President Carter is pretty good about signing books: he wants to make sure everyone gets one. He canceled the rest of his schedule tonight so he could sit here and sign them."

That was admirable on Carter's part, but it turned out to be a long evening: Carter signed books for every patron in line–more than two thousand of them. In the meantime, Christine and I tried keeping our two-year-old twins engaged by reading stories, playing games, and taking them for walks around the nearby stores. Directly outside the exit door of the stockroom was the parking lot (now sealed off with police tape) where Carter's limousine awaited. Secret Service agents let our girls take turns climbing on the backseat and playing inside the luxurious car.

As the evening wore on, I took Claire for a little walk through the bookstore to keep her occupied. She broke free of my grasp momentarily, ran around an aisle, and headed straight for Carter. The former president still sat at the table, signing books with his back to us; I caught Claire just as she ran up to Carter, who looked over with a smile when he saw my cackling little girl running from her daddy. Still, the sudden commotion she caused startled the Secret Service and police, but all relaxed quickly when they realized the cause.

It was 10:00 p.m. when Carter signed the last book. He then came back to the stockroom, where the agent in charge introduced us: "Mr. President," he said with great formality, "allow me to present Assemblyman and Mrs. James Rogan. Judge Rogan represents this district in the California legislature."

"I understand you're a friend of Bobby Salter's," Carter said as we shook hands.

Christine nudged me in the ribs, accentuating my own lack of clout. I said I knew Bobby well.

"And you admit to it?" he asked with a grin.

"Only for tonight, Mr. President," I responded.

That exchange ended the small talk. His staffer told him he'd be taking a picture with Dana and Claire: Carter said, "I'll get in the middle," and stepped between Christine and me (holding the kids). "Come on–let's get this over with," Carter commanded the photographer. Two pictures were quickly snapped of our group. "Okay, that's it," Carter announced, and then walked away. Christine later told me how annoyed she felt by his curtness, especially after waiting over three hours to meet him. I wasn't surprised: after seeing him many times before, I knew to expect abruptness.

The Glendale police officers working on his security detail formed a receiving line. Again, Carter was all business. He walked through the line, shaking hands quickly, but didn't pause to speak with any officers. Carter then sat at the wooden table and signed the stack of books before him hurriedly. As he was signing, I slipped out to the customer counter, bought three of the books, and returned with them. I handed them to Carter, who signed them for my family. With the last book signed, he walked out the rear exit to his waiting limousine without bidding anyone good-bye.[1]

"Let's get this over with": former president Jimmy Carter with (from left) Christine, Claire, Dana, and me, Super Crown Books, Glendale, California, February 8, 1995 (photo by William LaChasse)

Dana and Claire, who were up long past their bedtime to meet a former president, were asleep in our arms before we made it back to the car.

---

1   To his credit, during his post-presidential years, Carter proved to be a gracious signer through the mail. He signed several photographs and copies of his books for me in the decades since he left the White House.

37

Always Looking the Part

I n late 1995 I attended the annual "Sons of the Desert" banquet at the Hollywood Roosevelt Hotel. These dinners always proved a delight for us old film buffs, because the program consisted of the ever-thinning ranks of movie actors from the 1920s–'40s, who entertained and shared memories of their Tinseltown heyday at these affairs. Among those participating in this program were sisters Lassie and Peggy Ahern, who told stories about making their first silent film with humorist Will Rogers in 1923; Eugene "Pineapple" Jackson (who made his silent movie debut with Mary Pickford in 1925) sang and danced as he played the ukulele; Frank Coughlin, the only child star under exclusive contract to director Cecil B. DeMille, talked about appearing in *Gone with the Wind*; Dick Jones told the story of how Walt Disney picked him, at age ten, as Pinocchio's voice for

"The Lollipop Kid" Jerry Maren and me, Hollywood Roosevelt Hotel, October 28, 1995 . . .

the 1940 animated feature. A particular favorite was my friend Jerry Maren, one of the handful of surviving Munchkins at that time from the 1939 film *The Wizard of Oz*. That night Jerry sang the song he'd warbled to Judy Garland as he handed her a lollipop before she embarked down the Yellow Brick Road: "We represent the Lollipop Guild . . . and in the name of the Lollipop Guild [he bowed from the waist], we wish to welcome you to Munchkin Land!"

. . . and Jerry (center Munchkin), as he presented Dorothy (Judy Garland) her lollipop in *The Wizard of Oz*.

Seated at the table next to me was Ellen Corby, who began her career as a script girl for Laurel and Hardy and later became a film and television star in her own right. She appeared in dozens of movies, including Frank Capra's classic *It's a Wonderful Life* (1948); that same year she won an Academy Award nomination for her performance in *I Remember Mama*. In later years she charmed a new generation of fans as the beloved grandmother on the long-running 1970s television series *The Waltons*. Although confined to a wheelchair and with hands gnarled by arthritis, she wore a sweet smile on her face that never faded as she greeted scores of her fans at the banquet.

I was thrilled that evening when I learned my dinner partner was Anita Page. The frail, elderly, and utterly charming woman is remembered today only by serious film scholars–all of whom agree that Anita was the last of the great silent movie stars (and one of Hollywood's first international sex symbols). Considered in her day as one of the most beautiful women to grace the silver screen, she made her movie debut in 1925, and then signed a long-term contract with MGM. By 1928 she had rocketed to fame and eclipsed Greta Garbo as the star receiving the most fan mail (she averaged more than fifty thousand letters per month). Anita appeared opposite leading men such as Lon Chaney Sr., Buster Keaton, Ramon Novarro, Douglas Fairbanks Sr., Walter Huston, and a young newcomer named Clark Gable. She created an international incident in the early 1930s when the Italian dictator Benito Mussolini publicly declared Anita his favorite actress, and asked MGM executives to get him an auto-graphed picture. Despite heavy lobbying by the studio and the US State Department, Anita flatly refused to sign for the fascist.

The last of the silent screen stars: Miss Anita Page, the Hollywood Roosevelt Hotel, October 28, 1995...

She remained a top box office draw until 1934, when she retired from films.

When we met, Anita was almost ninety; she dressed with the over-stated elegance of the "Norma Desmond" character from *Sunset Boulevard*: heavy makeup, a vintage gown and mink stole, and silver, opera-length gloves that kept falling down her withered, slender arms. When she walked (she needed assistance on each side), her shoes kept slipping off her feet. But none of these sartorial difficulties took away from her saucy tone and the mischievous gleam in her eye.

Despite our prodding during dinner, Anita talked little about her bygone days in Hollywood; she was more interested in discussing life in the present. She did make one exception: when someone at our table mentioned that we dined in the historic ballroom where the very first Academy Awards ceremony was held in 1927, Anita cast a nonchalant glance around the room: "You're right," she nodded in agreement, "It was held here. I had a starring lead in a

...and in her prime: Anita Page, 1928

picture that year. I was nominated for an award, but I didn't win it. But that night—everyone looked so elegant. I wore a long, white, beautiful gown. Back then, the Academy Awards ceremony was just a dinner dance: nothing big or too special. We never expected it would grow to the degree it has."

"I remember they had a wonderful dinner served that night," she reflected, "but someone at a nearby table yelled at his waiter an accusation that the cook was serving canned peas. Although the waiters and chefs denied it angrily, it became a big joke, with everyone asking their waiters about the canned peas."

Our tablemates looked at one another in amazement: Anita had not only attended the first Oscar ceremony, but she was a nominee! We were impressed greatly; to Anita, it was no big deal.

It was a pleasure meeting and having her as my seatmate that night; we became friends and stayed in touch.

. . .

Eventually, Anita moved to a retirement home in Burbank (located in my legislative district). The complex's administrator invited me to attend their annual Christmas banquet, where I wanted to present Anita with a resolution from the state legislature proclaiming "Anita Page Day" in California.

At the banquet, and before Anita came down to the dining hall for the award, a nurse pulled me aside. She confided that she had started helping Anita get ready for the dinner more than eight hours earlier, because the retired actress required that much time to be "presentable" (as Anita termed it). "This is the first time Miss Page has ever come down from her room to join the other

For dear Jim Rogan, to your
All Best wishes
And forever! Love Anita Page

Looking the part: Anita Page and me at dinner following the presentation of the "Anita Page Day" resolution, Burbank, California, December 15, 1995

residents," she told me. "She never wants to leave her room and join in any community activities, because she says it takes too long to get ready. I keep telling her, 'Miss Page, you don't need to go to all this trouble! Just come down and meet everyone. They'd be delighted to get to know you.' But she always refuses politely."

Later that evening, after I presented the legislative scroll to Anita, we had dinner together and I raised the issue. "Anita," I told her, "don't worry about getting dolled up just to go downstairs to a meal! Go as you are–nobody cares. They have movie and bingo nights, regular entertainment, parties, and lots of other social activities. You need to come down and mingle more often, and don't worry about how you look."

Anita gave me a long gaze, and then put her small hand atop mine. "Dearie," she said politely, "that might do for everyone else, but it would not do for me. You see, I'm a motion picture star, and I must always look the part."

And she always did.

...

Anita did start getting out more; sixty years after she retired from films, she returned to acting and appeared in a couple of low-budget thriller movies. She also started appearing at nostalgia shows, signing autographs and greeting new

generations of fans, until ill health forced her to curtail her activities.

Anita Page died at age ninety-eight of natural causes on September 6, 2008. She was the last surviving major star of Hollywood's silent film era, and the last known survivor among those who attended the first Academy Awards ceremony.

Anita Page, 1928

38

"What Doin'?"

Earlier in the year, former president George Bush's office invited my family to his welcoming ceremony at a private hangar when he flew to Los Angeles Airport. At the last minute, Assembly Republican leader Jim Brulte needed me in Sacramento because of crucial legislative votes on a key piece of legislation. Brulte promised that if I skipped the Bush meeting, he would make sure my family got a rain check; he made good on it when Bush flew into Mather Air Force Base outside Sacramento for a speech a few months later.

Mather was practically deserted when we arrived; the Pentagon had shuttered the base a couple of years earlier due to budget cuts. A lone security guard at the entrance waved our car through the gate without checking our identification or inquiring as to our business. We drove past rows of empty barracks and down silent streets to the rear of the property, where we parked in front of the Trajen air support hangar. A dozen former Bush staffers, along with a couple Secret Service agents, stood along the tarmac, awaiting his arrival.

At 5:50 p.m. a small private jet landed on the airstrip behind the building. It taxied slowly and came to rest twenty yards from the hangar, where a Secret Service agent waited at the end of the red carpet now rolled out to greet the former chief executive. The pilot raised the hatch; a moment later, George Bush appeared at the door, shaking hands with the flight crew and presenting each of them with a souvenir presidential tie bar (similar to the one he wore) before exiting.

Bush stepped from the plane and waved to the small welcoming reception. Other than having more gray in his otherwise dark hair, Bush's appearance had changed little since leaving the White House a few years earlier. When he saw us standing with our twin daughters, he grinned and walked over to us. "This looks like it's going to be a *real* family picture," he said as he approached.

Former president George Bush arrives at Mather Air Force Base, October 6, 1995 (photo by William LaChasse)

Before Bush's arrival, I had rehearsed Dana and Claire in saying, "Hello, President Bush." They had developed some proficiency in enunciating the phrase (minimal complexity for three-year-olds, I guess). Now I prompted Claire to convey her greeting: "Claire," I asked as Bush shook her little hand, "can you say hello to President Bush?"

To Jim & Christine Rogan with best wishes, G. Bush

Claire Rogan releases her chokehold from the 41st president's neck: George Bush with the Rogan family, Mather Air Force Base, October 6, 1995 (photo by William LaChasse)

Claire's eyes lit up. "Hi, Bush!" she called to him. "What doin'?" With that, she lunged out of my arms toward Bush, wrapped her arm around his neck, pulled him cheek to cheek against her, and then planted a big kiss on his lips! Bush roared with laughter and shrugged off Christine's apology for Claire's aggressive affection: "I'm sure you understand little girls, Mr. President," she said. Turning to Claire, Christine reminded her that "President Bush is a daddy, too."

"And a grandpa!" Bush added.

When Bush greeted Dana, he was in for more of the same. Dana hugged him with both arms and pulled his head into her shoulder. He appeared to delight in the attention from our overly affectionate kids, and we appreciated greatly his sweetness toward them.

After introducing my family to him, Bush pulled me aside for an update on my congressional race. He expressed his longstanding regard for my predecessor, congressman Carlos Moorhead, and asked me to pass along his respects when next I saw him.

"You'll love Congress," he told me. "It's a great honor to serve there." Then, turning to Christine, Bush asked her, "And how do you feel about Jim running?"

Christine's smile belied her initial reservations. "I'm behind his decision," she said.

"You'll love Congress": former president George Bush giving me campaign advice, Mather Air Force Base, October 6, 1995 (photo by William LaChasse)

"Good," Bush added. "I know about your last Assembly race, Jim. You had a tough one, but it sounds like you went through the worst of it. You'll do just fine from here on in."

Before leaving, I asked Bush to autograph for me an engraved vignette of the White House, signed by previous presidents I'd met. Bush studied the abbreviated signature of President Richard Nixon–signed "RN."

"Old RN," Bush said with a sigh. "I've seen that version of his signature many times in the past when I worked for him. This will be a nice memento to pass along to the girls someday."

As Bush grasped Christine's hand during our good-byes, he told her, "Hang in there. We need good people in government, like your husband."

...

After winning a seat in Congress, I had the honor of getting to know President Bush better. He showed great interest in my career, and helped out in many ways—including hosting a fund-raiser (with his wife, Barbara) for me in Houston during my final reelection effort. By the end of that race, one might have thought I was a member of his family by the concern and interest he showed in my campaign. I have more stories to tell about him, but I'll save them for my next book of anecdotes from Congress.

Although many conservative Republicans don't rank George Bush among our greatest presidents, there is no denying he was one of his generation's great patriots, and one of my generation's great gentlemen.

39

Losing Stinks

Back in the early 1990s, a reporter doing a profile piece on me asked for my list of contemporary politicians that I admired. She expressed shock when my list included one of the leading liberals in the Democratic Party: former Massachusetts governor and 1988 Democratic presidential nominee Michael Dukakis. When asked why I included a man whose name was anathema to Republicans of that era, I replied, "Because Dukakis is one of the few men I can name in politics prepared to lose an election because he stood by his principles. I may have disagreed with those principles, but I admire his integrity greatly." I cited as examples some positions he took in his race against George Bush that he knew were political losers; because of it, Bush beat Dukakis handily.

Although I met Dukakis a few times before and during his White House run, I didn't know him personally. That opportunity came after he returned to private life. When the newspaper published the interview I gave, I sent him a copy with a note expressing admiration from a Republican who, I regretted telling him, was a former Democrat who changed parties during his donnybrook with Bush.

Governor Michael Dukakis campaigning for the 1988 Democratic presidential nomination, the Sportsmen's Lodge, Los Angeles, California, August 25, 1987

Coincidentally, a few days later, I left for a judge's conference in Boston; upon arrival, a student intern working for Dukakis called me at my hotel. He said Dukakis had received my letter and tried to call me at my court, but was told I'd already left for Massachusetts. The student said Dukakis wanted to invite me to his speech at the Kennedy School of Government at Harvard. I accepted the invitation gratefully, and asked him if I needed to contact any Dukakis staff member at the site. He laughed at the suggestion: "I'm his staff, and I won't be there–I have a midterm tomorrow." Here again was a lesson of politics I've seen repeated frequently: a national leader going from the pinnacle of power to commanding a staff (in this case) consisting of a grad student working for extra credit.

Governor Michael Dukakis addressing students at the Kennedy School of Government, Harvard University, Cambridge, Massachusetts, July 15, 1993

I arrived at the Kennedy School ninety minutes early, which got me a front row seat for Dukakis's speech in the ARCO Forum for Public Affairs. The room filled quickly, with late-arriving students finding standing-room-only spots in the balcony two floors above the platform. Sitting there in a pinstriped suit and wing-tip shoes amid hundreds of college kids in T-shirts, shorts, and flip-flops, I felt old and out of place. When Dukakis arrived, his apparel did nothing to alleviate my self-consciousness: he wore an open-neck Hawaiian print shirt, khaki slacks, white gym socks (with a big hole in one ankle), and sneakers. Obviously, I didn't get the wardrobe memo.

When Dukakis ambled into the room, the audience broke into spontaneous applause as he took a seat on the platform. A student offered a brief introduction before Dukakis stepped to the podium; using no notes, he kept his talk as casual as his dress. "Let's get something straight at the outset," Dukakis warned with a grin. "I do not claim to be an expert in politics. If I knew anything about politics, we would be having this meeting in the East Room of the White House!" The audience laughed and applauded. Dukakis promised to stay until five o'clock: "That's when I have to go to my favorite Greek barber down the street and get a haircut."

Although Dukakis covered a range of domestic and international issues, his primary theme was to encourage young people to enter politics at the ground level:

"When I was a law student down the road," he recalled, "I remember a young US senator named John F. Kennedy coming to talk with us and saying he wanted to run for president. Kennedy uplifted and encouraged us. And aside from myself, who later went on to become governor and a presidential candidate, my other classmates included Senator Paul Sarbanes, our first EPA director Bill Ruckelshaus, and United States Supreme Court Justice Antonin Scalia. By the way, Scalia was as conservative in law school as he is now on the Court. But he made it onto the Supreme Court–for better or for worse!"

Dukakis urged the students not to fear starting at the bottom by running and losing, citing as examples his own experience, as well as that of President Bill Clinton:

> Clinton came home from law school at Yale and ran for Congress unsuccessfully. In politics, you have to be prepared to lose. Clinton and I were both young governors with good national notices who were nonetheless thrown out of office after one term. We had the distinction, along with Minnesota governor Rudy Perpich, of being the only governors defeated for reelection that came back and later won. We called ourselves "the Retread Club."
>
> Keep in mind that "Dukakis" was not a household name when I first ran for statewide office. I served in the legislature for eight years before I decided to seek the 1970 Democratic nomination for lieutenant governor. One of my aides said I needed name recognition, so we made up ten thousand bumper stickers saying simply, "Dukakis 70." My aide slapped one of those on his car and drove across the state. He pulled into a gas station (in those days the attendant pumped the gas for you) and the guy asked my aide, "What the hell is a Dukakis?" My aide replied, "It's a rare bird–there are only seventy of them left in existence."

During the question period, a student asked if Dukakis had any future political plans.

"I doubt I will ever be a candidate for office again," he responded. "[New

York Governor Mario] Cuomo likes to say, when he is asked similar questions, that 'Bill Clinton will be reelected in 1996, so by the year 2000 guys like Cuomo and Dukakis will be on Medicare.' After twelve years as governor and a prior run for the presidency, what is there left to run for? This doesn't mean I won't stay active in politics and try to help when I can."

When asked about the man that vanquished his White House effort five years earlier, Dukakis said, "Truthfully, I thought George Bush would be a better president than he was. I say that with all due respect. He just never seemed to connect with the people. I don't think he had a clue what ordinary Americans needed." When one student suggested that the programs a Dukakis administration might have created were now implemented by President Clinton, he replied, "Let's just say I'm sleeping a lot better with Bill Clinton in the White House than I did when George Bush was there, and I'm sleeping a hell of a lot better than I did when Ronald Reagan was there!"

As the program drew to a close, I raised my hand (without identifying myself when Dukakis called on me). I mentioned that I read a few years ago that during a discussion between two losing Democratic nominees, Walter Mondale had asked George McGovern how long it takes until the pain of losing the presidency goes away; McGovern had replied, "I'll let you know." I asked how Dukakis dealt with the loss personally. He paused for a moment, and then answered candidly: "Look," he said, "losing stinks."

"Aside from the deep personal disappointment, you're damned tired after an eighteen-month national campaign," he elaborated. "Plus, millions of people who believed in you feel let down. I received thousands of letters after the election from people saying they cried themselves to sleep. You feel a tremendous sense of disappointment, but you can't dwell on it. You move on. A friend said that losing an election builds character; I'm just sorry I couldn't let my character-building end after my 1970 loss for lieutenant governor!"

Dukakis closed his speech with this final observation about running for the presidency:

> When you run for president, people recognize you wherever you go. Last year I
> visited my son and grandchild in Venice, California, where my wife, Kitty, and
> I stayed at a bed-and-breakfast near the beach. If any of you have ever been to

the Venice boardwalk early in the morning, you know there are a lot of strange people who hang out there. One morning I went out for a power walk. Two guys who looked like they hadn't slept in a real bed for months were eyeing me up one side and down the other. One guy finally said, "I know you! You ran for president!" I kept walking by and nodded in agreement. He turned to his friend and said, "Do you know who that guy is? That's Jerry Dukakis!"

At the conclusion of his talk, students surrounded Dukakis to shake his hand, get an autograph, and pose for pictures with him. Dukakis tarried happily, and demonstrated his multilingual talents by chatting at length in Spanish with one student from Mexico, and even greeting a Korean student in his native tongue.

Governor Michael Dukakis meeting a student after his speech at the Kennedy School of Government, Harvard University, Cambridge, Massachusetts, July 15, 1993

When I introduced myself, Dukakis winced: "Jim," he said, "I'm so sorry– I didn't know that was you when you asked the question." He put his arm around my shoulder and pulled me off to the side for a quick private chat. He asked me questions about my judicial conference, what I'd seen in Boston–even details regarding the recent birth of my daughters. His patient graciousness overwhelmed me, especially since so many students remained, waiting to meet him. I insisted he get back to business; as we shook hands, he said he wanted to keep in touch. When we returned to the waiting assemblage, a student handed me his camera and asked me to take his picture with Dukakis. While I aimed the camera, Dukakis pointed to me and told his young admirer, "You don't know who is taking that picture–That's Jim Rogan–a very important judge in California."

Appreciating the greatly exaggerated sentiment, I told the student, "I have to do things like this when I'm asked–I'm up for reelection next year!"

Dukakis was still mobbed by well-wishers and showed no signs of breaking away when I left the Kennedy School. I looked at my wristwatch: it was almost five thirty. The Greek barber would have to wait for another day.

. . .

That day at the Kennedy School was more than twenty years ago, and Mike Dukakis and I have remained friends since. From grabbing an occasional lunch at UCLA when he comes west to teach, to me speaking to his class, and from taking congratulatory calls from him when I won elections (and getting a much-appreciated cheer-up call when I lost a big one), to him cooking leftovers for me one late night in his Brookline kitchen, I've come to know Mike as a man of great kindness and personal charm. There isn't a touch of imperiousness in his genetic code. Behind the scenes he's a regular guy; he's nothing like the stiff and emotionless drone that some in the press (and everyone in my party) portrayed during his presidential race.

My favorite memory of Mike shows both his humility and his sense of humor: it occurred in March 1996, when I was Assembly majority leader in the California legislature and running for a seat in the House of Representatives. A couple of months earlier, I had received a note from him telling me he'd be teaching at UCLA for the winter semester and suggesting we get together.

One morning Mike called my office manager, Denise Milinkovich, and asked if I was free for breakfast the next day. When she told him she'd clear my schedule, Mike said, "Great—I'll drive out from L.A. to Glendale to meet him."

"Oh, no, Governor," she protested, "that won't do. He'll insist on driving out to see you. He won't want you driving all this way to see him." Mike cut her off, telling her it was his choice, and that he didn't mind driving. Under protest for the protocol lapse, Denise set up breakfast the next morning in the coffee shop of the Glendale Red Lion Hotel (now the Hilton). Mike then asked how much time we'd have; she said we could meet for breakfast at 7:30, and my schedule was clear until my late morning meeting with local school board members. "Sounds great," Mike told her. "And if Jim doesn't mind, maybe I can tag along with him to the next meeting and give him a quiet boost with the teachers."

Would I mind? I couldn't pay for that kind of help!

The next morning, I stood in the hotel lobby, talking with a couple of our local city council members, when I saw the elevator doors open. Mike stepped out (again dressed casually) and crossed the lobby. Many patrons gave him a surprised double-take; some walked up and asked if he really was him. He greeted each person warmly, and then joined me. A waiter seated us at a rear table of the restaurant; we ordered coffee, split an English muffin (neither of us were big breakfast eaters), and had a chance to catch up in many areas. As usual, Mike was disinclined to talk much about himself; he was filled with questions about my congressional race, my experiences as majority leader, my family, and how politics impacted Christine and our girls.

When I saw an opening, I steered the conversation to his presidential race, mentioning that Christine and I had crashed his Biltmore Hotel party in June 1988 on the night he won the California primary (and his delegate count put him over the top for the presidential nomination). He reminisced that his victory speech that night in the Biltmore ballroom had special meaning for him: twenty-eight years earlier, he and some of his buddies had hitchhiked across the United States to reach Los Angeles for the 1960 Democratic National Convention; he heard fellow Brookline native John F. Kennedy speak in that same ballroom when he beat Lyndon Johnson for the presidential nomination.

"Jim—you're the best, despite your party!" Breakfast at the Red Lion Hotel: Governor Michael Dukakis and me, Glendale, California, March 1, 1996 (photo by Greg Mitchell)

As for his own White House run, he said that after winning reelection to the governor's office in 1986, he gave no thought to running for president. However, after the Iran-Contra scandal rocked the Reagan–Bush administration, it got him thinking: "I told my staff I'd look at running for six months, and then make a decision. Ultimately, I decided to give it a try."

"The night I accepted the presidential nomination at the Democratic Convention in Atlanta was a thrill," Mike added. "It was a great night, but by the next day it was back to work." What surprised me most about Mike's experience in seeking the presidency was that he found the overall process less than exhilarating: he was on the go constantly for almost two years, giving thousands of interviews on the same subjects over and over. "After you've tried to answer the very same questions fifty different ways, you grow incredibly bored," he said. But the worst part for him was the sense of isolation while running: when he became governor, he declined all security and often rode the subway alone to work. "But once you sign on to the Secret Service as a presidential candidate," he lamented, "your life as you know it ends. You become surrounded by a huge wall, and nobody can penetrate it. It's terrible."

When discussing his defeat, Mike showed a dispassionate frankness: "I hated to lose the White House, but you don't brood about it. You get over it. In '88 we were way ahead of Bush. After my convention, I decided to run a campaign on the high road and not engage in character assassination–type politics. As you now know, my strategy failed. I was tarred with Willie Horton wherever I went.[1] The Bush campaign did their best to work me over at every opportunity. I didn't respond properly, and that cost me the election."

As the time drew near for me to head to my meeting with the local school board members, Mike volunteered to accompany me. I concocted an idea for a great practical joke and called my chief of staff, Greg Mitchell, who moonlighted as a professional Bill Clinton impersonator. I told Greg to rush over to the Red Lion with his Clinton makeup. Soon Greg arrived, and we all piled into his beat-

---

1   In the 1980s, Horton was a prisoner serving a life sentence for murder in Massachusetts, where state law provided for weekend furloughs for inmates. After obtaining a pass, Horton assaulted, robbed, and raped a victim. Dukakis didn't create the program (in fact, it started under a Republican governor in 1972), but he had supported it. The Bush campaign used the Willie Horton case in an unending barrage of blistering negative attacks against Dukakis.

The coconspirators: Greg Mitchell, aka "President Clinton," (before he applied his makeup) and Governor Michael Dukakis, Red Lion Hotel, Glendale, California, March 1, 1996

up red Mustang for the drive over to the Burbank Department of Water and Power.

We arrived about fifteen minutes late for the meeting, with the increasingly impatient board members awaiting me in the conference room. I had Mike and Greg stand just outside the door while I entered the room alone and apologized for my delayed arrival: "This meeting is so important to me that I decided to swing by my district office and pick up my chief of staff and my legislative director," I said. Then I called my coconspirators into the room one by one as follows: "You all know my chief of staff, President Bill Clinton." With that, Greg entered the room to laughter. Everyone there knew Greg, and also knew he worked as a Clinton impressionist.

Now came the payoff: "I don't think any of you have met my legislative director, Governor Michael Dukakis." Mike then rounded the corner and entered the room, still dressed in his casual shirt, khakis, and sneakers. For a moment there was silence as the board members studied my "staffer." Then they all broke out into uproarious laughter.

"Hey!" said one board member, "you actually do look a little bit like Dukakis. But you're too short—and your nose is too big!"

Now it was our turn to laugh—and nobody laughed harder than Mike Dukakis. As he started speaking in his distinctive baritone voice, I watched the faces of our prank victims change from mirth to confusion to shock. After a few moments, they understood that as unlikely as this far-fetched scene appeared, he was the real McCoy.

"I just wanted to come by and say hello with my pal Jim Rogan," Mike said. "You have a great guy in your assemblyman, but I still don't know where he gets his politics!"

"From being left out in the sun too damned long!" I answered.

As the jolt wore off, the board members lined up to meet Mike; he posed for pictures and signed autographs for them before it was time to head back to UCLA to teach his class. We packed him back inside Greg's old beater Mustang, I said good-bye, and then returned to my meeting with the board members. They were still in such shock that it took a while before anyone remembered why they had requested the session in the first place!

...

Governor Mike Dukakis continues teaching college courses, and continues inspiring new generations of students. I can think of no better example of public service than the one set by their professor.

After the shock: Governor Michael Dukakis and me with the Glendale and Burbank school board members, Burbank Department of Water and Power, March 1, 1996 (photo by Greg Mitchell)

40

Man Talk

After meeting for the first time the new governor of Texas, George W. Bush, I gave my legislative staff an assessment of the former president's eldest son:

1. He was very amiable.

2. Unlike his father, he was a serious supply-side/limited-government Reagan conservative.

3. If he ever ran, he'd never win the White House.

Today, conservative activists think I got two out of those three predictions wrong. So sue me. Besides, who'd trust my political judgment? Back then I also thought I could win a US Senate race from California—as a conservative Republican!

It was early 1996. George W. Bush was the recently-elected governor of Texas, and I was the new majority leader of the California State Assembly and also a GOP candidate for Congress. I received a call from the California Republican Party office asking me to introduce Bush at a breakfast organized in his honor. (Bush's staff wanted him to start making connections with members of the Southern California GOP donor base.)

The day before the event, I received a somewhat panicky call from a Party staffer: "We're charging a nominal fifty dollars for a reception and breakfast with Bush and his wife, but we have almost no takers. We want you to bring about thirty people—we'll comp them. We just need to have more bodies in the room so it won't be an embarrassment." In later years, when hoards of people spent tens of thousands of dollars to rub elbows briefly with President and Mrs. George W. Bush, I remembered how we couldn't give away tickets to an intimate breakfast with them.

The event was held in the penthouse of the Regency Club in the Westwood section of Los Angeles. The Bushes arrived ahead of schedule that morning (a hallmark during his presidency; Bush almost never kept an audience waiting). He must have received my picture in a briefing file, because when he got out of his car, he walked over and greeted me with a cheery, "Well, hello, Mr. Majority Leader!" His wife, Laura, was as charming a person as I'd ever met, with eyes so deep green that they looked as though they might glow in the dark. I escorted the Bushes to the foyer, where I introduced them to the assembled guests (both paid and comped). We mingled for half an hour, and then he and Laura joined me at the reserved speaker's table for breakfast, along with Los Angeles Dodgers owner Peter O'Malley. A fitness buff who ran seven miles daily, Bush passed on the fare of greasy sausage, hash browns, and eggs, and instead asked for a fruit plate.

It didn't take long for Bush (a former part-owner of the Texas Rangers) and O'Malley to became engrossed in a lengthy (and exclusive—to them) discussion relating to baseball team ownership. During their two-man powwow, I tried to crack into their conversation by interjecting my own ballpark experiences ("Hey, I've been to a few Dodgers games," or "I sure love those big Dodger Dogs they sell at the park. Hey, Peter, do you guys use Gulden's or French's mustard on them?"), but after a while I gave up and let them have their fun. Still, I felt that my grandfather who raised me—a longshoreman on the San Francisco docks for forty-five years—would shake his head in dismay at the sight of the menfolk talking baseball while Laura and I shared stories and swapped photographs of our children.

Actually, we had commonality on this domestic topic: the Bushes and the Rogans both were parents of twin daughters. When Laura drew her husband into the discussion of the challenges of raising twin girls from a dad's perspective, I told Bush I appreciated his pain: mine were only three; his were fourteen. "Mine won't want a driver's license for years," I said, "and yours are almost there."

"I'm not worried about the driver's license," Bush quipped as he sipped his coffee. "I'm worried about the boys starting to call for them!"

Listening to the man-talk: Texas governor George W. Bush and me, Regency Club, Los Angeles, April 19, 1996

Eventually, Bush and I settled into a political discussion. He said I was crazy to leave the bench for politics. I replied, "Look who's talking–you left baseball for politics!"

Bush chuckled: "Yes, that's true, but I'm having the time of my life as governor. I really get to make an impact on people's lives." He then brought up my recent legislation, Assembly Bill 888 (signed into law as California's Sexually Violent Predator Act). He wanted all the details of how I drafted and got it passed; he said he wanted to propose a copycat bill to the Texas legislature. I had one of my staffers retrieve a copy of the bill and legislative analysis, and I gave it to him for his later review.

Bush asked me about my current congressional race, and I gave him the lay of the land insofar as I was running as a Republican in a Democratic district (which grew increasingly Democratic each day). I told him the national and state Democratic Party had targeted me for defeat, and I'd have an uphill climb to keep it in the Republican column. Bush said he'd be back to California several times between now and November, and offered to come out and help me. Of course, I was delighted to accept.

After the program began, I introduced Bush for his speech. He returned the favor by urging everyone to help me go to Washington in November to join the great GOP revolution led by House Speaker Newt Gingrich. Speaking from a prepared text, Bush expressed optimism that presumptive GOP presidential nominee Bob Dole had a strong chance to win the White House that November: "Bob Dole is so strong in Texas that he should abandon Texas. He has it won. He should focus his fire on California, where he can win." He then gave a brief syn-

opsis of his goals for moving Texas forward economically by adopting free-market conservative principles.

At the end of the program, I introduced Bush to my legislative and campaign staff. When he met my chief of staff, Greg Mitchell (the Bill Clinton professional look-alike), Bush laughed aloud: "Hey, let's get a picture together!" he insisted. "We

Texas governor George W. Bush addressing an intimate audience at the Regency Club, Los Angeles, April 19, 1996. In the background (to Bush's far left): me, Los Angeles Dodgers owner Peter O'Malley, and future First Lady Laura Bush. (Photo by Greg Mitchell)

can relive the 1992 election [when Clinton beat Bush's father for the presidency]." After Greg posed with him, Bush made me promise he'd get a copy of the photo.

"I want to show this to Mother and Dad," he said.

I walked Bush to his car; he thanked me for coming and for introducing him around. "I'll be back to help you later this year," he promised as he gripped my hand.

Reliving 1992: Texas governor George W. Bush and Greg Mitchell, Regency Club, Los Angeles, April 19, 1996

. . .

During the course of my 1996 congressional campaign, we contacted Bush's office many times trying to set up an event with him, but his staff never returned our phone calls. I didn't take it personally: governors have bigger issues on tap than helping with out-of-state House races.

The next time I saw George W. Bush, I was in my second term in Congress, and he was asking for my support in his 2000 presidential run.

. . .

Despite my confident prediction in 1996, four years later voters elected George W. Bush the forty-third president of the United States. And, of course, California voters never elected me to the US Senate. When it came to my political prognostications that day, as they say in baseball, I was 0 for 2.

41

One for the Team

In 1972, US Senator Bob Dole gave me his autograph when I was a kid. In 1996, as the Republican presidential nominee, he flew to California and campaigned with and for me a few times when I was my district's GOP congressional nominee. His running mate, former congressman Jack Kemp, did the same. No appearances they did meant more to me than those in the closing days of the race, when both showed up even though my home state was a lost cause for the national ticket.

Elected to the House of Representatives in 1962, Dole advanced to the Senate in 1968. When I first met him, he served as chairman of the Republican National Committee during the Nixon administration; later he became the 1976 GOP vice presidential nominee. Dole ran for the presidential nod unsuccessfully in 1980 and 1988; in 1996, he secured the prize and faced off against incumbent President Bill Clinton. Despite enormous odds and trailing badly in polls, Dole barnstormed the country gamely for the ticket.

A former college and professional football player, Jack Kemp entered Congress in 1970 and quickly became a darling of the conservative wing of the GOP. He ran unsuccessfully for the 1988 Republican presidential nomination; after the dust settled, President George Bush selected Kemp as his secretary of housing and urban development. Dole picked Kemp as his vice presidential running mate in 1996 to help unite his Party's right flank.

I thought Dole's selection of Kemp was smart politics, but I found it curious personally. Two months before the nominating convention, I spent an afternoon with Kemp in Sacramento when I introduced him at a Repub-

At the Burbank airport: GOP presidential nominee Bob Dole and the Rogan family, October 17, 1996 (photo by William LaChasse)

campaign button I'd given him at the airport. "Jim," he asked, "will you pin this on my lapel? I want to wear it for our rally." Dole couldn't accomplish the simple task without asking for assistance: this hero had lost the use of his right arm fifty years earlier from grave wounds received by German machine gun fire in World War II.

While awaiting his cue, Dole paced back and forth; he sprayed throat lubricant into his mouth repeatedly, telling me that as the national campaign neared an end, he feared his voice wouldn't hold out.

When the rally began, escorts led us from the holding area to the front of City Hall. Standing with Dole, awaiting my signal, I saw many of my

Campaign volunteers passed out this trigate Dole-Kemp-Rogan badge at our Glendale Rally, October 17, 1996

young nieces and nephews outside in the crowd. When they saw Dole and me, they began pointing and jumping up and down with great excitement. Meanwhile, backstage, just before hitting the stage, Dole's coordinator told me that once everyone gathered on the platform, he wanted me to go to the microphone, make my remarks, and then introduce California attorney general Dan Lungren (to introduce Dole).

The crowd roared loudly at each introduction; I was one of the last to take the stage before Dole. As I stepped from the doors with my cue, Dole patted me on the back. "Okay, Jim," he said encouragingly, "let's go do it!" I stepped out into sunshine and cheers. A sea of American flags, pom-poms, and Dole and Rogan posters waved across the crowd of more than three thousand. Two large banners proclaimed "California is Dole Country" and "Dole's Golden Rule: You Earned It, You Keep It." Secret Service and police sharpshooters were atop the roof of the courthouse across the street (where I once served as the municipal court's presiding judge); dozens of television and still cameras were trained on the stage from a riser erected nearby.

As the band played and the crowd's enthusiasm grew, Lungren told me how impressed he was by the energy: "This is great; he's been getting crowds like this all around the state." A deafening cheer rang out when Dole appeared; as he walked to the stage, his coordinator rushed over and whispered for me to hold off introducing Lungren: "We've had a change of plans," he said. "Don't do anything until I go check. I'll be right back." Meanwhile, the band's music pulsated as the crowd's roar grew. Dole stood onstage, flashing a thumbs-up and waving. Amid this electricity, Lungren leaned over and asked, "Aren't you supposed to introduce me?" I told him that was the original plan, but Dole's aide had called a signal change and said not to start. "Oh, forget him!" Lungren said. "There's too much excitement going now. We need to keep it going!" With that, he gave me a shove toward the podium.

Standing at the lectern, I saw two smoky teleprompter screens before me, with Dole's prepared remarks ready to scroll for him. On the podium sat a three-ring binder with his speech typed in large font (I was a bit surprised that at this late stage of the game, Dole still used a written text to give a stump speech to the party faithful). After motioning the crowd to silence and welcoming everyone, I made a brief pitch for my congressional campaign before introducing Lungren, who in turn presented the nominee.

Dole began by urging my election to Congress, and graciously referenced my campaign several times during his speech. He hammered on President Clinton's lack of ethics and the growing number of White House scandals. Deriding Clinton's twenty-eight visits to California since becoming president, Dole said, "He comes to California and drops money from the federal treasury the way you and I leave tips at the restaurant!"

While Dole spoke, I saw Christine behind the security barrier directly below the stage. She held Dana and Claire by the hand; I walked offstage, gathered the girls in my arms, and carried them back with me so they could be part of the Dole rally from the best seat in the house. The twins acted as if they were at Disneyland: each time the crowd cheered, they waved pom-poms. Soon I noticed the photographers started training their lenses away from the candidate

Claire and Dana in my arms, showing their support for the Dole–Kemp ticket, Bob Dole rally, October 17, 1996 (photo by William LaChasse)

to the happy twin girls in my arms. Lungren also saw this diversion; he whispered to me with a chuckle, "Shameless . . . you're shameless!"

"I'll rent them to you, Dan, when you run for governor."

Dole ended his speech: "California is not Bill Clinton country. It's still Reagan country! And on November 5, it's going to be Dole–Kemp country!" With that, several loud pops from confetti guns showered the crowd with a thick, heavy stream. Dole called over to me: "Come on, Jim," and raised my arm in a victory pose before we climbed down to shake hands with the crowd. Dole signed scores of autographs and posed for pictures; at one point he got ahead of me, and a Secret Service agent asked me to catch up to him: "The senator is talking to your nieces and nephews, and he wants to take a picture with all of you."

As our procession moved down the rope line, I noticed my young nephew,

Andrew Apffel, back in the crowd with tears in his eyes. I walked back and asked him what was wrong. "All of my brothers and sisters got an autograph except me," he said. When I told Dole that Andrew got overlooked, Dole went back and turned Andrew's tears into a smile. (If a very proud uncle may brag for a moment, that teary-eyed boy is, at this writing, Corporal Andrew Apffel, United States Marine Corps, on active duty overseas).

When it was time to go, I thanked Dole for coming to Glendale and giving my campaign this huge boost. "Jim," he replied, "you can repay me by winning this election. I'll see you in Washington." As Dole left, I looked back and saw Dana and Claire playing on the confetti-covered stage. The press photographed their antics almost as much as they covered Dole's exit.

. . .

With only five days before the election, the national GOP campaign arranged a hastily scheduled rally in my district with vice presidential nominee Jack Kemp at Woodbury University in Burbank. When I arrived at the rally site, organizers told me I'd be introducing Kemp to the large crowd of supporters assembling (despite the threatening rain clouds forming overhead). I was already onstage with the other candidates and local officials when Kemp's motorcade arrived shortly after 2 p.m. Jack and Joanne Kemp, along with actors Chad Everett, Billy Barty, and Bo Derek, emerged from the lead bus and made their way to the platform.

Once onstage, Kemp greeted each of us; a woman in the crowd threw him a football and a pen, which he autographed for her and tossed back.

I got a laugh from the audience when I introduced the nominee, saying, "I told them the first Republican National Convention I ever attended was in 1972 when I was just fourteen. I remember listening to one of the most dynamic speakers of the convention; he impressed me greatly . . . It was a freshman congressman from Buffalo [with the audience anticipating Kemp's identity, I looked back at the silver-haired nominee] . . . a youthful, vigorous guy with dark chestnut hair!"

I got my next laugh when I reminded everyone of the topic of Kemp's speech that long-ago evening: "And I'll never forget that stirring speech he gave–seconding the nomination of Spiro Agnew for vice president!" As the audience roared over Kemp nominating Agnew (who later resigned the vice presidency in disgrace), Kemp called out from his seat, "Your memory's too good, Jim!" getting another laugh.

Like Dole before him, Kemp urged the crowd to elect me to Congress, referencing my race several times in his remarks. He talked about growing up in Los Angeles, and meeting his wife, Joanne, at nearby Occidental College (where both were undergraduates). Kemp then kicked the Clinton administration for its unending scandals, and closed with this explanation of the entrepreneurial differences between the two parties:

Here I am introducing 1996 GOP vice presidential nominee Jack Kemp, Dole–Kemp Rally, Woodbury University, Burbank, California, October 31, 1996 (photo by William LaChasse)

"We are the party of civil rights. The Democrats want minorities to ride in the front of the bus, which is their constitutional and God-given right. We want to unlock the capital and credit to let minorities not only ride in the bus; we want them to own the bus—and the hotel—and the restaurant!"

When he finished, Kemp reached into a box filled with foam "Dole–Kemp" footballs and started tossing them to the crowd. He locked arms with the candidates for a victory pose, and then jumped off the stage to shake hands along the rope line.

. . .

On election eve, Kemp and I repeated this drill at a Long Beach rally. I finished out the evening going to multiple campaign events.

Finally, on November 5, the long race ended and the balloting began. That afternoon, as America voted, Kemp called me from his campaign plane to wish me luck. "This time tomorrow, Jimmy, you'll be the next congressman from the Twenty-Seventh District," he told me optimistically. I tried to return the cheer.

"More important, Jack, is that this time tomorrow you'll be the next vice president of the United States."

Kemp snorted at my glowing optimism. "Yeah, well, hmmm, anyway . . ." He turned the subject back to my campaign and me.

Kemp knew.

. . .

Bob Dole and Jack Kemp failed in their bid to unseat Bill Clinton by almost nine points; they lost my home state of California by a whopping thirteen points. Meanwhile, I won election to Congress that same day by squeaking out 50.1 percent of the vote in my Democrat-heavy district.

After I moved to Washington, I saw Bob and Jack in town occasionally (both did later events for me when I ran for reelection as an incumbent). Whenever I needed any help from either man, politically or advice-wise, they always were there. I asked Bob and Jack in later years why they came to California repeatedly so late in the 1996 race to do rallies like the ones with me, when they knew they'd never win California. Both told me the same thing: they wanted to try and help the down-ticket candidates. Most nominees running behind would have blown off the loser states—and us.

When it came to California in 1996, Bob Dole and Jack Kemp both took one for the team—and because of it, I went to Congress. I'm forever grateful to them.

. . .

After the election, Bob Dole and Jack Kemp returned to private life: Dole joined a prestigious Washington law firm, working as a political and legal consultant—and occasional TV pitchman.

Bob Dole giving my congressional race a big boost (from left: Los Angeles county supervisor Mike Antonovich, Senator Bob Dole, California attorney general Dan Lungren, me, candidates Susan Brooks and John Geranios, and Robin Dole (daughter of Bob Dole), Glendale, California, October 16, 1996 (photo by William LaChasse)

Jack Kemp served as chairman of his Washington-based Kemp Partners consulting firm and continued his involvement in charitable and political work until his death from cancer on May 2, 2009, at age seventy-three.

Home stretch rally (from left: Joanne Kemp, 1996 vice presidential nominee Jack Kemp, me, State Senate candidate Paula Boland, Congressman Howard "Buck" McKeon), Dole–Kemp campaign rally, Woodbury University, Burbank, California, October 31, 1996 (photo by William LaChasse)

42

Bad Rap

When I served in political life, we conservatives always accused the national mainstream media of having a double standard when covering Republicans and Democrats. Nowhere was this imbalance more evident during that period than in their treatment of Vice President Dan Quayle (1989–1993). A veteran of both houses of Congress, Quayle had built a solid reputation among his Senate colleagues when George Bush tapped the forty-one-year-old as his 1988 running mate.

Almost from the moment Bush announced the selection, the press pounced on Quayle, claiming that his Vietnam-era US Coast Guard service was akin to draft-dodging, and that his twelve years in Congress showed a lack of experience for the job. Once elected, they double-downed on Quayle, magnifying every minor verbal gaffe as proof of their collective assessment. Of course, when the Bush–Quayle ticket ran for reelection four years later against Democrats Bill Clinton and Al Gore, these same press complaints evaporated when it came to the Democratic challengers—despite Clinton taking well-documented pains to avoid all military service during Vietnam, and Senator Gore having almost the same amount of prior congressional service that Quayle had when Bush picked him.[1] I cannot think of any modern political figure more thoroughly

---

1 A more extreme (and recent) example of this double standard was the mainstream media's total lack of interest in these same "qualifications" when Senator Barack Obama declared his candidacy for president—with barely two years of congressional service under his belt and no military record.

and unfairly treated by the mainstream media than Dan Quayle.

After the Bush–Quayle ticket lost reelection in 1992, Quayle returned to his native Indiana, contemplating his future. He made no secret of his interest in a Clinton rematch in 1996, but a serious illness placed his White House ambitions on hold. Instead, he relocated to Arizona, hoping to establish a Western political base to strengthen his chances for a later presidential run. This move coincided with my first congressional race, and I was delighted to receive his offer to campaign for me in my district.

Welcome to Burbank: That's me greeting former vice president Dan Quayle at Burbank Airport, October 19, 1996 (photo by William LaChasse)

With only two weeks to go until Election Day, my campaign staff and I drove out to Mercury Terminal at the Burbank airport to pick up Quayle, whose small private plane taxied and landed at 1:45 p.m. He climbed out with his jacket slung over his shoulder; when I thanked him for coming to help, he laughed. "Don't thank me, Jim. I should thank you. You've done me a big favor. My family and I just moved to Arizona, and the moving vans arrive today with the boxes. So Marilyn [Mrs. Quayle] gets to unpack them, and I get to come to Southern California!"

Dan and I hit it off immediately: he was friendly, warm, engaging, and very unpretentious. While driving through Burbank, I briefed him on my race as we headed to our first stop. The day before, his office had called and said that when he campaigns he likes to drop in on a local diner to shake hands. When they asked if I would mind doing it with him today, we made arrangements to visit Connie Barron's family restaurant on West Burbank Boulevard. I called Connie ahead of time and asked casually if she would mind if I dropped by with a "pal." When I then told her the name of my guest, she said she almost fainted!

When Dan and I pulled in front of Barron's Family Restaurant, we found a group of reporters and fans waiting outside with cameras. Dan hopped out of the van, tossed his jacket on the seat, and rushed across the street to greet each person there. He enjoyed a leisurely time at the restaurant, having coffee and shaking hands with customers, posing for photographs, and signing autographs for kids. Connie and her customers were delighted by his surprise appearance.

During the later ride to my Glendale fund-raiser, I asked Dan when he knew he was under serious consideration for vice president by George Bush in 1988. He said it was a few weeks before the GOP convention:

Former vice president Dan Quayle campaigns with me at Barron's Family Restaurant, Burbank, California, October 19, 1996 (photo by William LaChasse)

I was at a golfing tournament with my daughter. My secretary called me on my car phone and said George Bush called twice that day. I told her to tell him to call me when I got to the office. A few minutes later my secretary again called to say Bush had called for the third time. When we finally spoke, he said he wanted to consider me. I asked for a day to discuss it with my wife, Marilyn; I called Bush the next day and told him it was okay. I knew it was serious, because there was no other reason for him to call me. I hadn't even endorsed him for president. I didn't know him all that well. I had been to his home a few times with other members of Congress, but to be candid, we weren't friends. We were from two different generations.

As the Republican Convention grew closer, I knew it was between Bob Dole and me. One morning I heard Dole being interviewed on TV, popping off about how undignified the whole process was of being considered for the second spot. When I heard that interview, I turned to Marilyn and said, "Well, that's it. I guess it's us." Bush called me and said he wanted to introduce me to a national audience in New Orleans [the GOP convention site]. Marilyn and I were unprepared for how our quiet lives were about to change. Suddenly we were surrounded by hordes of Secret Service agents and reporters. I wasn't really nervous about standing before the convention to deliver my acceptance speech. I was more pumped up than nervous. It was quite a night in my life. The rest, of course, is history.

Our conversation was interrupted when the van came to a stop at the former home of my in-laws (1521 Melwood in Glendale); tonight it would serve as the location of our joint event, but it also held another special memory for me—in 1988, my wife, Christine, and I exchanged our vows in the rear yard of that house.

Local Republican officials awaiting our arrival welcomed Dan as our van pulled up to the gate. We made our way inside through a thick crowd of supporters. When I introduced him to my family, he told Christine how important it was for me to run and win: "But you need to know how very different your lives will be once you go to Washington," he warned her.

Former vice president Dan Quayle campaigning for me, Glendale, California, October 19, 1996 (photo by William LaChasse)

After a forty-five-minute photo-op line, Dan and I went out to the rear yard, where a couple hundred supporters cheered for us when we emerged from the house. I introduced Dan, who gave a rousing stump speech on my behalf. His off-the-cuff remarks were light, fun, and very complimentary when urging my election to Congress. At the end of the program, television reporters awaited us for interviews.

Driving back to the airport, we continued our conversation about his career. I asked if on the day he became a freshman congressman he ever considered the possibility that he might be vice president one day. "No," he said. "But after two terms in the House, I grew bored. We were in the minority and didn't get to do very much. I decided to run for the Senate and move up or out. I ran against a very popular three-term incumbent, Birch Bayh. I beat him in the 'Reagan Revolution' of 1980, and then we Republicans were in the majority. It was much better. If you keep the Republican majority in the House in 1996, you will see what I mean.

"You'll find once you get to Congress that there is not a lot of raw talent back there," he told me. "You'll wonder for the first few months how you ever got there, then spend the rest of your life wondering how most of them got there!"

When we arrived at the airport, Dan gave me his new home telephone number: "Call me if I can do anything else for you. Also, have Christine call Marilyn; she'll tell her what to expect as a congressional wife." When I told him Christine would balk at picking up the phone and calling the former vice president's wife, he took my home number. "Then I'll have Marilyn call her," he said—and a few days later, she did.

I walked Dan back to his plane, shook his hand, and thanked him again for all the help. "I'll see you in Washington, Jim," he called out as he climbed aboard the flight back to Arizona. "You are in for the greatest time of your life!"

. . .

Once I got to Washington, I stayed in touch with Dan. He not only helped my races with a personal appearance and a fund-raiser; he also contributed financially to my campaign. After my work as a prosecutor in Bill Clinton's impeachment, when the national Democrats made me their number-one target for defeat in the 2000 election, Dan came out and addressed the California

Republican State Party convention. He opened his keynote dinner speech by signaling me out in the audience, calling me a hero for fighting for the rule of law, and led the cavernous hall in giving me a standing ovation.

The last time I spoke with Dan, he called to tell me he planned to run for the presidency in 2000 and asked for my support. My heart sank: I had committed already to Texas governor George W. Bush. I told Dan I picked Bush because I thought Bush could win the White House, and I didn't think Dan could overcome the obstacles he inherited, even though many of them were earned unfairly. He was gracious and said he understood.

In later years, I've often thought about that phone call. I don't think my political analysis was wrong, but I've wished I could relive the moment. If that were possible, I'd have endorsed Dan. I know my endorsement back then didn't mean anything to anyone else, but it meant something to Dan—because he thought enough about it to ask me for it personally.

Besides, as I noted in the opening chapter of my book on Clinton's impeachment (*Catching Our Flag*, WND Books, 2011), after being one of the first House members to endorse Bush, I met with him in Washington one week after the Clinton impeachment trial ended. Putting his arm around my shoulder, he filled me with praise: "You did a great job in the impeachment trial, Jimmy, and I'm really proud of you. I'm going to do all I can to help you win in 2000 and keep your seat." To cement our connection, Bush pulled me in closely and whispered in my ear, "You avenged my father," a reference to candidate Clinton defeating President George H. W. Bush in 1992. When we met again a few months later, Bush repeated the same theme with the same arm thrown around my shoulder. "I'll be there to help you," he pledged to me. "We'll have a great campaign. We'll campaign a lot together in your district."

During the 2000 general election campaign, Bush (by now the GOP presidential nominee) brought his campaign to my district twice. Both times, my reelection team organized the rallies and turned out the thousands of volunteers to greet him. Both times his campaign called at the last minute with a message from the governor: *he respects you deeply for your role in impeachment; you did the right thing; thanks for putting together the rally, but don't come:* "We don't want you at the rally, on the stage, or in the photograph," I was told. I honored each request, assuming it came from staff rather than from the grateful candidate who pledged to help me for doing the right, but unpopular, thing. Still, it stung later to learn that at each of those rallies, Bush stood on the stage and looked out upon a sea of hundreds of "Rogan for Congress" signs waving in his face. In all his speeches and press interviews in my district, Bush never once mentioned my name or asked anyone to help me. As someone told me later, "It was like he came into the district of a congressman under indictment."

When Dan Quayle pledged his support to help me, he followed through on every level. He stood by me.

I should have done the same for him.

43

Vignettes from the Mailbox

W hen I was a kid, I not only spent years pestering famous politicians for autographs, advice, and information about their careers when we met in person; when I couldn't meet them, I did it through the mail. Back in 1968 (when I was eleven), I wrote President Lyndon Johnson and asked for an autograph. I never thought a president would write me back, but he did. Soon the postman delivered mail to me almost daily from someone who at one time was a major player in Washington.

As time went by, I took advantage of these opportunities to ask my subjects to share memories of the people and events from their past. The hundreds of responses I got over the decades have, for the most part, been donated to archivists at the US Congress or to The Richard Nixon Presidential Library Foundation. I kept a small selection of them, however, and some favorites that remain are included in this chapter. Writing this book now gives me a chance to impart these stories–some of which came from people alive when Ulysses S. Grant was still considered presidential timber.

. . .

Over the years, I asked a number of former political leaders to share their recollections of the various presidents they knew and with whom they served.[1]

---

[1]   I left the capitalization and punctuation in these letters as the various authors used it.

Senator John Sparkman (D-AL) (1899–1985), the 1952 running mate of Democratic presidential nominee Adlai E. Stevenson, served in Congress from 1937 to 1979. He offered these insights of President John F. Kennedy's inauguration, over which he presided as the cochair of the 1961 Presidential Inaugural Committee:

> I have very clear memories of the Inaugural of President Kennedy. On the morning of the Inaugural Day I went by the home of Speaker Rayburn of the House of Representatives and he and I went together to the home of President-elect and Mrs. Kennedy in Georgetown. We took them in the car with us to the White House for a courtesy call on President Eisenhower, after which we went to the Capitol together.
>
> At the Capital Mrs. Sparkman and I gave a luncheon for the new President and Mrs. Kennedy and others closely connected with the inauguration. Following the luncheon we went to the Inaugural Stand, where first Vice President Lyndon Johnson was administered the oath of office, followed by the Chief Justice of the United States administering the oath to President Kennedy. Following the inauguration President Kennedy delivered the Inaugural Address. It was one of the most beautiful speeches I ever heard in which he pronounced that lasting statement "Ask not what your country can do for you, ask what you can do for your country."
>
> Following the luncheon and the Inaugural I escorted President and Mrs. Kennedy to the White House for the Inaugural Parade. I knew President Kennedy quite well, having served with him in the Senate. We were good friends and I respected him highly. President Kennedy sent me a large photograph in color showing our ride together in the parade. The photograph was signed by both President and Mrs. Kennedy. The President wrote on the photograph: "John, you got us into all of this."[2]

Senator Burton K. Wheeler (D-MT) (1882–1975), the 1924 running mate of Progressive Party presidential nominee Robert M. LaFollette, served in the US Senate from 1923 to 1947. When I received this letter from him, his secretary paper-clipped a little note to it and apologized for his signature. She said Wheeler was blind and in his nineties; he dictated the letter to her, and he

---

2   April 14, 1970

insisted on signing it for me personally. She said she had to place his hand on the paper so he would know where to pen his name:

> I knew a good many candidates for the Presidency, but not too many Presidents. I met Harding in Butte, Montana when he was on his way to Alaska. I was introduced to him as a newly elected Senator. He said, "I don't know whether to congratulate you or to commiserate with you!" He died on that trip. He was a weak President.
>
> I knew Calvin Coolidge. He was honest and made a good President considering the problems that he had to face at that time, which were somewhat minor compared to those of today.
>
> I knew Herbert Hoover. He was an able individual, but a very poor politician, and as a result wasn't a very successful President. I talked with him as I did with President Coolidge on a number of occasions.
>
> I knew President Roosevelt. I was the first Senator to come out publicly for his nomination. He was a master politician and knew how to manipulate various groups and play them like a master musician. He advocated some very fine legislation. I handled quite a good deal of it including the Utility Holding Company Bill which I put through the Senate with one vote. I handled the Wheeler-Case bill, the Wheeler-Howard Bill and the Transportation Act of 1940, in addition to some other minor bills for him. A great many people said I hated him because I disagreed with him on the Court fight and on the war issue. I didn't hate him. Personally I liked him. He had a charming personality. On one occasion William Randolph Hearst was criticizing him to me and I said, "Why don't you go to see him." He said, "I am afraid to. Everybody who goes to see him gets taken right in."
>
> I was selected by the Democrats and Republicans who were opposed to Roosevelt's program of packing the Supreme Court, and I led the fight against it, and we succeeded in defeating the legislation. That was his most serious defeat during the time he was President. After that in 1939 he sent for me and asked me to handle the Railroad Transportation Act. I finally agreed to do so and it became known as the Transportation Act of 1940. After that I disagreed with Roosevelt on the war issue. I said that I was opposed to getting into the war unless we were attacked. Of course when Japan attacked us, I said we would have to lick them. There was no question but what Roosevelt wanted to get us into the war. Even Churchill, in some of his memoirs, said that in his conversations with Roosevelt, Roosevelt assured him that we would get in even if he had to create an incident.

I knew Truman intimately. I was Chairman of the Senate Interstate and Foreign Commerce Committee and he was a new member. And he would tell you today if he were alive that I helped him when he first came there more than anybody else. He was a close friend of mine at all times. He was not a great Senator but was looked upon as one who belonged to the lower echelon.

I knew Eisenhower. He had a wonderful personality and I felt he made a good President, not a brilliant one.

I knew Nixon but only casually. I think he did right in resigning. It was hard for me to believe much that was said about him until after his admission that he had lied to Congress, to the people and to his own lawyers. I know President Ford just casually. I know very little about [Ford's nominee for vice president, Nelson] Rockefeller except that he is a very rich man, and that he was elected and reelected as Governor of New York. I don't know of any reason why he shouldn't be confirmed.[3]

Senator Claude Pepper (D-FL) (1900–1989) served in the US Senate from 1936 to 1951, when he lost a primary for reelection. Pepper returned to Congress in 1963 as a member of the House of Representatives, where he served until his death in 1989:

I came to the Senate at the beginning of the second term of President Roosevelt and enjoyed a close and warm friendship with him. I think he was one of our few greatest Presidents. What he did to save our country from economic collapse, to build the forces of freedom in the world, and to win World War II, was a monumental achievement. It could not have been excelled by anyone. His impact upon our government and nation will long endure.

President Truman, as Churchill said, deserves much commendation for his ability to make decisions and to take and maintain firm positions. He did not accomplish in the domestic field as much as Roosevelt or Johnson, but in general he pursued a wise and aggressive course. He made some mistakes in foreign affairs, as when he, after World War II, failed to support the efforts of many people in Southeast Asia to keep the French from going back into Vietnam as a colonial power. If that had happened, we might not have had the tragedy of Vietnam that we are lamenting today.

President Johnson achieved more in domestic policy than any other Presi-

---

3   April 5, 1974, and October 7, 1974

dent except Roosevelt, his friend and mentor, but he made a tragic mistake in enlarging the war in Vietnam and in fighting it–or allowing the generals to fight it the way we did.

President Eisenhower was an honorable man, but having no experience in politics did not achieve, as President, comparable to his achievements as Commander of the Allied Forces in World War II.

President Nixon's record and character are well known to you without my having to make any comment. His influence upon public life in America has been vastly contaminated. President Ford is an honorable and candid man who means well. It's too early to make an appraisal of his Presidency.[4]

Senator Margaret Chase Smith (R-ME) (1897–1985) served in Congress from 1940 to 1973, becoming the first woman in America to serve in both houses. She ran unsuccessfully for the 1964 Republican presidential nomination:

My first opportunity to meet a president was when I visited Washington as a graduate from Skowhegan High School in 1916 and was introduced to and shook hands with President Wilson. I met President Coolidge but I knew Mrs. Coolidge personally. It was my privilege to have dinner with President Herbert Hoover at his home in the 1960s. He called personally one day and asked if I would do this as he would like to talk with me. The only other person present was one of his assistants. I was a great admirer of President Hoover and this meant a great deal to me.

As you know, the Roosevelts spent a great deal of time in Maine at their summer home in Campobello, now a part of the international conference center. He gave us much to be thankful for when he showed the vision and courage necessary to bring us out of that deep, deep depression.

President Truman, a longtime member of the US Senate and an historian, gave us much to be thankful for in as much as he was an historian, studied issues confronting him, making decisions that he remained with. President Kennedy was an attractive young man; but because of his assassination, had too little service to be judged. President Johnson was one of the outstanding leaders of the US Senate.[5]

---

4   April 30, 1975

5   July 1, 1991

Senator Charles McC. Mathias (R-MD) (1922–2010) served in Congress from 1961 to 1987:

> About my recollections of presidents, I might start with the first I met, Calvin Coolidge. In February 1929, when I was six years old, my father drove from Frederick, Maryland, to pay a farewell call on President Coolidge before he left the White House on March 4th. It is a commentary on the changing times that presidents then had the leisure for such social courtesies. He took me with him and on the trip tried to explain why we were going to visit. When I heard that the President was moving I asked if his furniture was packed. No, my father replied, a president took only his "wardrobe" when he left the White House. To me, at that age, a wardrobe was a massive mahogany cupboard and I pictured the President struggling with it. When we reached the Oval Office the early spring sunlight was flooding the green carpet, which I can still see with the inward eye. I do not recall the conversation except that when we were leaving my father started in the wrong direction. I can plainly hear Coolidge's clipped Yankee voice saying "Please go out the other door."
>
> My introduction to President Herbert Hoover took place a relatively short time later under very different circumstances. The President's full name was Herbert Clark Hoover and the Clark family had lived on a farm in Carroll County, Maryland. Since the site was a short distance from Washington the President wanted to visit the house of his ancestors which he had never seen. My father had helped to make the local arrangements so he was invited to join the President's party. We met the White House limousine at the designated rendezvous where Mrs. Hoover invited me to ride with her and the President to the Clark farm. Sometime later the President sent me one of the then new, smaller size dollar bills which he had autographed and which I still have. Because Frederick, Maryland, is situated between Washington and Shangri-La (now Camp David), I had occasional glimpses of President Roosevelt and President Truman. Beginning with President Eisenhower, I have had substantial contact with every succeeding president up to George Bush. Those stories will have to wait, however, for another occasion.[6]

Senator Charles Percy (R-IL) (1919–2011) served in the US Senate from 1967 to 1985, when he lost a bid for reelection. Often mentioned as a potential presi-

---

6   July 3, 1991

dential or vice presidential candidate, Percy never sought national office. He wrote me of two presidents with whom he was intimate (Eisenhower and Ford), and then threw in for good measure his recollections of meeting the legendary prime minister of Great Britain, Winston Churchill:

In 1958, I was President of Bell & Howell Company, and I was the Illinois state finance chairman of the Republican National Committee. The election year of 1958 had not been a good one for the Republican Party, and we were concerned about what we could do to rebuild our party. Following the election, I decided I needed a vacation, so I was skiing in Sun Valley, Idaho when I received a telegram from President Eisenhower asking me to attend a meeting of Republican leaders at the White House early in 1959. Our group met with the President, and when he asked for suggestions, I proposed that we set up a Commission on National Goals. The Commission would be headed by a prominent person, and the members would be selected from both Republican and Democratic parties. Once the goals were outlined, the Republican Party could establish a committee that would indicate how Republicans thought they might achieve those goals. I also hoped that the Democrats would do the same. I thought that this would be good for the country and that the committees could come up with an answer to the question "Where should we be as a nation by 1976–our bicentennial?"

President Eisenhower was enthusiastic and invited me back to the White House the next day. It turned out that he was working on his State of the Union message and wanted to add to it a request to set up the Commission on National Goals. We spent the day working on this part of his speech, and after we had finished, he invited me back to the White House residence section for a friendly chat. I'll never forget that talk we had together, because it was then that I became aware of the President's humility and learned of his loyalty. He was talking about his brother Milton Eisenhower, who was President of Johns Hopkins University. President Eisenhower put his arm around my shoulder and said, "Milton is the brightest of the Eisenhower brothers. He was the one who really should have been President, not I." He also made me an offer, and over the years I learned of his loyalty. He told me that he hoped that I would run for public office myself one day, and that he would support me "be it the highest office in the land." He truly meant it and did indeed support my political career through the years.

The State of the Union message was given, and it included a request for the Commission. President Eisenhower asked me to head the Commission, but I had to refuse. I was too much of a Republican to head a non-partisan group such as this, though I gladly accepted his invitation to be the Chairman of the Republican Committee on Programs and Progress. This was the group that published a report on what we thought our party ought to do to achieve the goals of the Commission. After nine months of work, our report, "Decisions for a Better America," was published. I have always thought it was my work on this Committee that caused me to be named Chairman of the 1960 Platform Committee of the Republican National Convention which led to my full-time entry into politics.

I first met Jerry Ford in Peoria, Illinois in 1949, when we were both elected as two of The Ten Outstanding Young Men of the Year by the United States Junior Chamber of Commerce. He has proved the wisdom of their choice since then. His 1976 campaign theme of candor, honesty and openness is exactly the theme that I think deserves high priority.

Both Jerry and I look upon a swimming pool, lake, ocean or river as the best possible place for exercise, and both of us would like to be able to swim every day of our lives. The exception was when Jerry became President and had to leave his home, which had a pool, to move to the White House where President Nixon had removed the pool. While he was waiting for a new White House pool to be completed, I mentioned to Jerry that as I swam in my own small pool in Georgetown, I said to myself, "Now, if I lived at 1600 Pennsylvania Avenue, I wouldn't be able to do this."

Winston Churchill was the most impressive foreign politician that I ever met. I never knew him during his term in office, but I met him later in Washington when he came to visit President Eisenhower. I also once found myself seated next to Churchill on a plane flying from London to the south of France. I told him that years before, a London collector of rare books had put together a complete set of all of the writings of Winston Churchill, from his earliest work to his latest, and had bound these in red leather. I had bought the complete set which was my most treasured possession, because as a public official it inspired me. But, I admitted to him that the stories of his early difficulties in school had also been a source of great satisfaction to my son Roger, who early in life was not particularly a good student either. I recalled that he had told of doing so poorly in school that he was not permitted to continue in Greek. He was required instead to continue his courses in English. I mentioned that he had concluded his autobiography with the words "Thank God I was forced to learn how to speak and write the English language." I told him that many of us were also appreciative of this. A smile settled over his face as he seemed to reflect upon his love of the English language and what he had done with it over the years to advance his own political cause and to save his beloved England.[7]

Stansfield Turner (1923–), a retired admiral and former director of the CIA, shared this recollection of his mentor and former Annapolis classmate, President Jimmy Carter:

> In December of 1974, I was passing through Atlanta on Navy business. I asked for and had an appointment with then-Governor Jimmy Carter, who had been a classmate at the Naval Academy many years before. What impressed me first about our meeting was that it took him only about one minute to dispense with the normal pleasantries of "How are you" and "What have you been doing." For the next 29 minutes he interrogated me up and down about the state of our military preparedness. What he was doing was stretching my thinking into areas I had not considered, but which would be of concern to a president. It was an exciting and challenging experience for me, one that left me mentally drained at the end.
>
> At the completion of my thirty-minute interview, the Governor led me to the door, and as we parted said he wanted me to know that in two days he would be declaring his candidacy for the presidency. I said "Good luck, Jimmy" and left with very little thought that he would actually become president. Nor did I have the slightest idea that his becoming president would change my life in the dramatic way it did—from Admiral to Chief of the CIA.[8]

. . .

I corresponded over the years with many former candidates for the presidency and their running mates. A few recollections of historic campaigns of bygone days follow.

As noted earlier, Senator Burton K. Wheeler ran as the 1924 vice presidential nominee of the Progressive Party along with presidential candidate Robert M. LaFollette (1855–1925). Although losing to the Republican nominees Calvin Coolidge and Charles Dawes, the LaFollette–Wheeler ticket carried Wisconsin and 17 percent of the popular vote against Coolidge and Democratic nominee

---

7   August 30, 1991

8   July 31, 1991

John W. Davis. A few months before his death at age ninety-two, Wheeler shared this vignette from the 1924 race:

> To recall the events during the 1924 LaFollette–Wheeler Progressive Party campaign would take too long, but I did open the campaign on the Boston Commons. LaFollette and his friends felt that the man they had to beat was [Democratic Party nominee] John W. Davis. I disagreed with him and told him the man he had to beat was Calvin Coolidge, and I insisted that my first speech in the campaign would be my attack upon the Republican Party and the candidate, which I did in my opening speech, and I continued to do so throughout the campaign.
>
> LaFollette thought that we would be elected, but I never felt we would, and I told him that we would be lucky to get 5 million votes. We were given close to 5 million, but in some places our votes were not even counted.[9]

In an earlier chapter, I shared my story of calling multiple times on the telephone former Kansas governor Alf M. Landon (1887–1987), the 1936 GOP presidential nominee vanquished by Franklin Roosevelt in his drive toward a second term. Landon offered these thoughts regarding his 1936 battle:

> I am sorry I do not have any campaign literature or materials to spare. I did not save it at the time, and am only now making a collection for my own grandchildren. [Author's note: a few years after Landon's death, a grandchild sold at auction the collection Landon had assembled–so much for family sentimentality.]
>
> I made three main issues in 1936 that are still hot ones: First, that inflation was like a whirlpool and, once we got sucked into it, it would keep getting bigger and bigger all the time. Second, the political corollary of a planned economy meant increased centralization of political power in the national government. Third, [we] need a long-range national land use policy.
>
> I made the usual "swing around the circle" as it was called then, in a special train from coast to coast. I had many visits with President Roosevelt.[10]
>
> [Today, at age 84] I am feeling fit as a fiddle. I go horse-back riding three or four mornings a week for between four and six miles.[11]

---

9   April 5, 1974

10   December 12, 1974

11   August 16, 1971

The 1936 GOP presidential nominee, Alf Landon, wrote out and signed for me his presidential campaign slogan: "That leadership along the trail which we have loved long since, and lost awhile, has come to us again."

The man who helped crush Landon's presidential ambitions was Roosevelt's national campaign manager–political kingmaker James A. Farley (1888–1976). Before FDR's White House run, Farley managed the New York gubernatorial campaigns of Al Smith in 1922 (Smith became the 1928 Democratic presidential nominee), and Roosevelt in 1928 and 1930. Farley was a one-man political dynamo; he revolutionized polling data, and cobbled together the religious and ethnic coalitions that form the base of the modern Democratic Party to this day. During Roosevelt's first two terms, Farley served simultaneously as the chairman of the Democratic National Committee as well as in FDR's cabinet as postmaster general. Considered a presidential dark horse candidate himself in the 1940 election cycle, Farley and Roosevelt's relationship dissolved that year when FDR broke the two-term tradition every previous president respected.

Farley wrote and told me his side of the famous schism between the two former allies and longtime friends:

I disagreed with President Roosevelt on the third term and resigned as Postmaster General. He resented this very much and I only saw him on a few occasions after I retired as Postmaster General the last week in August, 1940. I did support him openly in 1940 and 1944, although I did not make any speeches, but everyone knew that as a regular Democrat, I would support the Democratic candidate.

I was never a candidate for the presidency–there was no boom for me, but the Gallup Polls will show that I was always second to Mr. Hull [FDR's first Secretary of State] . . . I was for Secretary of State, Cordell Hull for President.[12]

Another leader left in the dust by the Roosevelt campaign juggernaut was Ohio governor and US senator John W. Bricker (1893–1986), the 1944 GOP vice presidential running mate of New York governor Thomas E. Dewey. Running for a fourth and final term, Roosevelt beat the Dewey–Bricker ticket (four years later, Dewey again stood as the GOP nominee and lost the presidency to Harry Truman). Bricker gave me these observations on his 1944 campaign:

My name came before the 1944 Republican Convention originally as a candidate for the nomination for president. A combination of New York and California and other states that were subject largely to New York control prevented my having the number of delegates to be nominated. I did know most of the Republican leaders of the country and did accept at their insistence the nomination for vice president. I had no reaction [to my nomination] because I was advised beforehand how it would come out. I was willing to do what I could for the Party and what I believed to be in the best interest of the country. I therefore accepted nomination for the vice presidency and campaigned vigorously for the election.[13]

Mr. Dewey should have won in 1948, but the 1944 campaign was a very difficult one against Mr. Roosevelt in the middle of a war. We did carry Ohio for Mr. Dewey in 1944 and he lost it in 1948.

Mr. Roosevelt was a very appealing man. In fact, he invited me on his train when he visited Ohio rather than the Democratic candidate against whom I was running. We both later carried the state.[14]

---

12   December 20, 1971

13   June 21, 1972

14   February 3, 1975

Historians debate to this day whether John F. Kennedy actually defeated Richard Nixon for the presidency in 1960. In the closest election in American history, official results showed Kennedy's victory margin was just 0.1 percent. With allegations of chicanery pouring out of Chicago and other key areas, Republican leaders nationwide demanded that Nixon contest the results formally in the hours and days following the balloting.

Herbert G. Klein (1918–2009) was Nixon's campaign press secretary that year. (Klein later served as press secretary for Nixon's 1962 race for governor of California, national communications manager for Nixon's presidential campaign of 1968, and White House communications director in the Nixon administration.) When I asked Klein why Nixon chose ultimately not to contest the election, he wrote and shared the backstory on that subject that he said was little known by most people:

> On the Saturday following the 1960 election, I was in Key Biscayne with Nixon and Bob Finch and then-Col. James D. Hughes and our wives. The full impact of "officially" losing the election to Senator John Kennedy finally had settled in. [Nixon] was too depressed for conversation.
>
> We went to dinner at a local restaurant, and as we arrived the maître'd told me there was a call for Vice President Nixon. I took the call which was from former President Herbert Hoover. Joe Kennedy [JFK's father] had called him to find out if the Vice President would accept a call from Senator Kennedy [which led ultimately] to a meeting between the two. The former President gave me the President-elect's telephone number in Palm Beach.
>
> I gave the message to Mr. Nixon and he immediately perked up and began discussing the problems of a country divided by a 50-50 vote. He then went to a public phone booth and called President Eisenhower in Augusta, GA. About this time the maître'd's phone rang and I picked it up, and it was John Kennedy. We had a conversation while Mr. Nixon talked to President Eisenhower. Senator Kennedy complimented me on my work. Five minutes later, Mr. Nixon called Senator Kennedy and arranged a meeting for the following Monday.
>
> The Vice President then decided not to prolong the turmoil by challenging the election results. [Later, Nixon and Kennedy] met in Key Biscayne and made plans to preserve national unity between the future President and the new leader of the loyal opposition.[15]

---

15   December 3, 1991

In another of America's closest elections, Nixon came out on top when he squeaked by Hubert Humphrey in 1968 by a mere 0.7 percent. Hubert Humphrey's running mate that year, Senator Edmund S. Muskie (1914–1996), went on to serve as secretary of state under President Jimmy Carter.

1968 Democratic vice presidential nominee Edmund Muskie with me, Washington, DC, September 1975

After he retired from politics, Muskie sent me this wonderful handwritten letter sharing the story of how Humphrey selected him for the second spot on the 1968 Democratic ticket:

> Hubert first indicated his interest in a flight from Washington to Maine to attend the Maine Democratic Convention in May 1968. I was surprised and flattered but skeptical that political realities would permit him to choose a running mate from a small state like Maine.
>
> I remained skeptical until the day after his own nomination in Chicago. He asked me to come to his room in the Conrad Hilton Hotel. The invitation convinced me that I was about to be selected—which of course proved to be the case.

As to my reaction, I was exhilarated and enthusiastic–notwithstanding the depressing events of the convention. We ended the campaign in the same spirit–and almost won! It was one of the greatest experiences of my life to be associated with Hubert Humphrey in such a venture![16]

First page of Senator Edmund Muskie's letter to me, describing how he became the 1968 Democratic vice presidential nominee, December 9, 1982.

---

16   December 9, 1982

Another close election occurred in 1976 between President Gerald Ford and former Georgia governor Jimmy Carter. Ford lost to Carter by only 2 percent; to his dying day, Ford blamed former governor Ronald Reagan's GOP primary challenge for costing him the election.

Before he became president, Reagan wrote me several letters regarding his 1976 challenge to Ford. The final in the series included a curious denial of what he wrote me in the first letter!

Two weeks after President Nixon resigned the presidency and Vice President Gerald Ford succeeded him, Reagan pledged his support to Ford for a full term in 1976:

> Since President Ford is our Party's new standard bearer who will undoubtedly run for re-election in 1976, I have no intention of challenging him for the nomination. It's never been more important for us to stand united; only so we can heal the wounds of Watergate and enhance our chances for an election victory. I am confident a Republican can win... in the next presidential election.[17]

A year later, things had changed dramatically. Now as a former governor, Reagan wrote me from his home in Pacific Palisades:

> Dear Jim,
> It was good to hear from you and I'm particularly grateful for your expression of support for my possible candidacy for national office. While the decision will be down the road a ways, the Committee which has recently been established in Washington will be a great aid to me in my assessment of who can best lead the Party to victory in '76 and lead the nation beyond that. If we use a scale from 1 to 10, I would say I'm an "8" in leaning toward seeking the nomination. I want to thank you for your kind offer of assistance if and when the time should come.[18]

After Reagan declared his candidacy against Ford in late 1975, I again wrote Reagan at his private address and asked him various questions about the

---

17   August 22, 1974

18   September 5, 1975

campaign. In one query, I quoted directly what he'd written me in 1974 about planning to support Ford, and asked him how he reconciled the abandonment of that pledge. I assumed that if Reagan made the statement to me privately, he had also made it to others publicly–and the press would grill him over it. Instead of getting an explanation, I got a denial. In a two-page letter dictated while on the campaign trail, Reagan wrote:

> First of all, I do not remember having made a statement pledging to support President Ford unequivocally. What I did say on several occasions was that I'd hoped and prayed that he'd do such a good job that my candidacy would not even be necessary and, as most Americans, I was sincere in giving President Ford my complete support when he took over the awesome duties of the Presidency. That was a year and a half ago. In the meantime, however, as all the public opinion polls have indicated, the rank and file of our party does not seem convinced that he is our party's best choice as standard bearer. My decision to challenge him for the nomination was only made after talking with people all over the country and being convinced that my candidacy would give them a voice in the coming primary elections.
>
> Number 2: 1976 is an unusual year. President Ford was appointed to the job by a man who left office in disgrace. As a matter of fact, President Ford has never won or even run in a statewide election. I intend to run in almost all of the primary states, all of which I will try my best to win. How many victories are essential to my own campaign, I don't know.
>
> Number 3: I'm not interested in the vice presidency nor am I interested in leading a third party ticket. If I get nominated, I will look for a running mate who shares my philosophy.
>
> And, number 4: It's hard to say which of the Democratic contenders would be the most formidable but I do think Hubert Humphrey has the best chance of being nominated. I do feel he can be defeated by a Republican.[19]

My friend, former Massachusetts governor Mike Dukakis, shared this comment regarding what it was like for him to stand before the cheering delegates as he accepted the Democratic presidential nomination in 1988:

---

19   January 14, 1976

The Atlanta convention was a very special day for me, for Kitty and for our family. It was the culmination of over a year's work; thousands of hours of campaigning, and the coming together of so many of the people who put their hearts and souls into our primary effort. Would that we had done the same effective job in the final! Unfortunately, we peaked in Atlanta. But it was a great moment, one made even more poignant by the memories of my Dad, who would have been so proud of his son and of his adopted country.[20]

. . .

Within weeks of George McGovern's loss to Richard Nixon in November 1972, the Watergate scandal started unraveling; in August 1974, Nixon resigned the presidency in disgrace. A few leaders from that time shared their opinions with me on the unprecedented wound from which America sought to recover.

US senator Sam Ervin (1896–1985) served in the Senate from 1954 to 1974. He worked on two historic investigative committees: the hearings in 1954 that led to the downfall of Senator Joseph McCarthy and—most notably—he chaired the Senate's investigative "Watergate Committee," uncovering information that helped lead to Nixon's resignation. After he retired from Congress, Ervin wrote me from his home in Morganton, North Carolina: "While the Watergate was a great tragedy, it eventually taught the American people that we have the wisest system of government on earth. It particularly shows the wisdom of the Founding Fathers in separating the powers of the President, the Congress, and the courts. When the president proved faithless to his constitutional obligations, the Congress and the courts remained faithful to theirs."[21]

The man Nixon defeated narrowly for the presidency in 1968, Hubert H. Humphrey (1911–1978), offered this insight in a letter dated just a few weeks after Nixon's resignation:

I believe Mr. Nixon's resignation was in the best interests of the Nation. We must now turn to the duty of solving the difficult problems before us. The responsibility for governing, the task of rebuilding faith in government and confidence in our political institutions now belong to Gerald Ford and the Congress. I have pledged my full cooperation in achieving these goals.

---

20   April 23, 1992

21   February 1, 1983

These have been difficult times for our country. We should take this time to reflect on the meaning of these events, but we as a Nation should not despair, because the Constitution has met and survived one of its greatest tests. We should have pride in our political system, and vow to preserve the traditions which have been upheld.[22]

Alf Landon, the 1936 GOP presidential nominee who addressed Nixon's nominating convention I attended in 1972, offered this terse assessment: "I said from the first that Watergate was a scandal that must be cleaned to the bone. It is—not only by President Nixon's resignation, but also the judicial proceedings covering all the parties involved in that stupid and disgraceful criminal affair."[23]

Two days before Nixon resigned, the House and Senate Republican leadership—Senate GOP minority leader Hugh Scott, House GOP minority leader John Rhodes, and former GOP presidential nominee Barry Goldwater—trekked from the Capitol to the White House for a private meeting with Nixon. The press later reported that the trio demanded Nixon's resignation for the good of the country and the GOP. In a letter to me dated just three weeks after that historic meeting, Congressman Rhodes (1916–2003) discounted the media's version: "[T]he meeting of August 7 was set up at the President's request so that Senator Hugh Scott, Senator Barry Goldwater, and I could apprise him of the impeachment situation in the Congress. The meeting was relatively brief, as the President seemed to have a fairly accurate view of his own situation and only wanted us to confirm his impressions, which we did. At no point did we discuss the President's options. His decision to resign was one which he arrived at on his own."[24]

After Nixon signed his resignation letter and bade the White House staff good-bye on August 9, 1974, he boarded *Air Force One* for the final, lonely ride back to California. Accompanying him on that flight into exile was his White House press secretary, Ronald Ziegler (1939–2003). Almost two decades later, Ziegler wrote me and described that trip home and its aftermath:

---

22   September 24, 1974

23   December 12, 1974

24   August 28, 1974

I was one of the first men that President Nixon told that he had made the decision to resign his office. He said it was clear that he had lost the ability to lead the people of his country. Leadership in a democracy is grounded on freely received public support. President Nixon knew that because of "Watergate" he had lost the ability to obtain or rally support for his presidency. He felt it was time to remove the turmoil surrounding this tragic episode from the agenda of the nation's leadership. . . .

I flew out to San Clemente and into self-imposed exile, with President Nixon, in 1974. I did not know what to expect–how this man who had been disgraced, who had resigned from office, would deal with that circumstance.

The first morning in San Clemente, I looked out the office window of what was called the Western White House, and saw former President Nixon walking across the compound from his home in a suit and tie. Not in a sport shirt, nor unshaven, not beleaguered, however, obviously feeling and showing the strain of the terrible position that he had placed himself in and the agony he felt because of it.

He began to use his mind in a disciplined way, focusing on his shortcomings, the mistakes of his administration, analyzing his own actions and the actions of other men. He talked about his achievements. He looked back–to learn from his shortcomings how he could strengthen himself, on a personal basis. He chose to survive and not to destroy himself. I learned from that experience that no matter how extensive an individual's humiliation or failure might be, that only they can destroy themselves. President Nixon clearly chose not to. Today he has written seven excellent books on foreign policy and on politics, is listened to as he speaks out from time to time on national and world affairs, and is living a quiet and healthy life in the East, enjoying his grandchildren.

I have always felt very fortunate to have had the opportunity to serve our Country in that capacity. It was also a privilege to be able to know a leader of our country on such a personal level. The President was always most considerate of and interested in my family and my own activities. The opportunities made available, knowledge gained and lessons learned have helped to shape my life both personally and professionally.[25]

---

25   July 17, 1991

. . .

A number of former Members of Congress wrote and shared recollections and advice for a budding young political aficionado:

E. L. Mecham (R-NM) (1912–2002) served as the fifteenth, seventeenth, and nineteenth governor of New Mexico; after he lost his bid for reelection in 1962, Senator Dennis Chavez died suddenly and Mecham appointed himself to the vacant Senate seat. Defeated for election to the term in 1964, he retired to New Mexico until President Nixon appointed him to the federal bench. Mecham shared this humorous anecdote–as well as a rare historical artifact for my collection:

> The only memento I have of my time in the Senate–two years–is a pen that was used by President Johnson to sign the legislation creating the [1964] Civil Rights Act. [Author's note: in 2000, I sent this historic pen to the Smithsonian's American History Museum in Washington, where it has remained on continuous display since.]
>
> I was a peon at the time, being next to the last in seniority on the Republican side, and filling out the unexpired term of the late Senator Dennis Chavez with slight expectation by anyone of election. The Senate timetable was heavily burdened by the civil rights and federal aid to education legislation. I was also trying to mount an election campaign and spend as much time as possible in New Mexico without neglecting the Senate business, so I did miss out on quite a bit of the side play, significant and otherwise.
>
> Two of the more lasting memories are Ralph Yarborough's efforts to get a quorum for a subcommittee hearing to start consideration of the civil rights legislation. He would call a session with no quorum, get on the phone, send pages, and even go into the hall to try to find a subcommittee member to lure in. One such was Strom Thurmond who was resistant to Ralph's effort to pull him into the session. Strom decided the invitation had gone far enough so he offered to wrestle Ralph in the hall of the beautiful Old Senate Office Building, with the loser to abide by the wishes of the other. Ralph agreed and Strom then threw him in about three seconds. Ralph complained that Strom had a head start and wanted another fall. Strom agreed and quickly threw Ralph again, helped him up, brushed him off, and walked away.
>
> The other was after the Supreme Court's opinion banning prayer in public schools. The rumor went around that it would be applied to the Senate. At the opening of the next [Senate session], after prayer, Dick Russell and

Everett Dirksen, the [Democratic and Republican Party] leaders, went down on their knees in the well of the Senate chambers facing the Supreme Court Building and began to Salaam Oh Ye Mighty Supreme Court. [Here was] one time the Senate rule against cameras and recording was soundly abused.[26]

House Speaker John W. McCormack (D-MA) (1891–1980) served in Congress from 1928 until his retirement in 1971. I wrote him often, and he always replied in longhand with a steep right vertical slant to his penmanship. On a beautiful engraved vignette of the US Capitol, McCormack penned for me his congressional philosophy: "Sometimes I think it might be well if we erect a large sign over Congress which contains this thought: 'Here the opinions of all Americans are heard and should be heard with equality.' As a result, the sense of their principles becomes the law of the land. And perhaps we should put it in more typical common language: 'Here your two cents does make a difference!'"[27]

Former US senator Sam J. Ervin, University of San Francisco, February 1975

---

26   July 3, 1991

27   August 30, 1973

I was a teenager when I met Senator Sam Ervin in 1975 (the Senate Watergate Committee chairman), and I took a photograph of him addressing a college audience. Later, when I mailed the picture to him for his autograph, I mentioned I hoped to go to law school one day. Ervin returned the photograph to this future lawyer with his advice inscribed on the border: "My father, who was an active practitioner at the North Carolina Bar for sixty-five years, gave me this sage advice: 'Salt down the facts; the law will keep.'"

. . .

One letter in my archives came from an unlikely writer: James Earl Ray (1928–1998), the convicted assassin of Dr. Martin Luther King, Jr. Decades after King's murder, when I was a county prosecutor, I read an interview with Ray where he appeared to disclaim responsibility for the dastardly shooting. I wrote him at Brushy Mountain Prison in Tennessee and asked if he now denied responsibility for King's murder. I never expected a reply, but a couple of weeks later, a typed letter on a sheet of yellow legal paper arrived at my office, with the bold signature of King's killer at the end:

> 5 July 1988
> Inmate #65477
> Petros, TN 37845
>
> In re to the MLK case, I've denies [*sic*] responsibility before the courts, and before the Congressional Committee that investigated the case. I don't deny or admit anything to the news media since I don't think I owe the media any explanations about anything. I know the newspapers quoted me as denying responsibility last April but that was their own words. Most everything (records), connected with the case have been classified, e.g., the Congressional Committee classified 185 cubic feet of its files following the investigation. . . .
>
> I worked on a book about the case for five years then let an editor finish it up. I've enclosed a clipping about it in case you or anyone would be interested in it.[28] [Author's note: a few months later, a package came to my office from Brushy Mountain Prison. Ray had sent me an inscribed copy of his book on

---

28   July 5, 1988

the Martin Luther King assassination; it remains perhaps one of the most macabre and peculiar volumes in my personal library.]

. . .

I'll close this chapter with a couple of favorites. One letter came from the legendary entertainer Bing Crosby (1903–1977). I grew up a fan of Crosby's records, movies, and television specials. My favorite Crosby vehicles were the classic "Road" films he did with partner Bob Hope (made between 1940 and 1962). When I grew up in San Francisco, Crosby lived in a mansion in nearby Hillsborough. I saw him in concert twice. Near the end of his life, I wrote him a letter, told him I was a fan, and sent him a set of photographs I took at his 1976 live concert with his family. He wrote me a delightful reply:

> Thanks for your letter. I am pleased to know you have been a longtime supporter of mine, and also of the work of my erstwhile partner, Mr. Hope. He's a very deserving lad, and I like to hear nice things said about him, because it encourages him in his work!
>
> Glad to know that you have some of my albums, also. You asked me what my favorite "Road" picture is. I guess I would have to say "The Road to Utopia." Had some good songs in it, and I thought some of the gags–particularly the visual gags–were quite well conceived and executed.
>
> Also glad you liked "Going My Way." [Crosby received the Best Actor Oscar for his performance in that film]. That was a big boost for me and my career. Of course, the big thing that happened to me was Irving Berlin writing a song called "White Christmas." This really has been a sustaining influence for me and for my work. . . . I hope this finds you in good health and spirits. Always your friend, Bing

The final letter I'll share came from former US senator Ralph Yarborough (D-TX) (1903–1996). Some years after he left politics, and when I was a kid, he wrote me a longhand letter urging me to keep up my interest in politics and giving me advice if I ever succeeded in my political ambitions. "Never fear defeat," he said. "Never compromise yourself, serve always with the best interest of the people and the nation in mind, even if it means defeat . . . Never do a dishonorable act."

The closing line of Yarborough's letter has particular significance to me, and in its own way, it is now a relic of constitutional history. Twenty-five years after Yarborough penned the advice for me, I stood in the chamber where Yarborough had served decades earlier and delivered the final lines of my closing argument in the impeachment trial of President Clinton. My final words to the United States Senate—and to a live worldwide television audience, were these:

> From the time I was a little boy, it was my dream to serve one day in the Congress of the United States. My constituents fulfilled that dream for me two years ago. Today, I am a Republican in a district that is heavily Democratic. The pundits keep telling me that my stand on this issue puts my political fortunes in jeopardy. So be it. That revelation produces from me no flinching. There is a simple reason why: I know that in life, dreams come and dreams go, but conscience is forever. I can live with the concept of not serving in Congress. I cannot live with the idea of remaining in Congress at the expense of doing what I believe to be right.

Senator Ralph Yarborough's letter to me (1975), which I referenced in my closing argument to the United States Senate in the impeachment trial of President Clinton (1999)

I was a teenager when a distinguished member of this body, the late senator Ralph Yarborough of Texas, wrote and gave me this sage advice about elective office. He told me to put principle above politics, and to "put honor above incumbency."

I now return that sentiment to the body from which it came. Hold fast to it, Senators, and in doing so, you will be faithful both to our Founders and to our heirs.

44

A Last Good-Bye

The first famous person I ever saw in my life was California governor Ronald Reagan. You may recall in the earlier chapter, "My Governor," how I stood outside the gate of the San Francisco Opera House as he drove by and waved to me on the occasion of the twenty-fifth anniversary of the signing of the United Nations Charter in 1970. Since he was my first encounter with fame, and since he had such a profound impact on my life (personally and politically), I thought it appropriate to close this book of reminiscences with a final story about him.

...

In a handwritten letter dated November 1994, former President Ronald Reagan informed the world that he suffered from Alzheimer's disease, an incurable neurological illness that depletes the brain cells. I knew he had it before the formal announcement. While a member of the State Assembly, Reagan's long-time press secretary and aide Lynn Nofziger campaigned for me in my Southern California district. As we ate a late evening dinner at a local Mexican restaurant, Nofziger told me that he'd dropped by Reagan's office that morning to see his old boss, but wouldn't be returning. Confused by the comment, I asked why.

"Because," Nofziger said, "he didn't know me. I had to keep telling him who I was. Something's wrong. I don't want to see him this way, so I won't be going back."

Shortly thereafter, lobbyist (and Reagan son-in-law) Dennis Revell visited my office in Sacramento. When I told him the disturbing news from Nofziger,

Revell shook his head sadly and delivered a similar report about his father-in-law:

> Recently we had a family dinner when someone started talking about some
> major event of the Reagan presidency. He sat looking confused and inter-
> rupted by saying, "You're all talking about something like I should know
> what this is all about." At first we thought he was kidding, and then it sunk
> in that there was something wrong. Finally, Maureen [Reagan's daughter]
> took his hand and said, "Dad, you were president of the United States. You
> served two terms in the White House." He looked dazed.
>
> "I was president?"
>
> Maureen led him to the window and pointed out the Secret Service
> agents stationed outside. "Dad, those are Secret Service agents. They guard
> you because you were president."
>
> "I was president?"
>
> A few minutes later, he was back to normal and engaged in the conver-
> sation as if nothing happened. That's when Nancy decided to call and make
> the doctor's appointment.

After the Alzheimer's announcement, Reagan maintained a public schedule
at first, but as time wore on, the disease took its toll. He made fewer visits to his
Century City office, and withdrew slowly from view.

Two years later, Republicans won a majority in the California State
Assembly for the first time in almost thirty years. The first official act of Speaker
Curt Pringle was to move Reagan's formal Capitol portrait from the basement
to a place of honor at the entrance hall of the Assembly chamber. As the new
majority leader, I authored a resolution honoring Reagan on the occasion of
his eighty-fifth birthday. When I called Reagan's office to make arrangements
to have the framed scroll sent to him, I received a surprise invitation: would I
like to come by and deliver it to the president in person? However, the invitation came with a caveat; his aide told me that Reagan has "good days and bad
days, and if it's a bad day, you'll have to just drop it off with his secretary." I
understood completely.

I had another reason for wanting to see Reagan one last time: to tell him
how much I owed him personally. As I explained earlier, had Reagan not given
me his speech notes when I waited three hours for him outside the Boundary
Oak restaurant in 1973, I would not have finished law school. This meant I

never would have become a lawyer, a gang murder prosecutor, a judge, a state legislator, majority leader, and in a few more months be on my way to Congress. I wanted to apologize for selling them to finance my education, but mostly I just wanted to say thank you.

I *needed* to say thank you.

. . .

When I mentioned later to Dennis Revell that I might see Reagan soon, he told me that his cognitive abilities are unpredictable. "It's like he's on a staircase. He goes along okay in a flat pattern, and then there is a sudden, big drop. Then he goes along okay at that level, and then another big drop." He warned that the meeting might not happen.

. . .

The day before my scheduled meeting with Reagan, my Assembly colleague Tom Woods approached me on the chamber floor. He told me that he and his wife, Alice's, single greatest ambition was to shake hands with Ronald Reagan, and he asked if they could accompany me. I didn't expect Reagan's staff to approve a group visit, but they granted permission for the additional visitors—providing everybody understood that the meeting may or may not occur, depending on how Reagan was doing that day.

On March 21, 1996, accompanied by Tom and Alice, we drove to Reagan's office at the Fox Towers Building in Century City. An aide greeted us at the desk and brought us back to the suite outside Reagan's private office. Several Secret Service agents lingered in the hallways, looking bored; the office staff had been slashed: the frantic activity I saw on previous visits was gone. All was now still.

While waiting in the reception area, his aide said that Reagan no longer made any public appearances: "He still visits the office occasionally, but only because the doctors think it is helpful if he is brought around familiar surroundings. He doesn't 'work' here anymore. About the only physical activity he gets is to golf now and then. We're all trying to keep his mind active."

As we talked, I saw a concerned look cross her face suddenly. "What're those?" she asked, pointing to the leather-bound copies of Reagan's autobiography that both Tom and I carried. We told her we brought them in case Reagan could sign them for us. The aide explained quite firmly that when meeting Reagan, *nobody* was allowed to ask him to sign anything. She said that these days, if Reagan signs something, they prefer to allow him to do it privately. The unspoken message was clear: they didn't want to embarrass Reagan if he couldn't complete the task, and we told her we understood completely. The aide collected our books and said she'd try to get them signed after our appointment.

As the aide ushered us into Reagan's private office, Alice Woods walked through the door first. When she saw Reagan standing next to his desk–still ramrod straight but now with graying hair, eyeglasses, and two hearing aids– she gasped in excitement: "Oh, my goodness! It's him!" He shook hands and greeted each of us with a sweet, slight smile. His voice sounded hoarse, but it was still clearly identifiable as the one that moved a generation, and moved history along with it.

So as to minimize any concerns of his hovering staff, I did most of the talking; I told Reagan I had just become the first Republican majority leader of the California Assembly in twenty-eight years–the first since he won election

Here I am presenting President Reagan with a resolution from the California State Assembly on the occasion of his 85th birthday, Office of Ronald Reagan, Century City, March 23, 1996

as governor in 1966. I said that our first official act was to move his painting to the honored place in the Capitol outside our chamber. "That's wonderful," Reagan replied. "I'm deeply touched by all you fellows have done." When I handed him the framed resolution, he took it and studied it at length: "Oh, my," he said. "It's beautiful."

"It's just something to add to the warehouse filled with these things that you've collected over the years, Mr. President," I told him.

Tom and Alice posed for a picture with their lifelong hero, and then it was my turn. As Reagan took my hand, he whispered several times, "Thank you . . . thank you . . . This was very beautiful."

Reagan then took my arm and led us over to the credenza and bookcase behind his desk. "This is my 'photo corner,'" he said as he pointed to signed portraits of German chancellor Helmut Kohl, British prime minister Margaret Thatcher, Pope John Paul II, Japanese Emperor Hirohito, President Eisenhower, and others. As we admired his impressive collection, Reagan said, "This way, you get in the photo all these . . ." and then his voice became still. Reagan closed his eyes briefly, and then tried again as he pointed to the framed collection: "You know, these fellows here . . ." He couldn't finish the sentence. I started admiring the photos aloud, trying to ease him away from the awkward moment.

Sensing his aide's growing angst, I thanked Reagan again and told him our caucus dedicated our 1994 victory to him, and that we planned to do the same in November when we held the majority. We shook his hand and said good-bye. As I stepped from his office, I glanced back. There he stood, straight and tall, with a sweet, grandfatherly look on his face.

I wanted to thank him—to tell him what those speech notes he gave me meant. To tell him how that three-hour wait for him outside the Boundary Oak restaurant changed my life forever.

It wasn't to be. And I knew I'd never see him again.

. . .

Our final good-bye: former President Reagan and me, Office of Ronald Reagan, Century City, March 23, 1996

After we exited Reagan's office, his aide said she'd go back and try to get our books signed. As she stepped inside and closed the door, I told Tom she was probably going to run the books through the autopen and have them machine-signed. That wasn't a problem for me under the circumstances. I grew surprised, and then saddened, when I realized she really was getting them signed. The sadness came from what I could hear her saying in a loud voice to the great man behind the door: "Mr. President, we'll have you sign these books for your two guests that just left . . . Sir, if you'll hold the pen . . . That's good . . . Now, on the first one, write, 'To'– *T . . . o . . .* 'James'–*J . . . a . . . m . . . e . . . s.*'"

And so it went for the next ten minutes as Reagan inscribed my book, and then Tom's. As much as I delighted in having the book signed, my heart sank listening to her guide each pen stroke. Surprisingly, when she returned the books to us, his script (so familiar to me over the years) remained clear and strong.

Just before leaving the office, I ran into another longtime Reagan staffer, my old friend Peggy Grande. We chatted briefly, and then she stepped into Reagan's office, carrying a folder with the presidential seal. She closed the door behind her; through the door I could hear her telling her boss in a loud, slow voice, "Mr. President, I have some things for you to sign." And then the painful process I had heard a few minutes earlier began again.

. . .

My 1973 Boundary Oak experience, where I got those coveted speech notes, was the first time I waited three hours for Ronald Reagan. It was not the last.

Caisson with military honor guard carrying the body of former president Ronald Reagan to the Capitol Building, Washington, DC, June 9, 2004

I waited three hours for him one more time: it was on a hot, muggy afternoon in downtown Washington, DC, more than thirty years later. At the first sight of the American and presidential flags leading his procession, I

The riderless horse with the boots of her fallen leader facing backward in the stirrups (per military custom); funeral procession of former president Ronald Reagan, Washington, DC, June 9, 2004

remembered Reagan's initial grimace, followed by a smile and a twinkle in his eye, when he handed over that stack of note cards to a glib kid in a parking lot.

Now, on this particular day, as I stood on Constitution Avenue with my family and watched his flag-draped casket and the riderless horse pass in front of me, I remembered what Ronald Reagan did for America and for the cause of freedom.

But mostly, I stood there and remembered what Ronald Reagan did for me.

APPENDIX

This sheet bears some autographs of political leaders I collected as a boy in the early 1970s; many of their accompanying stories are included in this book. How many signatures can you identify?

Engraved White House vignette signed for me by seven presidents of the United States: Richard Nixon ("RN"), Gerald R. Ford, Jimmy Carter, Ronald Reagan, George Bush, Bill Clinton, George W. Bush

"With memories of a great house that belonged to us"

I collected on this engraved vignette of the White House the signatures of eleven First Ladies of America—an unprecedented grouping: Bess Truman, Mamie Eisenhower, Jacqueline Kennedy, Lady Bird Johnson, Patricia Nixon, Betty Ford, Rosalynn Carter, Nancy Reagan, Barbara Bush, Hillary Clinton, Laura Bush

To Jim Rogan — Happy Birthday! Just keep celebrating your 39th! Ronald Reagan

As I remember him: When I was majority leader of the California State Assembly, former president Ronald Reagan delivered to my office this special 39th birthday present in a leather folder, August 1996

ACKNOWLEDGMENTS

This is my third book venture with my old friend Joseph Farah, editor-in-chief, chairman, and founder of WND. Technically, it's our fourth writing venture: over a quarter century ago, when I was an unknown deputy District Attorney in Los Angeles County, the editor of my local newspaper (Joe Farah) asked me to write an op-ed. I did, he published it, and that got me started on the road to Congress. Once again, Joe, I am honored to be part of your bizarre habit of publishing books written by me that so few people buy! Joe and WND published my second book (our first book together), *Catching Our Flag*, in 2011. This year Joe, his wonderful wife, Elizabeth, (chief marketing officer and cofounder of WND), and their fantastic team at WND Books are betting the Daily Double on me. They not only reissued my very first book, *Rough Edges*, as a tenth anniversary edition in April 2014; a few months later, they published the book you now hold in your hand. How much more blessed can an author get? Deepest thanks to Joe, Elizabeth, and the WND crew who brought this project to life: editorial director Geoffrey Stone; production coordinator Aryana Hendrawan; creative director Mark Karis (who resuscitated successfully the 1970s lime green on the book's dust jacket); proofreader Thom Chittom, copyeditor Renee Chaves, typesetter Ashley Karis, marketing coordinators Michael Thompson and Amanda Prevette, and PR consultant Tamara Colbert.

Unending thanks to Speaker Newt Gingrich and my literary agent Jillian Manus, both of whom combined years ago to make an author out of me and continue to give me more encouragement than I deserve.

My mother, Alice Rogan, was (in the words of a lifelong friend) "one tough old broad." She smoked two packs a day for over sixty years; the daughter of a longshoreman, she swore like a sailor, lived off junk food, said whatever was on her mind, made it to almost seventy-nine, and was gone in an instant without discomfort or fanfare. Had she lived a few months longer, she would have loved getting a copy of this book–and she wouldn't have cared what the rest of you thought about it. No son could have had a scrappier cheerleader in his corner. Life with you was never conventional, Mom, but it was rarely boring. Teri, Pat, John, your many grandkids, and I miss you each day.

On those long-ago excursions to annoy famous people, I usually dragged someone along for the ride; my most consistent co-conspirators were my junior high school classmates Dan Swanson and Roger Mahan, and my kid brother Pat. The four of us share many great memories from the stories in this book. Thanks to each of you, and of course, if any of your memories conflict with mine, please keep your version to yourself! By the way, our hanging out to get autographs and advice didn't hurt any of them. Today Dan is a senior partner at the law firm of Gibson Dunn and Crutcher in Los Angeles; Roger is a senior policy analyst for the Budget Committee of the U.S. House of Representatives, and little brother is director of engineering operations at Levi's Stadium (home of the San Francisco 49ers).

To Jim Dunbar, veteran KGO-San Francisco newsman and National Radio Hall of Fame inductee, thanks for letting a gaggle kids hang out and meet your famous political guests many decades ago instead of doing what the law required you do–report us to the truant officer!

Now and then I let a handful of friends read all or portions of the manuscript to gain their input and point out my unending trail of typographical and grammatical errors. Thanks to the following people for undertaking this duty: Ann Anooshian, Linda Bonar, Wayne Paugh, the Honorable Chris Evans, Trudy Kruse, Roger Mahan, the Honorable Chuck Poochigian, and the Honorable Scott Steiner. Also ongoing thanks to my attorney, Paul Meyer, who is counting on my literary flights to finance a new sunroom off his patio.

Finally, love and continued hugs to the three leading ladies in my life: Christine, Dana, and Claire. Once again, I'm done hogging the computer for now.

–J.R., Orange County, California, July 8, 2014

INDEX

Page numbers in italics refer to graphics.

Index

Index

Thank you for choosing to read

'And *then* I met...'

If you enjoyed this book, we hope that you will tell your friends and family. There are many ways to spread the word:

Share your thoughts on Facebook, your blog, or Tweet
"You should read #ANDTHENIMET by James Rogan // @worldnetdaily"

Check out all of James Rogan's books at GoingRogan.com.

Send a copy to someone you know who would benefit from reading this book.

Write a review online at Amazon.com or BN.com
Subscribe to WND at www.wnd.com
Visit the WND Superstore at superstore.wnd.com

WND Books

A **WND** COMPANY • WASHINGTON DC • WNDBOOKS.COM

 WND Books

PRESENTS

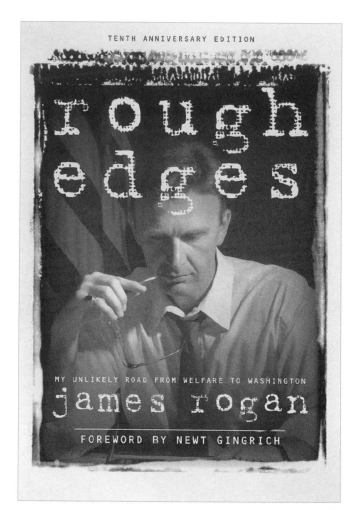

As one of the leading members of the House Judiciary Committee that impeached President Bill Clinton, James Rogan's place in the pantheon of conservative heroes remains secure. But that is just part of an amazing life story that contains more drama than found in ten lives. *Rough Edges* is chock-full of wild tales, humor, and fun. Rogan tells an engaging story that will make you laugh and cry, and is perhaps the most honest political memoir ever written.

WND Books • A *WND* COMPANY • WASHINGTON DC • WNDBOOKS.COM

PRESENTS

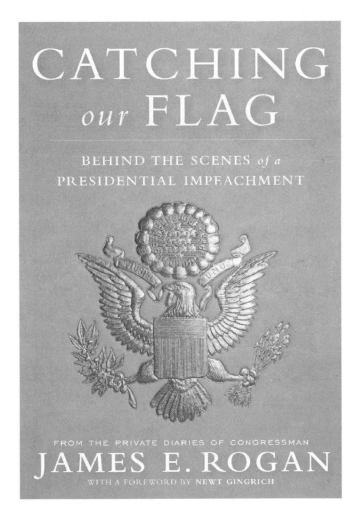

It has been more than a dozen years since the media force-fed America and the world a steady diet of Monica Lewinsky's blue dress, a wagging presidential finger and the parsing of phrases like "the meaning of 'is.'" Now, Jim Rogan has opened this archive for both modern readers and for history by penning the ultimate insider's story on what led a very reluctant House of Representatives to impeach a then-very-popular American president.

WND Books · A **WND** COMPANY · WASHINGTON DC · WNDBOOKS.COM

No publisher in the world has a higher percentage of *New York Times* bestsellers.

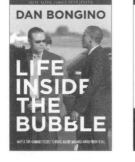
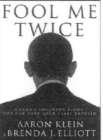

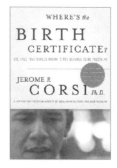

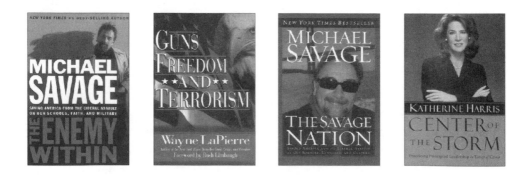